I0021021

DevOps Unleashed with Git and GitHub

Automate, collaborate, and innovate to enhance your
DevOps workflow and development experience

Yuki Hattori

DevOps Unleashed with Git and GitHub

Copyright © 2024 Packt Publishing

Group Product Manager: Preet Ahuja

Publishing Product Manager: Vidhi Vashisth

Book Project Manager: Uma Devi

Senior Editor: Romy Dias

Technical Editor: Irfa Ansari

Copy Editor: Safis Editing

Proofreader: Romy Dias

Indexer: Tejal Daruwale Soni

Production Designer: Ponraj Dhandapani

Senior DevRel Marketing Executive: Linda Pearlson

DevRel Marketing Executive: Rohan Dhobal

First published: April 2024

Production reference: 1210324

Published by Packt Publishing Ltd.

Grosvenor House
11 St Paul's Square
Birmingham
B3 1RB, UK

ISBN 978-1-83546-371-0

www.packtpub.com

Foreword

I have known Yuki Hattori from the InnerSource Commons Foundation for several years where, upon arrival, he stood up a local community for the foundation in Japan within a couple of months. He is one of the experts bringing Git and GitHub to teams. He is one of the rare people I know who can bridge the gap between collaboration best practices developed within open source and corporate structures.

Git and, by extension, GitHub have evolved into vital tools in software engineering – not only in the open source world but also in professional engineering teams ranging from development to operations. Both tools, however, shine in particular when adopting not only the technology itself but also the processes, cultures, and ideas that they were built upon.

More than two decades ago, open source was still the new kid that everyone was skeptical about. Even though several open source projects were already vital ingredients of several products, professional teams remained skeptical as to whether and how processes from the open source world could carry over to professional engineering. Over time, though, open source communities showed how to build bridges across not only teams but corporations, and not only floors but time zones and nation-states.

While you are trying to get started with DevOps collaboration, what are your strategies to reduce the friction between silos and help you thrive with a different team?

After reading Yuki's book you will know how to apply these lessons to bridge the silos in your organization. You will understand how collaboration means gaining together by sharing the work to create a sound technological basis. The book will also give you an understanding of the tools that enable this collaboration. With InnerSource, it shows you a set of collaboration patterns that complement Git and GitHub, making their application much more effective within your organization.

Benefit from standing on the shoulders of giants: after reading this book, not only will you be able to build bridges within your organization, you will also have gotten a glimpse of how easy it can be to benefit from being more involved in the open source projects you use in your stack on a daily basis.

Isabel Drost-Fromm,

Founding Director of the InnerSource Commons Foundation, member of the Apache Software Foundation

To Xinlei, the source of joy and strength in my life

Contributors

About the author

Yuki Hattori, an architect at GitHub, showcases his hands-on expertise in DevOps and technical advice for enterprise clients. He began as a software engineer and progressed to cloud solution architect at Microsoft, overseeing cloud architecture and DevOps. A strong advocate for open source culture within an enterprise, he champions InnerSource adoption, serving as a board member of the InnerSource Commons Foundation. This nonprofit role drives global InnerSource adoption, breaking down organizational silos for innovation.

I want to thank the people who have been close to me and supported me, especially my wife, Xinlei, and my parents, Ken and Yumiko.

About the reviewers

Daniel Cho is a solutions engineer at GitHub Japan and has worked in various roles within the IT industry over the past 11 years, ranging from support to project management to pre-sales. He has presented at various local events in Japan and has also assisted with webinars that target a broader audience in Asia. His background in chemical engineering has helped give a different perspective throughout his years within the technology industry and he currently works closely with both traditional technology companies and non-technology companies to increase awareness of GitHub.

Yasuki Takami has worked supporting application development culture/infrastructure for more than 10 years, with 6 years specifically dedicated to DevSecOps culture acceleration in organizations. He started his career as an infrastructure engineer supporting developers' efficiency and moved forward to support organizations in being more efficient and agile-like decision-making while building SaaS-based products in the market. He thinks it is more important to be secure than efficient to sustain DevOps organizations and culture.

I'd like to thank my family and friends, who understand the time and commitment it takes to research and test data that is constantly changing. Working in this field would not be possible without the supportive DevOps/InnerSource community that has developed over the last several years. Thank you to all of the trailblazers who make this field an exciting place to work each and every day. We are grateful for everything you do!

Sebastian Spier has worked as an individual contributor, agile coach, team lead, product owner, and director of engineering. Over his 15 years in the software industry, no matter the role or team, effective cross-team collaboration has been key for him to get things done at organizations of any size. Having seen first-hand how DevOps transforms the way that software is built and delivered, it is one of his key objectives to reduce the barriers between departments and teams so that they can jointly ship software in the most efficient way possible, continuously reducing the lead time to business impact.

Yoichi Kawasaki is a technology professional with extensive experience in software development, cloud computing, and technology advocacy, having worked with leading technology firms for over 20 years. Currently, he is employed by Postman as a technology evangelist, where he is responsible for driving Postman's adoption in Japan. Beyond his professional engagements, he is an avid contributor to the tech community, speaking at conferences and meetups, co-authoring a book, and writing numerous technical articles focused on DevOps tools and developer productivity.

Table of Contents

3

Advanced Git Usage for Team Collaboration   59

Part 2: GitHub Excellence and CI/CD Fundamentals

4

Elevating Team Collaboration with GitHub   103

5

Driving CI/CD with GitHub   163

Part 3: Beyond DevOps

6

Enriching DevOps Implementation   195

7

Accelerate Productivity with AI   227

8

Reflection and Conclusion   247

Index   251

Other Books You May Enjoy   260

Preface

Let's dive into the world of DevOps with this essential guide, crafted for developers, operations professionals, and DevOps enthusiasts eager to master Git and GitHub. This book transcends mere theory and instructional content; it's a treasure trove of practical wisdom and real-world applications, setting you on a path to mastering these crucial tools in modern software development and operations.

What sets this book apart:

- **Git fundamentals unveiled**: Begin your journey with a solid grounding in Git basics. Understand its pivotal role in version control and collaborative software development, a foundational step for any aspiring DevOps professional.

- **Exploring GitHub's advanced facets**: Progress to the sophisticated functionalities of GitHub. Learn how it empowers continuous integration/delivery (CI/CD) and streamlines workflows, bridging the gap between development and operations.

- **Hands-on DevOps strategies**: Move beyond the basics with practical insights and real-world scenarios. Witness Git and GitHub in action across various DevOps processes, from enhancing collaboration to integrating security practices seamlessly into your development cycle.

Git and GitHub for DevOps is more than a book; it's a comprehensive toolkit. Packed with expert tips, hands-on exercises, and insightful case studies, it's the ultimate guide for anyone striving to excel in the dynamic world of DevOps.

Have you ever experienced a situation where you thought, "*Oops, I made a mistake! This is embarrassing*"? Even if it wasn't really embarrassing, did it cause you to feel a little low or nervous?

Even though we're advised to learn from our mistakes, we all want to avoid errors whenever possible.

The good news? The more you fail, the more you learn. There's no such thing as learning without failure. Now, for some bad news. Git and GitHub, which you will learn about, are fundamentally systems designed to record changes. They are not built to easily hide your mistakes. In some circles, being proficient with Git is taken for granted, and not being able to use GitHub can even call into question your qualifications as an engineer. What's worse, mistakes in automated DevOps pipelines can directly lead to production failures. A minor slip-up could be the gateway to much bigger errors. In a technological ecosystem that thrives on collaboration and rapid development, these tools and methodologies underpin modern engineering practices. Your desire for a comprehensive understanding of Git, GitHub, and DevOps is well-placed.

And this is the book that will meet that desire. It's a book that empowers people in development teams to communicate effectively within their teams, teaching the fundamentals of modern team development to continually refine your products. Ultimately, it's a book that will significantly enhance your developer experience.

But let's be clear, perfection is a myth. However, excellence is undoubtedly achievable. In that way, this is not only a book about avoiding mistakes but also about embracing them and establishing a process, workflow, and culture that permits errors. It's about understanding how to react, adapt, and grow when they inevitably happen. This is the essence of a thriving DevOps culture.

What's essential is your openness to learn from your missteps, to communicate with your team openly about them, and to find collective solutions. Every mistake you make and learn from brings you one step closer to becoming not just a competent engineer but also an invaluable team player.

I hope you will find this book not just a guide to mastering Git, GitHub, and DevOps, but also a mentor in your professional growth. As you turn these pages, you'll encounter real-world scenarios, practical exercises, and insights that will illuminate the path ahead. You'll learn how to navigate the complexities of team collaboration tools, manage code in a shared environment, and streamline your development process.

Welcome to a journey of continuous learning, improvement, and collaboration. Welcome to the world of Git, GitHub, and DevOps mastery.

Who this book is for

This book is a comprehensive guide for those stepping into the dynamic world of DevOps, specifically tailored to cater to diverse roles within the industry. The book's target audience encompasses the following:

- **Upcoming DevOps professionals**: If you're an engineer embarking on your first DevOps project, this book is designed for you. We understand the apprehension of making mistakes. This guide will arm you with the skills and confidence to use Git and seamlessly integrate it into your team proficiently.

- **IT administrators and infrastructure engineers**: As the industry moves toward managing cloud configurations via Git, this book is a vital resource for infrastructure engineers accustomed to manual management. It provides the necessary guidance to adapt to this new paradigm, enriching your traditional IT and infrastructure skills with essential coding and cloud computing knowledge.

- **Product managers and product owners**: This segment includes non-coding professionals who are integral to product development. If you're using GitHub for team communication but lack operational knowledge of Git and GitHub, this book will demystify these tools for you.

What this book covers

Chapter 1, DevOps and Developer Experience – Entering the World of Modern Development, introduces DevOps and developer experience, highlighting their significance in modern software development. It provides foundational knowledge about these concepts, tools such as Git and GitHub, and their role in enhancing development processes.

Chapter 2, Getting Started with Git, offers a practical introduction to Git, emphasizing both its basic usage and the communication aspects essential for team development. It covers file management, branching, and the principles of collaboration in a Git-enabled engineering environment.

Chapter 3, Advanced Git Usage for Team Collaboration, focuses on advanced collaboration techniques. This chapter teaches how to manage commit history, handle complex branches, and resolve merge conflicts. It underscores strategies for effective code base management to boost team productivity.

Chapter 4, Elevating Team Collaboration with GitHub, explores GitHub's role in DevOps, going beyond its identity as a code hosting platform. It covers GitHub features crucial for teamwork and collaboration, transitioning from traditional systems to modern DevOps practices.

Chapter 5, Driving CI/CD with GitHub, is an in-depth exploration of GitHub Actions. This chapter covers its core concepts, workflow optimization, and advanced deployment strategies such as blue-green and canary deployments, as well as feature release strategies.

Chapter 6, Enriching DevOps Implementation, takes a comprehensive look at DevOps, discussing the importance of metrics, the integration of security practices (DevSecOps), and strategies for scaling collaboration within organizations.

Chapter 7, Accelerate Productivity with AI, focuses on AI in software development. This chapter delves into tools such as GitHub Copilot and best practices for coding with AI assistance, including effective prompt crafting and AI-friendly programming principles.

Chapter 8, Reflection and Conclusion, reflects on the transformations brought about by technologies such as Git, GitHub, DevOps, and AI in software development, and considers the future impact of AI on software engineering practices.

To get the most out of this book

This book will involve working with commands in the terminal to understand Git more fundamentally. It is a good idea to have a beginner's level understanding of terminal commands.

Software/hardware covered in the book	Operating system requirements
Git	Windows, macOS, or Linux
GitHub	Windows, macOS, or Linux

You will need a working environment with the latest Git version and a GitHub account to not only read this book but to really experience it.

Instructions for installing Git can be found in the book's Git Repository (a link is available in the next section).

If you are using the digital version of this book, we advise you to type the code yourself or access the code from the book's GitHub repository (a link is available in the next section). Doing so will help you avoid any potential errors related to the copying and pasting of code.

Download the example code files

You can download the example code files for this book from GitHub at https://github.com/PacktPublishing/DevOps-Unleashed-with-Git-and-GitHub. If there's an update to the code, it will be updated in the GitHub repository.

We also have other code bundles from our rich catalog of books and videos available at https://github.com/PacktPublishing/. Check them out!

Conventions used

There are a number of text conventions used throughout this book.

`Code in text`: Indicates code words in text, database table names, folder names, filenames, file extensions, pathnames, dummy URLs, user input, and Twitter handles. Here is an example: "For `release` preparation, a release branch is created from the `develop` branch."

A block of code is set as follows:

```
name: Node.js CI
on:
  push:
    branches: [ "main" ]
jobs:
  build:
```

When we wish to draw your attention to a particular part of a code block, the relevant lines or items are set in bold:

```
on:
  push:
    branches: [ "main" ]
```

Any command-line input or output is written as follows:

```
$ git checkout main
$ git merge --no-ff add-feature
```

Bold: Indicates a new term, an important word, or words that you see onscreen. For instance, words in menus or dialog boxes appear in **bold**. Here is an example: "By clicking **Explore workflows**, You will get to the marketplace page and can look for GitHub Actions."

> **Tips or important notes**
> Appear like this.

Get in touch

Feedback from our readers is always welcome.

General feedback: If you have questions about any aspect of this book, email us at customercare@ packtpub.com and mention the book title in the subject of your message.

Errata: Although we have taken every care to ensure the accuracy of our content, mistakes do happen. If you have found a mistake in this book, we would be grateful if you would report this to us. Please visit www.packtpub.com/support/errata and fill in the form.

Piracy: If you come across any illegal copies of our works in any form on the internet, we would be grateful if you would provide us with the location address or website name. Please contact us at copyright@packt.com with a link to the material.

If you are interested in becoming an author: If there is a topic that you have expertise in and you are interested in either writing or contributing to a book, please visit authors.packtpub.com.

Share your thoughts

Once you've read *DevOps Unleashed with Git and GitHub*, we'd love to hear your thoughts! Scan the QR code below to go straight to the Amazon review page for this book and share your feedback.

https://packt.link/r/1835463711

Your review is important to us and the tech community and will help us make sure we're delivering excellent quality content.

Download a free PDF copy of this book

Thanks for purchasing this book!

Do you like to read on the go but are unable to carry your print books everywhere?

Is your eBook purchase not compatible with the device of your choice?

Don't worry, now with every Packt book you get a DRM-free PDF version of that book at no cost.

Read anywhere, any place, on any device. Search, copy, and paste code from your favorite technical books directly into your application.

The perks don't stop there, you can get exclusive access to discounts, newsletters, and great free content in your inbox daily

Follow these simple steps to get the benefits:

1. Scan the QR code or visit the link below

https://packt.link/free-ebook/9781835463710

2. Submit your proof of purchase
3. That's it! We'll send your free PDF and other benefits to your email directly

Part 1:
Foundations of Git, GitHub, and DevOps

This part on modern software development begins by introducing DevOps and developer experience, underscoring their importance in today's development landscape and offering foundational knowledge and theories. Then, it provides a hands-on introduction to Git, covering its basic functions and highlighting the communication aspects vital for team collaboration, including file management and branching. Finally, the discussion deepens to encompass advanced Git methodologies tailored for team collaboration, such as managing commit histories, handling complex branches, and resolving merge conflicts, all aimed at enhancing team productivity and effective code base management.

This part has the following chapters:

- *Chapter 1, DevOps and Developer Experience – Entering the World of Modern Development*
- *Chapter 2, Getting Started with Git*
- *Chapter 3, Advanced Git Usage for Team Collaboration*

DevOps and Developer Experience – Entering the World of Modern Development

In this chapter, we will cover two main topics. First, we will address what DevOps is, the main subject of this book. Next, we will delve into developer experience, a strategy essential for maintaining and continually achieving success in DevOps within an organization. Within this context, we will also introduce the tools, Git and GitHub.

This chapter serves as a compass for those about to embark on learning about DevOps, tools, and collaboration practices for DevOps. It will establish foundational knowledge on the positioning of these concepts and practices and how they can enhance your development process.

We will cover the following main topics in this chapter:

- DevOps – Accelerating the development cycle by reducing friction
- Developer experience – A strategy for developer excellence
- Git – Where code collaborations begin
- GitHub – The AI-powered developer platform

DevOps – Accelerating the development cycle by reducing friction

Let's get started by learning the DevOps fundamentals.

The world of technology has various terms. At times, such terms can be abstract, and people tend to apply various interpretations to a specific framework. DevOps is no exception. Additionally, when referring to DevOps, considering perspectives from an individual, team, and the entire organization can sometimes make it unclear how various components interact with each other.

We will review the basics of DevOps, clear up misconceptions, and touch on some of its typical practices. Now, before we dive into what DevOps is, let's talk about how things used to be in the past.

Background on DevOps

Back in the day, software was essentially something you installed. So, for a product development team, all you needed were engineers who could develop and test it. Speaking of testing, it was all about squashing bugs before the release. Just imagine it for a moment; it was similar to the release of early video games, much like the **Nintendo Entertainment System (NES)** era. Once a game was shipped on a cartridge, there was no opportunity for updates or adding new features. Bugs that shipped with the game remained with the consumer forever. However, with the emergence of the Apache HTTP Server and the shift toward network communication, the need arose for IT Operations to manage this new paradigm.

In many cases, the IT Operations team specialized in IT operations. Their tools, culture, and even their objectives were different from those of the development team. The development team wanted to add features, while the IT team considered system stability their top priority. This was a contradiction.

Moreover, in the divided world of these two teams, when it came to deployment, it felt like tossing code over the wall. Developers would toss a perfectly deployable artifact to the IT Operations team on the other side of the wall. However, for some reason, the IT Operations team would receive something incomplete and non-functional for the production environment, leading to exhaustion as they struggled to deploy and maintain it somehow:

Figure 1.1 – Engineers tossing code over the wall

In recent years, there has been remarkable technological advancement, and its influence has permeated well beyond the realm of software, touching virtually every industry. Why is this the case? This is because software development plays a pivotal role in the strategies of organizations, regardless of their size, in modern business management. Companies affected by this technological wave find themselves in a competitive landscape where the focus is on delivering swift, cutting-edge, and reliable products to their customers.

Despite the possibility of significant changes in market conditions and customer needs in less than a year, releasing software only a few times annually is not sufficient. We cannot afford delays in software releases due to friction between internal silos. A **silo** denotes an isolated system, process, or department that lacks integration or communication with other parts, potentially causing inefficiencies. We must find a way to streamline the process from product development to operation. This is where a completely new development methodology, organizational structure, and culture come into play.

DevOps emerges as a methodology born from this very scenario. It represents a fusion of development and operations, where development and operations teams collaborate as a unified entity to instill a shared culture, refine processes, and deploy tools, all in the pursuit of expediting releases, enhancing overall product quality, gathering customer feedback, and ultimately providing better and faster service to customers. This, in turn, leads to more effective market performance.

What is DevOps?

The term **DevOps** is a blend of the words **Development** and **Operations**.

So, is DevOps simply about fostering collaboration between the development and operations teams?

While that's part of the story, the reality is often more complex. There's usually a disconnect between these two teams, each having their unique priorities and objectives. Merely bringing them together may enhance their relationship and mutual understanding to a degree, but that's often insufficient for effective collaboration. In essence, DevOps transcends just integrating roles or teams; it represents a broader cultural shift within the organization. It is about aligning priorities, streamlining workflows, and, ultimately, breaking down silos that hinder effective communication and progress.

In brief, DevOps is the union of people, process, and tools to continually provide value to end users and is fundamentally a cultural shift:

Figure 1.2 – DevOps is the union of people, process, and tools

"I see. I understand. DevOps is all about people, process, and tools."

Many people think they understand it here and move on to implementing an automation pipeline for DevOps. But wait. Simply replacing these elements alone will not ensure the success of a DevOps initiative. For DevOps to be successful, you need to know more about what it is, what it is not, and why it is.

In reality, the definition of DevOps is quite broad. Consequently, the concept of *Dev*Ops*, an extended form of DevOps, has been rapidly expanding recently. Various derivative approaches such as DevSecOps and BizDevOps have been proposed, leading to a multitude of perspectives on what DevOps encompasses.

Unfortunately, there is no universally accepted, precise definition of DevOps, and how to do something called DevOps is answered differently by different people. Consequently, misconceptions and inaccurate interpretations about DevOps are common, often leading to disputes. And sometimes, people do not want to talk about it when it comes time to talk about doing DevOps, even though it is so important!

Figure 1.3 – DevOps is like the elephant in the room that often goes unaddressed

What is NOT DevOps?

Often, when defining what DevOps is, it might be easier to indicate what is *NOT* DevOps rather than trying to specify what DevOps truly is. Let's clear up a typical misunderstanding here.

DevOps is NOT just about a tool, technology, or product

There are numerous tools available in the market that can be applied to DevOps. Many cloud and tool vendors promote them by saying, "*With this tool, you can build a DevOps workflow*," or "*This tool is essential for a DevOps team.*"

When many people hear the term *DevOps*, some of them think of cloud technologies such as **Amazon Web Services** (**AWS**), Azure, and **Google Cloud Platform** (**GCP**), or technologies such as Docker and Kubernetes. Furthermore, Kubernetes' ecosystem also includes many components such as Istio, Flux, Helm, Envoy, and Prometheus. There are several platforms, including GitHub Actions, CircleCI, and Jenkins, that facilitate continuous, fast, and frequent releases. The world of monitoring tools is equally diverse. If you are not yet acquainted with these names, it might take some time to understand their nuances and benefits.

However, even if you master these tools and follow well-known architectures or success stories, that does not mean you have achieved DevOps. Because people and process always exist behind the tool, and just changing tools will not change them.

In reality, it is not uncommon to see waterfall-style development even while using tools branded with the name *DevOps*. Respecting existing complex company rules by inserting multi-step approval processes into automated workflows, restricting customer releases to once every 3 months to avoid changing accounting or security checks, or having the infrastructure team manage containers created by the app team using a platform built with the modern orchestration system, Kubernetes—doing all these things will only increase the operational burden and confusion rather than creating business value.

Ultimately, achieving significant business goals and transformations requires changes in people, organizations, and processes. Then, is DevOps about transforming individuals and organizations?

DevOps is NOT just specific individuals, teams, or roles

DevOps is a reality, but the term itself is somewhat of a buzzword. Companies hire engineers for these new activities with titles such as DevOps Engineer or DevOps Architect, and they even refer to their teams as DevOps teams. People who think they cannot do DevOps themselves may even make the mistake of trying to outsource DevOps to DevOps partners.

When you look at this situation, it might seem like DevOps refers to specific individuals, teams, or roles, but that's not the case. In many instances, these terms simply refer to roles such as super infrastructure engineers, super developers, or just cloud engineers.

Companies do this because, in order to respond quickly to evolving business needs and achieve rapid releases, they require new technologies and automation. Moreover, they often have to manage complex platforms that include both existing and new components. This includes making the most use of GitHub Actions, which is covered in this book. Areas that used to involve manual installation in the infrastructure domain, configuration through screens, or CLI operations now require to be under version control with Git and the configuration and management of automated workflows.

However, in practice, DevOps deals with even more complex matters. It is not just about mastering these tools and technologies or configuring roles for them. In reality, it requires strong leaders who can lead transformation within existing systems and organizations. Often, they engage in actions that go beyond the broad framework of DevOps. Many of the individuals I have seen who have truly achieved DevOps are pursuing larger goals rather than just the *implementation of DevOps*.

DevOps is essentially a journey to transform organizations that deal with a variety of complex technologies and products, and it is not about simply adding people with new skills to existing teams or changing team or job definitions.

So, if DevOps is not merely a tool nor solely about people and organization, does a process specifically termed DevOps exist?

DevOps is NOT just a process

DevOps teams often engage in iterative development over short cycles of 2-3 weeks, commonly called **sprints**, and hold stand-up meetings every morning. This is true, and by adopting DevOps, you may incorporate processes that adhere to Agile process and Scrum best practices. These are methodologies in software development that divide each functionality into smaller parts and drive development through numerous short cycles.

So, is DevOps an evolved concept of Agile or Scrum, or does it encompass them? The answer to this question is both *yes* and *no*.

DevOps broadens the scope to not just focus on software development like Agile, but also extends to the release of software, gathering feedback, and improvements. These principles and philosophies apply throughout the **Software Development Life Cycle (SDLC)**. Teams focus on the entire life cycle of the product, not just on developing new features or designing web components:

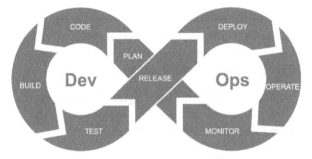

Figure 1.4 – The eight phases of a DevOps life cycle

However, the ultimate goal of DevOps is not to introduce a new process itself.

DevOps has a wide range of practices. Specific practices will be elaborated on from *Chapter 5* onward, but not all these practices can be equally applied to every team. For example, an environment that needs to deploy applications to numerous servers such as Microsoft is different from a situation where a small application is deployed to an EC2 instance. The practices to be applied also differ between a service with a user base of 1 million and a service with a user base of 1,000.

Let's consider Agile, quoting from Andy Hunt's blog:

> *Agile methods ask practitioners to think, and frankly, that's a hard sell. It is far more comfortable to simply follow what rules are given and claim you are "doing it by the book." It is easy, it is safe from ridicule or recrimination; you will not get fired for it. While we might publicly decry the narrow confines of a set of rules, there is safety and comfort there. But of course, to be agile or effective is not about comfort.*

This idea applies to DevOps as well. In order to frequently and swiftly release customer-centric developments, offer a reliable service, and ultimately make a significant impact on the business, you need to tackle problems from a broader perspective than just tools, people, and process.

DevOps is culture

So, DevOps is more than just a fusion of development and operations, specific roles, processes, tools, technology, or products. But, people often simplify it as people, process, and tools.

So, what is DevOps, really?

Let's turn to the words of Patrick Debois, a prominent figure in the DevOps community, for clarity:

> *My current definition of Dev*Ops: everything you do to overcome the friction created by silos ... All the rest is plain engineering.*

In today's era of cloud technology, both cutting-edge companies and traditional enterprises, along with start-ups, can readily access the same environments. Even AI-powered tools are available at an affordable cost.

Ultimately, what hinders your team and business progress is friction, and this friction often arises within silos that encompass people, process, and tools.

DevOps, at its core, represents a cultural shift and an approach designed to eliminate friction among the silos within an organization. It entails a shift in mindset, habits, and culture.

DevOps principles

So, what exactly constitutes a DevOps culture? Let's delve into the core principles of DevOps to gain a more comprehensive understanding of what this culture truly entails.

Customer-centric

Every action in every process should aim to provide value to the customer.

Focusing on the customer while building and maintaining software enables quicker and more relevant feature delivery. Short feedback loops contribute to fine-tuning the product in alignment with user needs, reducing risks, and maximizing value at the lowest possible cost. By focusing on the customer's needs, the ultimate goal becomes efficiently solving real-world problems, making it easier to prioritize tasks, manage backlogs, and streamline resource allocation, making operations efficient and cost-effective. Ultimately, this sets the stage for long-term business success by better meeting market demands and user expectations.

In DevOps, being customer-centric is not just a catchphrase; it is a necessity.

Creating with the end in mind

Understanding customer needs and addressing real-world problems should take precedence over operating on mere assumptions. This advocates for a holistic strategy where teams synchronize both developmental and operational tasks to satisfy customer requirements. This includes a grasp of the product's entire life cycle, from its inception and development through to its deployment and ongoing support, making certain that the final deliverable genuinely benefits the end users.

Neglecting customer needs from the beginning can result in a technically impeccable product that, nonetheless, misses the mark in terms of user satisfaction and problem-solving capability. This principle acts as a constant cue to align all technological endeavors with business goals and user expectations, ensuring that the final product is not only functional but also valuable and relevant to the audience.

Cross-functional autonomous teams

At the core of successful DevOps implementation is the indispensable strategy of forming autonomous, cross-functional teams. Unlike traditional engineering setups, where developers, operations, and **Quality Assurance** (**QA**) specialists operate in distinct compartments, DevOps champions the dissolution of these barriers. The key takeaway here is not just the formation of diverse teams but making these teams autonomous—capable of overseeing a product or feature from inception to delivery.

Why is this essential? The answer lies in agility and efficiency. When a team possesses a range of skills, from coding and testing to deployment and design—and even a nuanced understanding of the business—the speed of decision-making accelerates. This replaces the sluggish and cumbersome chain of command inherent in hierarchical systems with a culture of prompt, accountable action.

The elimination of these organizational bottlenecks not only speeds up the workflow but also cultivates a culture of ownership and accountability. The team does not have to wait for external departments or higher-ups to make decisions; they have the collective skill set and the empowerment to address challenges head-on.

By dissolving silos that often cause friction within organizations, autonomous, cross-functional teams serve as the linchpin for smooth DevOps operations. The result is a streamlined process that facilitates quick responses to changes and fosters a culture of collaboration and responsibility. This is not just a nice-to-have feature of modern engineering; it is a foundational strategy for any enterprise aiming to successfully implement DevOps.

Continuous improvement

Continuous improvement serves as the bedrock of DevOps, offering both technical and cultural advantages that are indispensable for modern software development and operations. On the technical side, it enables qualities such as reliability, adaptability, and efficiency of software delivery processes through ongoing analysis of performance metrics and utilization of automated workflows. These features not only make the end product robust but also contribute to resource optimization and quicker feature delivery. Culturally, continuous improvement fosters a collaborative environment, ensuring accountability, encouraging a learning culture, and ultimately aiding in the breakdown of organizational silos. It also aligns strategically with improved developer experience.

The importance of continuous improvement becomes even clearer when viewed through the lens of feedback loops, which act as the nervous system of the DevOps life cycle. These loops enable real-time monitoring and provide actionable metrics that feed directly into continuous improvement initiatives. By regularly assessing system performance, user engagement, and other **Key Performance Indicators (KPIs)**, organizations can quickly adjust their strategies and ensure long-term success. This dynamic, data-driven approach is essential in today's fast-paced technology landscape, making continuous improvement not just a best practice but a fundamental requirement for competitive survival.

Automation

In traditional development models, development and operations have often been two separate silos. The developers focused on writing code and building applications, while operations focused on deployment and maintenance. This disjointed approach often led to delays, inefficiencies, and friction between the two teams.

Continuous Integration/Continuous Delivery (CI/CD) emerged as the crucial bridge to connect these two worlds. With CI, code changes from multiple contributors are frequently merged into a shared repository, where automated tests are run to detect errors and inconsistencies as swiftly as possible. This encourages a more collaborative environment by making it easier to identify issues early in the development cycle. CD ensures the code is always ready for deployment, eliminating lengthy *freeze periods* where no new features could be added because a release was pending.

Manual processes are not only prone to errors but also act as a significant drag on speed and efficiency, the very issues DevOps aims to resolve. Before automation was broadly adopted, system admins would manually configure servers, a cumbersome and error-prone process. Also, developers would often find it challenging to replicate the ops environment for testing, leading to the notorious "*It works on my machine*" syndrome.

Automation, in this context, is not a luxury but a necessity. Automated scripts handle tasks from code testing to deployment, ensuring that the process is as standardized as possible, thereby eliminating many of the errors and delays associated with manual intervention.

Soaring to excellence in DevOps practices

The basic concept of DevOps has been covered so far. In fact, the concept of DevOps has been continuously evolving. Some concepts are positioned as *what should have been originally included* or *what was originally included but have not been discussed*. These may carry different labels than DevOps.

Let's look at some particularly important ideas within this context. These are beneficial concepts to incorporate into the culture of DevOps.

DevSecOps

DevSecOps is an approach that integrates security elements into the DevOps framework. In this methodology, security is considered a crucial aspect from the initial stages of development. The aim is to deliver software that is both efficient and secure in a timely manner.

Traditionally, security was often handled by separate specialized teams and was generally addressed in the final stages of the development cycle. Many instances occurred where vulnerabilities were identified post-development, causing delays in software releases. By adopting a shift-left approach to security, it is possible to significantly reduce the cost of corrections. In the DevSecOps context, **shift-left** refers to the practice of integrating security measures earlier in the SDLC, ideally during the design and development phases. By addressing security concerns from the outset, teams aim to identify and mitigate vulnerabilities more efficiently, reducing the costs and risks associated with late-stage fixes. The shift-left approach emphasizes proactive security rather than reactive, ensuring that applications are secure by design. The remediation costs for security issues that emerge during the operational phase can be prohibitively high. Moreover, this late-stage focus puts customer data at risk and can harm a company's reputation.

According to the **National Institute of Standards and Technology (NIST)**, addressing flaws during the production phase can be 30 times more costly, and this cost can escalate to 60 times more when dealing specifically with security-related defects:

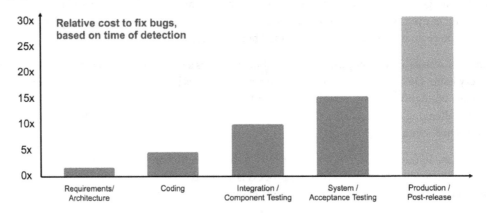

Figure 1.5 – Graph of the relative cost to fix bugs based on time of detection provided by NIST

What stands out in DevSecOps is the concept of treating security not as an endpoint but as a **continuous state**. For example, in the past, it was common to do static code analysis or check off security considerations in a security sheet during releases or technical adoptions. However, as release cycles have accelerated and technology continues to evolve rapidly, manually checking all security aspects each time has become impractical. DevSecOps addresses this issue by employing automated tools to ensure a continuous state of security. This allows for rapid response when new vulnerabilities are discovered.

In this sense, DevSecOps could be defined as integrating security processes and tools into the DevOps process, creating a culture in which developers can also consider security, treating security as a state rather than an artifact at a specific point in time, and creating a state in which processes, environments, and data are always preserved so that security and innovation can be compatible.

DevSecOps is particularly critical for companies that utilize **Open Source Software (OSS)**. Nowadays, most businesses actively use some form of OSS, and this software may contain unknown vulnerabilities. By incorporating DevSecOps principles and checking for these in workflows on a weekly basis, it is possible to detect these vulnerabilities early on and quickly make corrections:

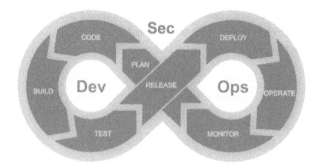

Figure 1.6 – DevSecOps emphasizes security within the DevOps life cycle

Overall, DevSecOps aims to incorporate security throughout the development-to-operations life cycle, facilitating more secure and efficient software development. This integrated approach allows for the coexistence of business and security.

Infrastructure as Code

Infrastructure as Code (IaC) is a methodology for managing and provisioning system infrastructure, including network configurations and server settings, through code. This is automated by specialized configuration management software. Traditionally, tasks such as server setup and network configuration were performed manually by humans, following procedural documents. This manual approach posed several problems, including the complexity and time-consuming nature of the tasks, a high risk of human error, and potential inconsistencies between procedural documents and the actual environment. These issues become particularly exacerbated in large-scale systems, making manual management unsustainable.

The adoption of IaC alleviates these challenges significantly. In an IaC environment, the state of the infrastructure is defined in code, which is then automatically applied by configuration management tools. This eliminates the need for tedious manual work and ensures high levels of reproducibility and consistency. Furthermore, since these tools handle the automated building and operation of the infrastructure, the processes become far more efficient and can be automated, allowing for more reliable and scalable system management.

Observability

Observability serves as a crucial component in managing modern software systems, especially within a DevOps framework that seeks to eliminate friction and enhance communication across organizational silos. Observability is often perceived as an evolved form of monitoring, but each serves its unique purpose.

In traditional monitoring, the focal point is to observe predefined elements of a system. Essentially, monitoring is rule-based. It involves setting predetermined metrics and benchmarks that, when breached, generate alerts. Monitoring is about keeping an eye on known issues—it is an approach that asks, "*Is my system working as expected?*" However, the scope of monitoring is typically limited to spotting where the problem has arisen. Not why it happened. This may only show the tip of the iceberg. It is going to take a long time to get the whole overview:

Figure 1.7 – The areas visible in the monitoring are just the tip of the iceberg

Observability, however, presents a more nuanced approach. It not only incorporates monitoring but goes beyond by offering a comprehensive insight into a system's overall health. In this model, it is less about watching for predefined issues and more about a deep-rooted understanding of what's happening inside your system. Observability invites you to look beyond the surface, enabling you to ask, "*What is the system's current state and why is it in that state?*"

Observability, conversely, relies on metrics, logs, and traces, often known as telemetry data, to provide a comprehensive and interrelated picture of system performance. In the realm of DevOps, monitoring is not just an isolated task for the operations team; it is a collective responsibility that involves both operations and development professionals. As systems have become more intricate, especially with the rise of cloud-native technologies and microservices, the importance of observability has been amplified. It offers a more holistic way of understanding how different components of a system interact, making it easier to spot bottlenecks, debug issues, and optimize performance:

Figure 1.8 – The three main pillars of observability are tracing, metrics, and logging

Traditional monitoring tools were often created to meet the requirements of particular organizational structures and needs, leading to a somewhat fragmented landscape of solutions. However, cloud-native environments require a more integrated approach. Observability tools are designed to provide this integration, offering a unified view of the system's state across diverse environments. This comprehensive understanding enables DevOps teams to streamline processes, mitigate risks, and more effectively contribute to their organizations' goals.

The next challenge

You now understand the basics of DevOps. This section has covered what it is and what it is not, and it also covered the DevOps culture. You have also reviewed the areas that make up DevOps, such as DevSecOps, IaC, and observability.

So, let's say you have either succeeded in DevOps or you are on the road to success and feeling good about it. What is your next challenge? That is, "*How can DevOps itself continue to be successful and grow within the organization?*"

Something like this could happen: "*We have a great DevOps team. It is not perfect yet, but the culture has changed a lot and we are getting great collaboration!*" Just when you think it is going to be perfect, the engineers who have grown are leaving in droves. They are looking for a better environment.

In many cases, the most skilled engineers on the team with the broadest knowledge will be doing the most complex operations behind the scenes. The most valuable engineers may end up doing those minor trivial tasks that they may not really want to do.

The fact is that most organizations do not have an environment in place for developers to work productively and happily. It could be the tools, or it could be the large number of non-essential tasks and too many tools.

Now, these are just examples, but to keep DevOps at its best and to grow it further, an organization needs to think about its developers over the long term. No matter if you are an individual contributor or a manager, you are also responsible for making sure that your team members feel good about their work so that you can have the best team possible. If you embody a good development experience, your team members will give you a good experience too.

Let's go back to the first question here: *"How can DevOps itself continue to be successful and grow within the organization?"*

One answer is to make developers happy—in other words, to create an environment where developers can do their best work. This is called developer experience.

Developer experience – A strategy for developer excellence

Developer experience, the term, goes beyond mere user experience and encompasses how developers within a DevOps team can be productive and satisfied with their work. This also works as an organizational strategy to make DevOps successful. If engineers are happy, there are no silos within the organization, and if the communication flows well, your DevOps will succeed. In that regard, GitHub is basically a platform for maximizing the developer experience, and Git is the means to that end:

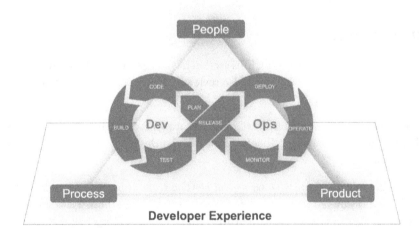

Figure 1.9 – Developer experience is a key strategy and foundation for successful DevOps

When you look at individual tools within the realm of DevOps, they may seem small. However, when viewed from the perspective of sustaining and achieving DevOps success, the connection between developer experience and how to use Git and GitHub becomes significantly stronger. Because that is where the essential developers' communication is taking place.

Developer experience is a strategy

The developer experience is essentially about creating an environment where developers can do their best work. If it is defined in the context of DevOps, the developer experience can be interpreted as a strategy for creating, growing, and maintaining the best DevOps culture as an organization. DevOps is all about culture. If your development team is dissatisfied, do not expect a thriving culture. Without a thriving culture, DevOps will not flourish.

According to GitHub, the concept of developer experience is represented by the following equation. This equation can be found in the article *Developer experience: what is it and why should you care?* (`https://github.blog/2023-06-08-developer-experience-what-is-it-and-why-should-you-care/`):

Figure 1.10 – GitHub's developer experience formula: how developer experience is represented on GitHub

Each element of the equation can be explained as follows.

- **Developer productivity**: This represents *efficiency* and *speed*. In other words, it reflects how efficiently and quickly a developer can complete tasks.

- **Developer impact**: This includes *impact, implementing code changes*, and *moving from idea to production*. It illustrates the extent of influence a developer has and how swiftly they can transform an idea into a real product or service.

- **Developer satisfaction**: This signifies achieving *high impact with low friction in the work environment, workflow*, and *tools*. It essentially measures how satisfied developers are with their work, how smooth their workflow is, and how effective the tools they use are.

Additionally, these elements are amplified by **collaboration**. The better the cooperation and communication within a team, the higher the productivity, impact, and satisfaction levels of the developers will be. Let's now explore how each of these elements works for the DevOps foundation.

Developer productivity

Boosting developer productivity presents a complex challenge. DevOps serves as a catalyst in smoothing organizational inefficiencies and ramping up the throughput of development teams.

Today's developers juggle a plethora of responsibilities: coding, code reviews, architectural planning, and, occasionally, infrastructure deployment. Some of these tasks occur at an organizational or team level, while others are individual endeavors. DevOps clearly emphasizes collaborative efforts, but it is crucial to also focus on amplifying individual performance—a dynamic that needs careful monitoring. The developer experience also covers this part.

Numerous businesses are currently struggling due to a lack of skilled engineers. However, consider this: in a 100-developer organization, if every developer could conserve 10 minutes each day, that would amount to nearly 17 extra hours. It is almost like adding two additional members.

However, measuring an individual engineer's productivity poses a challenging endeavor. Although quantifiable metrics such as the number of lines of code written or commits made may seem like reliable indicators, they often fail to provide a comprehensive view. Sometimes, a single well-thought-out line of code can be more valuable than 10 hastily composed ones. Tasks such as research and architectural design typically go unmeasured, further complicating the assessment. Relying exclusively on these narrow metrics could unintentionally cultivate a culture of micromanagement. When these metrics become evaluative benchmarks, there is a risk of promoting behaviors that emphasize noise over actual value. These metrics are covered in *Chapter 6*.

In the context of developer productivity, one perspective could also be to use AI in various development settings. The incorporation of AI into development workflows marks a transformative era. Tools such as GitHub Copilot serve as AI-powered coding assistants, supporting the code-writing process and thereby reducing both time and costs. Since the unveiling of ChatGPT in November 2022, AI's footprint in development has been expanding at an unprecedented rate.

Developer impact

In the realm of DevOps, the focus often centers on how teams influence customers and the overall business. Metrics in this area commonly begin with the product or customer, such as measuring the frequency of deployments. In contrast, developer experience zeroes in on the developer, emphasizing the impact they can make on both the code base and the ideas that eventually go into production.

Now, what is the difference between developer productivity and developer impact? For productivity, the measure of success would be to do more work in less time. On the other hand, it is very difficult to understand how to measure impact and what should be measured. Also, different teams have different definitions of impact.

The easiest thing to identify is something that can be quantified as a contribution to the eventual value of the product. For example, if a team is developing a new feature, the impact would be the number of users onboarded and the revenue generated from the new feature. Other examples can include downloads, requests, **Service-Level Agreements (SLAs)**, and so on.

I believe that engineer can become happy when a good DevOps culture is created. However, some may have thought, "*After all, it is all about money, isn't it?*" In fact, measuring the impact of developers is a matter of money.

If the engineer's impact is not measured correctly and the compensation is not appropriate to the engineer's market value, then the engineer's satisfaction with the job will go down. The scenario from here should not be hard to imagine. Many organizations are becoming more complex, and the impact is indirect, but even currently, not many companies are able to measure that indirect impact.

This ultimately aligns very strongly with the DevOps principle. After all, if the impact of the developer is to be measured, it is necessary to know the customer and the customer's state in the product and to create the product with the mindset of "*Create with the end in mind.*"

There are many possible metrics for developer impact, but the easiest to take include the time it takes for a developer to close a pull request and the span of time between receiving customer feedback and actually implementing it.

Developer satisfaction

Most importantly, developer productivity and its impact in this context is not intended for managers to manage and point out the productivity of individual developers, but rather to help developers accelerate their development in a more positive manner.

Organizations need to make sure that their engineers are satisfied through development and delivering value to customers by having the best environment, workflow, and tools in place.

While at the broader organizational level, in the context of overall optimization, it is necessary to ensure that the environment is broadly prepared to increase the productivity of all developers, at the narrower organizational level, it is necessary to develop strategies to increase developer productivity according to team, role, and experience. This includes minimizing lead times through DevOps practices that alleviate team bottlenecks while providing individual developers with the tools they need to perform optimally.

Collaboration

When it comes to fortifying developer experience for DevOps success, collaboration is the linchpin. It is not just about integrating the development team and infrastructure team and sharing some responsibility; it is about creating an environment where developers can thrive, contribute, and feel a sense of ownership and engagement. The ideal is a state of transparent collaboration where organizational silos are not just reduced but entirely eliminated. This free flow of ideas, best practices, and constructive criticism leads to a work environment that fuels developer experience.

For example, it is said that DevOps is not just about tools and practices; it is a culture, a philosophy, and a concept aimed at business and organizational success. In this context, Git and GitHub are often marginalized as *just tools* or *means of communication*. Such a viewpoint is sometimes true but often short-sighted. Adopting this perspective may limit your understanding to only individual aspects such as how to use GitHub Actions for CI/CD or how to use Git and Git branching strategies when you intend to learn Git and GitHub for DevOps.

When working in an organization or as a team, the team consists of individual contributors such as developers. Especially when developers work in a team or an organization, communication becomes extremely complex. The success of this dialogue is ultimately the key to enhancing the productivity of the team or individual. Git and GitHub are not just tools but platforms to share code, get feedback, integrate, and grow. The ability to communicate well in such environments is crucial to the success of DevOps.

One of the most powerful paradigms to facilitate this kind of collaboration is InnerSource. Borrowing from the open source collaboration model, InnerSource empowers developers within an organization to contribute to other teams' projects that they are not formally a part of. Just like in open source development, InnerSource encourages open communication, code sharing, and collective problem-solving, effectively reducing silos that often plague organizations.

The open source collaboration model itself serves as a testament to what can be achieved when barriers are broken down. By opening up a code base to the public, open source projects tap into a global community of developers, each bringing their unique perspective and expertise to the table. There's a mutualistic relationship between individual growth and collective progress, a symbiosis that DevOps teams should strive for internally. This open model brings with it the core tenets of transparent documentation, peer reviews, and a democratic approach to problem-solving, enriching the developer experience.

Transparency is key to this collaboration. When everyone from junior developers to team leads can access discussions, view code bases, and partake in decision-making, the walls between roles and departments start to crumble. This absence of silos naturally leads to quicker identification of issues, more efficient problem-solving, and a more unified vision.

Elements that amplify DevOps and developer experience

There are some ideas that can help make your DevOps more successful. It is the adoption of a decentralized contribution model and the concept of **Platform as a Product (PaaP)**. Yes, that's right: InnerSource and Platform Engineering. These will improve the developer experience.

InnerSource – Decentralizing the contribution model

InnerSource draws inspiration from the open source world, but it is designed to solve internal engineering challenges by applying open source practices within organizational boundaries. It allows cross-team collaboration and sharing of technical expertise, and most importantly, it aims to create a more transparent and inclusive culture. This approach closely aligns with DevOps philosophies of eradicating organizational silos and promoting a culture of collaboration and transparency. InnerSource also aims to create a cultural shift, a movement that is essential for boosting the developer experience.

Defining InnerSource

In essence, InnerSource is an approach to collaboration on software projects that happen within the confines of a single organization. The concept was popularized by companies such as PayPal to address silos and boundaries that often exist within large organizations. InnerSource encourages an open culture where anyone can contribute code to any project, and where processes and decision-making are transparent.

The four pillars of InnerSource

Let's delve deeper into the four foundational principles—*Openness*, *Transparency*, *Prioritized Mentorship*, and *Voluntary Code Contribution*:

- **Openness**: Openness removes barriers to entry for any engineer within the organization. Clear documentation, akin to README.md and CONTRIBUTING.md in open source repositories, makes projects easily discoverable and accessible. This level of openness enhances the developer experience by reducing friction, allowing engineers to easily switch contexts or teams. Even with the large number of microservices in a DevOps environment, for example, it is helpful to have this kind of documentation culture in place to facilitate collaboration.

- **Transparency**: When we talk about transparency in InnerSource, it is about openness in project decision-making. For instance, issue conversations and pull request reviews are done transparently, often documented, and easily accessible. This provides insights into why certain decisions were made, who made them, and the context around them. Transparency not only improves the project's quality but also significantly enhances the developer experience by creating a sense of ownership and involvement in the project.

- **Prioritized Mentorship**: In InnerSource, mentorship is not a sideline but a priority. The role of repository maintainer in InnerSource is also named Trusted Committer, taking into account the differences in activities related to internal restrictions.

  The role of **Trusted Committer** is crucial here. Trusted Committers are not just code contributors; they are advocates for the project, focusing on the quality and sustainability of the code as well as mentoring new contributors. They have a deep understanding of the repository and the organization, serving as bridges between the two. The Trusted Committer's mindset is one of openness, inclusivity, and a dedication to elevating others. This role is vital for maintaining a high level of developer experience by ensuring quality contributions and fostering a culture of continuous learning.

- **Voluntary Code Contribution**: The principle of Voluntary Code Contribution emphasizes that contributions are opt-in, leading to a culture where engineers feel a sense of ownership and responsibility toward the projects they engage with. It is a bottom-up approach, as opposed to top-down, allowing for a more organic, collaborative environment. The culture becomes self-aligned as engineers voluntarily engage, contributing to both the project and the organization's overall culture. Such a participatory environment significantly enhances the developer experience, offering opportunities for personal and career growth. It parallels the DevOps culture of collective ownership, where contributions are made to improve the system as a whole and not just individual components.

The complementary relationship between InnerSource and DevOps

By intertwining InnerSource with DevOps practices, organizations can create a holistic environment conducive to both customer-centric and developer-centric development. InnerSource offers tools to improve developer experience by focusing on cultural attributes—openness, transparency, mentorship, and voluntary contribution—that make engineers' daily work more engaging, meaningful, and satisfying.

Platform engineering

There are numerous cloud services available, especially from major public cloud providers. Particularly in the heart of the **Cloud Native Computing Foundation** (**CNCF**), the ecosystem around Kubernetes has dramatically evolved, encompassing over 1,000 projects. The proliferation of tools increases the cognitive load on development teams.

Platform engineering is an emerging approach in the tech industry that focuses on rationalizing developer experience and operational efficiency. It aims to implement reusable tools and self-service features, automate infrastructure operations, and thereby improve developer experience and productivity. In essence, the customers for platform teams are the development teams, and there is a particular emphasis on meeting their needs.

Fundamentally, platform engineering revolves around the construction and management of **Internal Developer Platforms** (**IDPs**). These platforms integrate various tools, services, and automated workflows to provide developers with self-service options. Essentially, they offer a *golden path* for developers, helping them navigate from development to deployment without getting bogged down by the complexities of infrastructure.

Platform teams often provide developer portals, such as Spotify's open source Backstage, reinforcing the idea of PaaP. The most important mindset is to consider the platform not merely as a tool but as a product aimed at internal developers—the customers.

The role of platform teams is multifaceted, from creating IDPs to establishing internal SLAs. They monitor team performance metrics and supervise a secure and efficient delivery process. An essential element in the toolbox of platform teams is IaC, coupled with robust CI/CD pipelines. These setups act as the central nervous system for code development and deployment, automating everything from setting up infrastructure to building, testing, and pushing code to various environments. This allows platform teams to focus on more valuable tasks and customer value rather than being bogged down by manual, error-prone operations.

At its core, platform engineering aims to reinforce the DevOps paradigm, improve developer experience, and fine-tune the operational aspects of software delivery. This approach aims to eliminate typical barriers that exist in large organizations and accelerate the journey from code to customer. In doing so, platform engineering fills a crucial gap in the modern DevOps landscape, ensuring not only operational efficiency but also fostering a culture of collaboration and shared responsibility.

Git – Where code collaborations begin

Managing code changes is a sophisticated challenge. Various team members continuously contribute to a unified code base that must remain functional at all times.

Git has transformed how software development teams work together. By being distributed and offering the ability to create branches, Git has become a vital asset in the DevOps toolbox. A **branch** is essentially a separate line of development, like a parallel universe, where you can work on new features or fix issues without affecting the main project. This enables teams to focus on multiple aspects simultaneously, making the development process more efficient and adaptable to rapid changes and rapid software delivery, a key requirement in a DevOps environment.

Git is more than just a tool for tracking changes in code—it is a catalyst for change within organizations. By providing a reliable way to collaborate, Git promotes better communication among teams. This aligns well with the overarching DevOps aim of breaking down barriers within organizations, thereby removing friction and making the process of building and deploying software more cohesive and streamlined.

Imagining the world without version control

Imagine a landscape where version control does not exist. Developers would struggle to manage changes in files, with no systematic way to track history. Every change would have to be documented manually, resulting in an endless sea of comments that obscure the real purpose of the code. In such a scenario, achieving rapid delivery as seen in DevOps would be nearly impossible. The lack of version control would introduce friction into collaboration processes. Also, file conflicts would become a common headache. Imagine working on a feature only to find that someone else has overwritten your file with their own changes—this kind of conflict could halt the development process. Without version control, you would also have to resort to strange naming conventions such as `v1`, `v2`, or `backup-foobar-20230930.py` just to maintain backups of older file versions.

The history of Git

Git, created by Linus Torvalds in 2005, reigns as the most popular **Distributed Version Control System (DVCS)** globally.

However, why was Git created? The simple answer lies in necessity. Linus Torvalds needed a **Version Control System** (**VCS**) that could do several things well. First, it had to be fast and efficient, letting developers work without slowdowns. Second, it needed to allow multiple developers to work on the same project without getting in each other's way. Third, it had to manage large code bases without a hitch. Beyond that, Torvalds wanted a system that would keep a reliable history of the entire project. He also sought the flexibility to support a nonlinear approach to development, one that could manage multiple branches and merge effectively. In response to these needs, Git was designed to be straightforward but also incredibly powerful in its capabilities.

What is a VCS?

So, what exactly is a VCS? A VCS is a system for monitoring code modifications throughout the SDLC. In projects with multiple contributors, tracking who altered what and when—along with any resultant bugs—is crucial. A VCS efficiently orchestrates this tracking process.

VCS technologies generally fall under two main categories—centralized and distributed:

- **Centralized**: In this setup, a single remote repository stores the project data, accessible to all team members. SVN and CVS are examples of this.

- **Distributed**: In a distributed model such as Git, every developer works with a local repository copy, applies changes there, and later syncs them with a central remote repository.

The following diagram shows how files are distributed and passed around when using Git. Git essentially allows you to have multiple remote repositories and a flexible distributed development structure, but typically, people create a single remote repository using a development platform such as GitHub, and developers often interact with the remote and local repositories:

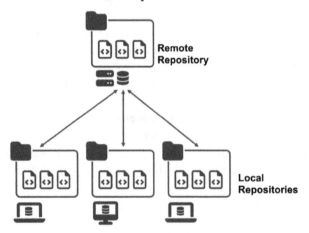

Figure 1.11 – Version control in Git is done in a distributed way,
allowing multiple people to collaborate simultaneously

The standout benefit of a distributed model such as Git is the autonomy it affords developers. This decentralized approach allows for more streamlined work, reducing the risk of code conflicts among contributors.

Security and integrity

For Git, ensuring the integrity of the source code is a top priority. In Git, each commit is assigned a unique hash value. This hash value is generated based on the contents of the committed code and its metadata. Therefore, if the code is altered, its hash value also changes, making it extremely difficult to tamper with history. Operations that affect branches or tags, such as merging or reverting, are also saved as part of the change history.

Adaptability

Git is highly adaptable and can accommodate a wide range of development workflows. Whether it is a small-scale project or an enterprise-level application, Git can adapt in various ways to track changes and facilitate collaboration among team members:

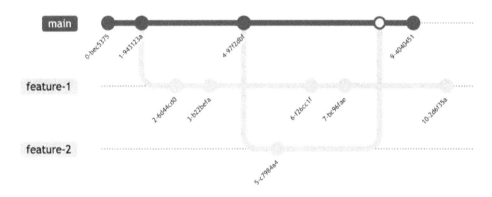

Figure 1.12 – Git manages code using branches, commits, and merges efficiently

Git is indispensable in modern development

Prior to Git's introduction, centralized systems such as SVN and CVS predominated. The rise of Git, however, has prompted a substantial shift toward distributed VCS options among both individual developers and organizations.

With the rise of cloud technology, the boundary between applications and infrastructure is blurring, and Git is no longer just for developers who write code but also for those who work on infrastructure.

In the world of DevOps, where seamless collaboration and communication are critical, Git acts as the backbone of the developer experience, supporting not just code management but also the workflow strategies that aim to improve collaboration.

In the realm of contemporary software development, version control is not optional—it is essential.

We will be covering all you need to know about Git in *Chapters 2* and *3*.

GitHub – The AI-powered developer platform

GitHub is the AI-powered developer platform to build, scale, and deliver secure software.

GitHub is often thought of as just a repository service, or sometimes as a repository service with attached CI/CD functionality. However, GitHub now offers a platform that covers the entire development life cycle, from writing applications to building and releasing. GitHub serves as the foundational platform for DevOps collaboration and automation. Through the lens of developer experience, it is the hub for InnerSource initiatives and houses code essential for platform engineering. Furthermore, this is empowered by AI. Whether you are writing code or reviewing it, GitHub's AI supports you in various scenarios.

The capabilities of GitHub can be divided into five main categories: **powered by AI**, **collaboration**, **productivity**, **security**, and **scale**. Let's look at each one in turn.

Powered by AI

The world is undergoing a transformation due to advancements in **Generative AI (GenAI)** powered by **Large Language Models (LLMs)**. This wave of change is impacting engineers as well, enabling developers to write code with the aid of AI. Not only can AI infer from existing code, but it can also translate natural language commands directly into code and even provide code explanations in natural language. When the AI revolution began, these functionalities were limited to simple code generation on editors. However, GitHub, as a platform, extends far beyond mere code generation, offering comprehensive support throughout the development life cycle.

GitHub Copilot – Your AI pair programmer

GitHub Copilot is one such AI-enabled service from GitHub. As of 2023, it stands out as a beloved service in Stack Overflow's developer survey. In the context of AI, what does productivity enhancement mean? It is evident that developers can write code faster and with improving accuracy. However, an engineer's job is not limited to coding; for example, research is also a critical element. Engineers frequently switch tasks from editor to browser or from editor to Slack, often multitasking. AI tools demonstrate their power not only in code generation but also in research and documentation tasks. These tools minimize engineers' need to multitask, allowing them to maintain flow. In other words, they assist in sustaining a **focus mode**.

The versatility of AI

AI does not just help with code; it assists with CI/CD configurations and the implementation of YAML files based on specific formats. Shell command implementations are also easy tasks for these AI tools. They are incredibly useful not just for application developers but also for platform engineers, boosting productivity on both individual and team levels.

The evolution of AI services is incredibly fast, and the latest information quickly becomes outdated. Therefore, this book will not delve into the specific services and features of GitHub Copilot, but *Chapter 8* will offer general advice on coding techniques using LLMs.

Collaboration

GitHub is a powerful platform designed to offer excellent collaboration experience for development teams.

The faster onboarding of new members is greatly facilitated by **GitHub Projects**, **GitHub Issues**, and **GitHub code search**. Specifically, GitHub Projects allows for the visual organization of tasks and their progress with Kanban, Roadmap, and Table views, while GitHub Issues clearly outlines specific problems or bugs. Furthermore, by labeling each issue, new members can quickly understand where to begin. This transparency and approach encourage organic collaboration. Additionally, GitHub code search allows for quick retrieval of past projects, discussions, and code, enabling new members to swiftly access existing knowledge and project history.

To ensure code quality, **pull requests** and **merge queues** are highly useful. Changes in the code are explicitly reviewed through pull requests. This process is made clearer and more efficient by the integrated view of review comments and code. Utilizing a merge queue ensures that reviewed changes are efficiently and safely merged into the production environment.

From a corporate culture standpoint, features such as pull requests, GitHub Issues, GitHub Discussions, and GitHub Enterprise's internal-type repositories effectively create *no silos through InnerSource* within an organization. By harnessing these features, there is a boost in transparent cross-team communication, evolving the development culture to become more open and bottom-up. It will also deter reinvention of the wheel. Embracing this InnerSource approach minimizes the redundancy of efforts and significantly adds to overall **employee satisfaction**.

Productivity

GitHub offers a variety of tools and features to be more productive.

First, GitHub has features for various automation flows and efficient DevOps. By using GitHub Actions, you can automate the process for CI/CD. This allows you to make stable changes to the product quickly while maintaining the quality of the code. GitHub Actions includes self-hosted runners and large runners, allowing you to adapt to restricted environments and high-specification machine requirements. This flexibility enables you to get software changes to market more quickly, contributing to improved **Time To Market (TTM)**.

Additionally, the Automation features of GitHub Projects improve work efficiency by automating a series of tasks. For example, you can automate the flow for issue items or the labeling of issues with built-in workflows. Of course, complex automation is also possible through GitHub Actions. GitHub Codespaces provides an online development environment, allowing you to code from anywhere. This enables development teams to collaborate efficiently remotely and significantly reduces the time and resources required to set up new members' environments. By using npm and GitHub Packages, package management becomes easier. By organizing dependencies, you can share and reuse code efficiently, speeding up the development cycle.

GitHub also offers GitHub Copilot, an AI pair programmer. It features a high-performance code completion function backed by the LLM, helping developers write code more efficiently. This improves code quality and dramatically increases developer productivity.

These features reduce the workload of developers who create the actual product's value, allowing them to focus on tasks that generate intrinsic value and contribute to **increased revenue growth**.

GitHub can streamline the development process and, by accelerating code quality and release speed, can more quickly bring to market products that meet customer needs, realizing **increased customer satisfaction**.

Security

GitHub is widely used as a platform for software development, but it also offers advanced experience in the realm of security. With the increasing importance of maintaining high-level security for applications, GitHub features become even more crucial.

For instance, the **Advanced Security** feature automatically detects vulnerabilities in the code, making it easier for companies and developers to reduce risks by addressing these issues promptly.

The platform also provides seamless management of security issues related to a project. Specifically, the **Security Overview** dashboard allows you to easily review all security warnings and settings, centralizing the management process.

In addition, GitHub's **secret scanning** feature automatically scans for any secrets or API keys mistakenly uploaded to GitHub, issuing warnings for them. For supported platforms, GitHub goes a step further by automatically revoking keys that are mistakenly uploaded to public repositories, and it can validate the activity status of a key. Simply detecting secrets often falls short of comprehensive DevSecOps requirements. This proactive approach not only identifies potential issues early but also significantly mitigates risks. Additionally, the **push protection** feature acts as a safeguard, preventing the accidental upload of sensitive information to GitHub.

The process of security policy creation and enforcement is also straightforward on GitHub. By setting up security policies and enforcing GitHub **Advanced Security** across repositories, it becomes easier for developers to maintain a secure coding environment. This leads to a more consistent set of security measures being applied throughout the organization or enterprise.

Lastly, let's talk about the supply chain. Nowadays, virtually every company is utilizing open source technology in some form. Many projects have hundreds of open source dependencies, which can potentially introduce security risks. What happens if a vulnerability is discovered in one of these dependencies? This is where Dependabot comes into play. It automatically identifies vulnerabilities in dependencies and proposes updates, helping to reduce security risks in the supply chain.

Overall, GitHub covers multiple aspects of security, offering developers and companies useful tools for creating and managing safer code in a shorter timeframe.

Scale

To scale a business, a scalable platform such as GitHub is essential. Trustworthiness, global access, and constant innovation are indispensable. With *more developers than any other platform*—over 100 million, to be exact—GitHub serves as a testament to its high level of trustworthiness and quality.

Next, as the **home of open source**, GitHub enables global reach. Developers and teams can share their code openly and collaborate with other developers around the world. The open approach of GitHub is the key to gaining access to diverse markets, engineers, and products.

Furthermore, the usage of GitHub not only allows users to develop their own software, but it also offers opportunities to leverage other projects and open source code to generate new ideas and solutions. This shows that GitHub is not merely a tool for code storage; it is a catalyst for innovation and collaboration on a global scale.

We will be covering all you need to know about GitHub in *Chapters 4* to *8*.

Summary

This chapter embarked on a journey to explore how DevOps revolutionizes the way we develop software. We talked about the importance of developer experience as a strategy for providing the best work environment in a DevOps team. We also delved into Git and GitHub, the backbone for collaboration in a DevOps setting.

Everything is connected and for a reason. The need for DevOps, the reasons for using Git and GitHub, and the importance of culture in shaping an organization's people, processes, and tools—all of these elements are interlinked. They collectively shape the form of a developer experience strategy, enabling developers in a DevOps team to perform at their best. What you will do will eventually come back to you, enriching you as a developer.

DevOps should be designed to allow for mistakes to occur in fast development. Each misstep is a step toward mastering DevOps, enhancing your skills, and making meaningful contributions to your team and organization. In essence, your journey through DevOps is a manifestation of everything we have discussed in this chapter.

So, let's take our newfound understanding and prepare to get hands-on. Up next, we will dive into the basic usage of Git, the VCS that serves as the backbone of DevOps culture and collaboration.

Further reading

- *The Secret Formula to Improve Developer Experience Revealed!*: `https://www.youtube.com/watch?v=mRqoVlhtVzA`

- *DevEx: What Actually Drives Productivity*: `https://queue.acm.org/detail.cfm?id=3595878`

- *Getting Started with GitHub for Startups*: `https://www.youtube.com/watch?v=K5zhNxnrVW8`

2

Getting Started with Git

Let's dive into learning Git. This chapter will touch upon the basic usage of Git. However, as explained in the previous chapter, this book is not just about introducing concepts and methods. It emphasizes communication and collaboration. Thus, while you will undoubtedly be able to master the basic usage of Git, you will also learn about the communication aspects behind it and how Git is used in team development.

In this chapter, we will first get a feel for the basics of Git by quickly going hands-on with the basics of file management and branching, and then we will cover how Git works. Then, you will get an understanding of the collaboration principles to be aware of when you are working with git as an engineer.

We will cover the following main topics in this chapter:

- Getting started with Git

- The anatomy of Git – A beginner-friendly explanation of how Git works

- Becoming a guru of Git communication

Technical requirements

The configuration instructions for proceeding with this section can be found in the following GitHub repository link. Please make sure Git and ssh tools are installed. For Windows users, it is recommended to use PowerShell. I also encourage you to get the most up-to-date information written about the different commands and environments:

```
https://github.com/PacktPublishing/DevOps-Unleashed-with-Git-and-
GitHub
```

Getting started with Git

In this section, we will proceed with how to use Git, assuming a scenario where you are working in an individual environment and simply building up a history.

Git basics – Begin with a hands-on experience

Before we delve into the details, let's start with some hands-on experience. It is likely easier to grasp the concept by trying it out rather than just only reading about it at first.

git config – Introduce yourself to Git

Now, there is something you need to do before you start a project. Introduce yourself to Git. To introduce yourself to Git, use the `git config` command:

```
$ git config --global user.name "John Doe"
$ git config --global user.email "john@example.com"
```

`git config` is a command used to set Git configurations at the levels of system, user, and repository. The level `system` applies to all users and all repositories. The level `global` applies to all repositories of a specific user. The level `local` applies only to a single repository.

To verify that your introduction has been registered, you can check with the `git congif --list` command:

```
$ git config --list
user.name=Your Name
user.email=Your Email
```

Now, the first task is done! Let's quickly move on to the basic operations of Git.

git init – Where your code journey begins

Just as every great journey has its origin, in the world of Git, your code's voyage starts with the `git init` command. The command is used to initialize a new Git repository and start tracking existing directories. When you run the command, it sets up a `.git` directory packed with all the goodies you need for version control. With that out of the way, you are all set to dive into Git's range of commands and start tracking and updating your project:

```
# Make a directory
$ mkdir handson-repo
# Change the current working directory
$ cd handson-repo/
$ git init
```

> **Important note**
>
> Another way is to pass a directory name as an argument, such as `git init handson-repo`; this will create the directory, so you do not need to run the `mkdir` command.

Now that the .git/ directory has been created, changes to files are saved under the .git/ directory, but Git does not automatically save files in the same way recent Microsoft Office products do.

In Git, saving is completed by executing the git add command, which consciously selects files to be saved from among those that have been edited, added, or deleted, and the git commit command, which registers those changes.

Next, let's add some code to the repository.

git add – Preparing your code for the spotlight

The git add command is your bridge between making changes in your working directory and getting them ready to be permanently stored in your Git repository. When you make changes to your files, Git recognizes that these files have been changed, but these changes are not automatically slated to become a part of the history. This is where git add steps in. This is the process of saving an office document, so to speak.

First, create a new file in your handson-repo directory:

```
# Making a README.md file
$ echo "# README" > README.md
```

The git status command shows the current state of your repository, showing which files have changes that are tracked and which ones are untracked. When you see the Untracked files message, it is Git's way of informing you that there is a file it has not been told to keep an eye on just yet. In our example, the README.md file is new to Git and is not registered; hence, it is labeled as untracked:

```
# Checking how Git recognizes the new file
$ git status
On branch main

No commits yet

Untracked files:
  (use "git add <file>..." to include in what will be committed)
    README.md
```

Newly added files are part of your project, but they have not been tracked by Git. To move them from the untracked status to a tracked status, you use the git add command:

```
$ git add README.md
$ git status
On branch main

No commits yet
```

```
Changes to be committed:
  (use "git rm --cached <file>..." to unstage)
    new file:    README.md
```

Now Git recognizes README.md as a new file, and it is now tracked. The state targeted for saving by the git add command is called **staged**. You might also hear the term **index** being used interchangeably with staging. Before files or changes are staged, they reside in an area often referred to as the **workspace**. This is essentially the environment where you are actively making changes to your files. Some might also refer to this area as the **worktree**. In short, in this process, you have staged the README.md file from worktree using the git add command.

> **Important note**
> git add has other options as well. You can include everything with git add ., include multiple files such as git add file1.md file2.md file3.md, or use a wildcard such as git add *.md to add all files with the .md extension.

Everything's in place; it is time to log your modifications into history.

git commit – Locking in your development progress

The git commit command records the changes you have staged with git add into the repository's history. This allows you to track changes over time.

Imagine you are playing a challenging video game. As you progress, you will often save your game to lock in your achievements. Similarly, when developing software, you will save your work using git commit. Each commit is a save point to which you can return later if needed.

To commit changes, you can typically do the following:

```
$ git commit -m "Initial commit with README.md"
```

Here, the -m flag is followed by a short, descriptive message that captures the essence of the changes you have made. Writing good commit messages is an art, as it aids in understanding the history and intent of changes.

Now, let's use the git status command again to see if all the changes in the current working directory have been saved:

```
$ git status
On branch main
nothing to commit, working tree clean
```

If the message nothing to commit appears, your changes have been incorporated.

Well, that is it; it is very easy to save a file in Git. Let's review it here. The edit, stage, and commit flow is still the same no matter how complex your project is:

1. **Edit files**: Make necessary changes to your files. For example, in this figure, two existing files have been edited for deletions and modifications, and another file has been added:

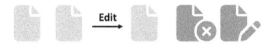

Figure 2.1 – Edit files

2. **Stage changes**: Decide which files or specific changes you would like to commit and stage them. For example, in this figure, out of the three edits, only the deletions and modifications are staged:

Figure 2.2 – Stage changes

3. **Commit changes**: Once satisfied with the staged changes, perform a commit to register them. Remember that every commit generates a unique commit ID:

Figure 2.3 – Commit changes

git log – Walking through the commit tree

Once you have made a few commits, you might want to look back and see the history of changes made in the repository. This is where the `git log` command comes in handy. The command displays a list of commits made in a repository in reverse chronological order, meaning the most recent commit is displayed first.

To try this out, use the following command:

```
$ git log
commit a16e562c4cb1e4cc014220ec62f1182b3928935c (HEAD -> main)
Author: John Doe <john@example.com>
Date:   Thu Sep 28 16:30:00 2023 +0900
    Initial commit with README.md
```

This will display a list of all commits, each with the following:

- **A distinct SHA-1 identifier**: This acts as a signature for the commit and can be employed in various Git commands to refer to that specific commit

- **Committer's details**: Showcases the name and email of the individual who executed the commit

- **Timestamp of the commit**: Displays when the commit was made

- **Commit message**: A brief and informative note capturing the essence of the alterations in the commit

In addition to the basic `git log` command, there are numerous options that allow you to tailor the output to your needs:

- `git log -p`: This option shows the difference (i.e., the patch) introduced at each commit

- `git log --stat`: This provides some abbreviated stats for each commit

- `git log --oneline`: This gives a more compact output, displaying each commit as a single line

- `git log --graph`: This visualizes the branch and merge history in an ASCII graph layout

- `git log --author="John Doe"`: This filters the commits to show only those made by a specific individual (in this case, "John Doe")

For example, it can also improve the outlook as follows:

```
$ git log --graph --pretty=format:'%x09 %h %ar ("%an") %s'
```

The output is as shown in the following screenshot:

```
*              4239830ee 5 days ago by "George Hattori" Merge pull request #617
|\
| *            939861113 7 days ago by "Jenny Park" Adding video
|/
*              e1390c6ff 8 days ago by "John Doe" Merge pull request #616
|\
| *            d94d94a0a 9 days ago by "Jenny Park" Updating banner
* |            c5eb9ceff 9 days ago by "John Doe" Merge pull request #615
|\ \
| |/
|/|
| *            563f44ee5 9 days ago by "John Doe" Update 2023 meetup bannar
| *            605b8ae57 9 days ago by "Jenny Park" Adding October event page
|/
*              5e8cc44d4 9 days ago by "George Hattori" Merge pull request #623
```

Figure 2.4 – Prettified git log

Now let's try the `git log` command with you at hand. First, update the `README.md` file and create a new `CONTRIBUTING.md` file:

```
$ echo "# CONTRIBUTING" > CONTRIBUTING.md
$ echo "# README\n\nWelcome to the project" > README.md
$ git add .
$ git commit -m "Set up the repository base documentation"
```

Once done, add a sample Python code:

```
$ echo "print('Hello World')" > main.py
$ git add .
$ git commit -m "Add main.py"
```

When it is confirmed in the log that it is properly logged, it is done:

```
$ git log --oneline
344a02a (HEAD -> main) Add main.py
b641640 Set up the repository base documentation
a16e562 Initial commit with README.md
```

In essence, the `git log` command is a vital tool for any developer. It helps you easily navigate through your code's history, whether you are searching for a specific change or merely revisiting previous work.

Now that we have reviewed what we have learned so far in examining the functionality of `git log`.

Working with branches – The cornerstone of collaboration

While the previous sections provide you with a robust understanding of how to initialize and manage a Git repository, the concept of branching takes this to a new level. While accumulating `git commit` only creates a liner history, `git branch` can be used to create a history of the parallel environment. Then, you can merge those multiple environments into one, which enables multiple people to work on them, giving you the flexibility to experiment with new features, bug fixes, or even totally *avant-garde* ideas without affecting the main codebase.

git branch – Understanding the basics of Git branch

When you initialize a Git repository, it automatically creates a default branch, usually called `main` (formerly known as master). When you run the `git branch` command, it will show the list of all branches in your repository, with the current branch highlighted:

```
$ git branch
* main
```

It is intuitive to think of a linear main branch like the following figure:

Figure 2.5 – git branch

You can create a new branch with the `git branch <branch name>` command. This command creates a new command from the current branch:

```
# Create a new branch named 'feature/new-feature'
$ git branch feature/new-feature
```

If you create a new branch, you can build a line with a different history and add commits to that branch, as shown here:

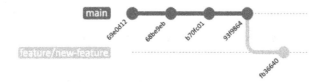

Figure 2.6 – Creating a new branch

Branch naming conventions are important for communication. A commonly used standard is to prefix the branch name with `feature/`, `bugfix/`, or `hotfix/`, followed by a brief description. This makes it easier for anyone to understand the purpose of the branch at a glance.

You can also create a branch from a specific branch or commit that is different from the one you are currently on. This is particularly useful when you need to create a feature or bugfix branch that should originate from a designated development or staging branch rather than from your current working branch:

```
# Create a branch from a specific branch
$ git branch <new-branch-name> <base-branch-name>
# Create a branch from a specific commit
$ git branch <new-branch-name> <commit-hash>
```

git checkout/git switch – Switching between branches

In your daily workflow, you will often need to switch from one branch to another, especially when working on multiple features or fixing bugs. When you have started work on multiple branches, gaining an awareness of the branch you are actively on becomes pivotal. In Git, the term **HEAD** refers to the tip of the branch you are actively working with.

Changing your current working branch is known as checking out a branch. The git checkout command facilitates this:

```
# Switch to 'feature/new-feature' branch
$ git checkout feature/new-feature
```

This operation switches the HEAD position, the tip of the branch, to a branch called feature/new-feature:

Figure 2.7 – Checking out a branch

The git checkout command results in the current position being the tip commit on the feature/new-feature branch, that is HEAD.

Recent versions of Git also offer the git switch command, which provides a more intuitive way to switch branches:

```
# Switch to 'feature/new-feature' branch
$ git switch feature/new-feature
```

Sometimes, you may find it efficient to create a new branch and switch to it immediately. Git provides a shorthand command for this, combining the functionality of git branch and git checkout or git switch.

To create a new branch and switch to it in one step, you can use the git checkout -b command:

```
# Create and switch to a new branch
$ git checkout -b feature/another-new-feature
```

This is equivalent to running the following:

```
$ git branch feature/another-new-feature
$ git checkout feature/another-new-feature
```

In recent versions of Git, you can achieve the same with git switch by using the -c option:

```
# Create and switch to a new branch
$ git switch -c feature/another-new-feature
```

Now you can not only save changes linearly with `git commit`, but also create parallel worlds with `git branch`, and move back and forth between parallel worlds freely with `git checkout`. Now, it is time to merge the two worlds.

git merge <Branch Name> – Merging branches

Once you have made changes in a branch and tested them thoroughly, you may want to integrate those changes back into the main branch or another branch. This operation is known as **merging**:

```
# First, switch to the branch you want to merge into
$ git checkout main
# Now, merge your feature branch
$ git merge feature/new-feature
```

Merging allows you to merge lines with different histories, as shown in the following figure:

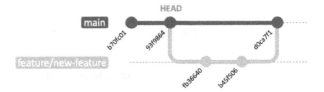

Figure 2.8 – Merging a branch

Merging can be a straightforward operation, but it can also get complicated if there are conflicts between the branches. In such cases, Git will require manual intervention to resolve the conflicts. Conflict resolution will be addressed in the next chapter.

git branch –d – Deleting a Branch

Once a branch has been successfully merged and is no longer needed, it can be deleted to keep the repository clean:

```
# Delete a local branch
$ git branch -d feature/new-feature
```

So, by this point in the hands-on tutorial, you should have understood the basics of Git and gotten a feel for it. You should now be aware of what is happening in your project and have learned how to use basic commands.

On the other hand, there is still a lot to learn for you to flexibly collaborate within a team. Going forward, you will learn those methods, but it is also necessary to understand how Git actually works in order to fundamentally understand those operations.

Knowing the mechanisms of Git deepens your understanding of what the commands are fundamentally doing, not only enhancing your proficiency in Git operations but also improving your communication in Git and GitHub and, consequently, in DevOps.

Let's take a look at how Git works.

The anatomy of Git – A beginner-friendly explanation of how Git works

Git is incredibly powerful, especially as projects become more complex. Up until now, our focus was on a straightforward history. However, where Git really shines is in its ability to handle large projects with a large number of contributors and manage the dynamically evolving code within a team seamlessly. We have come this far intuitively, working with Git operations as commands work. It is time to get down to the nitty-gritty. While it is helpful to have an intuitive feel for Git, by understanding how Git operates behind the scenes, we can harness its full potential.

The file lifecycle in Git

In Git, we learned in the previous section that saving changes is a two-step action, staging and committing, but Git actually handles files in four states.

Every file in your project can be in one of four states:

- **Untracked**: Files that are present in your directory but have not been added to Git's control. They are new files or files that Git has been explicitly told to ignore.
- **Unmodified**: These are files that have previously been added to Git and have not experienced any changes since the last commit. They sit quietly, monitored by Git but not requiring any immediate action. In other words, they are **committed**.
- **Modified**: Once you make changes to a tracked file, Git flags it as modified. At this point, the file has been altered since the last commit but has not been prepared (or staged) for the next commit.
- **Staged**: After modification, files can be staged, signaling to Git that they are ready for the next commit. The `git add` command stages your modifications. While these changes have been earmarked, they are not saved in the repository until you commit.

The following figure shows these status transitions. Files go back and forth between these states:

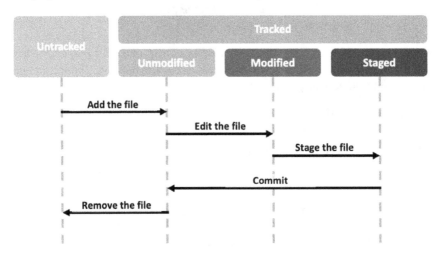

Figure 2.9 – Four types of the file status of Git

When you create or introduce new files to your project, they begin as **untracked**. By adding these files using the git add command, they transition to the **unmodified** status, signifying that they are now under Git's surveillance.

Subsequent changes to these tracked files will place them in the **modified** status. Before they can be committed, these changes need to be staged, moving the file to the **staged** status. Staging gives you a preview of the changes you are about to commit. Think of it as putting items in a box (staging area), and prepping them for shipment (commit). You decide which items (or changes) go into that box.

After staging, you can commit these changes using the git commit command. When you stage changes, especially through interfaces such as Visual Studio Code, it is typically as simple as clicking a button. Once you are satisfied with the staged changes, you commit them, permanently saving them to your project history.

Upon committing, these files revert to the **unmodified** status, waiting for future edits or changes. In other words, at this stage, the status can be said to have become **committed**. In Git, every commit you make records the current state of your project at that specific point in time. This recording mechanism is foundational to Git's capabilities, ensuring that every change is documented. This allows developers to navigate back to any specific commit, providing the flexibility to review or revert to previous versions as required.

Additionally, if a tracked file is removed from the directory, Git recognizes it as **untracked** until it is explicitly deleted from the repository.

This lifecycle provides developers with precise control over their project changes, allowing for strategic commits and ensuring clear, organized version histories.

Behind the scenes – Git's architecture

First and foremost, what is Git really? At its core, Git is a **key-value store**. Git's efficiency is one of its most striking features. By organizing data in this key-value structure, it swiftly retrieves the content of any commit using its unique key, the SHA-1 hash. This makes tasks such as branching and merging exceptionally fast. Let's delve further into these underlying workings. At the heart of every Git repository is the .git directory. This concealed directory contains the history of your code–commits, branches, configuration files, and more. You may recall from the initial stages of your Git journey, during the git init command section, that a .git directory is created.

A deeper dive – Exploring the .git directory

By running the ls command, you can see several sub-directory and configuration files. Among these, the objects directory is most relevant to our current discussion. This is the heart of Git's key-value store, housing the blobs (actual file content), tree objects (directory structures), and commits:

```
$ ls .git
COMMIT_EDITMSG   hooks     objects
HEAD             index     refs
config           info
description      logs
```

Now, let's peek into the objects folder. This is where the key-value store resides. The names of the folders, which are two alphanumeric characters, represent the first two characters of the commit ID:

```
$ ls .git/objects
2f    7e    b1    e3    info
34    a1    b6    e6    pack
4b    af    df    ea
```

Each commit or data piece in Git is uniquely identified by a key, the SHA-1 hash. This hash, a string of 40 alphanumeric characters, is something like b641640413035d84b272600d3419cad3b0352d70. This unique identifier for each commit is generated by Git based on the commit's content. These IDs you see include what you see when you run the git log command and match the changes you have made so far:

```
$ git log
commit 344a02a99ce836b696c4eee0ee747c1055ab846b (HEAD -> main)
Author: John Doe <john@example.com>
Date:    Thu Sep 28 18:41:41 2023 +0900

    Add main.py


commit b641640413035d84b272600d3419cad3b0352d70
Author: John Doe <john@example.com>
```

```
Date:    Thu Sep 28 18:41:18 2023 +0900

    Set up the repository base documentation

commit a16e562c4cb1e4cc014220ec62f1182b3928935c
Author: John Doe <john@example.com>
Date:    Thu Sep 28 16:35:31 2023 +0900

    Initial commit with README.md
```

If we open the b6 directory, we will recognize the structure of the key-value store, with the commit ID serving as the file name or the key. But what lies within these files? To find out, let's next take a peek inside with the `git cat-file` command.

> **Important note**
>
> In the case of this book, the first two characters of Hash are **b6**, but a different list should be displayed in your environment. Let's choose an appropriate hash and run the **ls** command:
>
> ```
> $ ls .git/objects/b6/
> 41640413035d84b272600d3419cad3b0352d70
> ```

git cat-file – Dissecting the inner workings

To inspect the contents of the value in the key-value store, the `git cat-file` command can be used. When passing the first seven letters of the commit ID as an argument, we get results showcasing the tree and parent, which refers to the ID of the parent commit:

```
# Passing the first seven letters of the Commit Id as an argument
$ git cat-file -p b641640
tree af4fca92a8fbe20ab911b8c0339ed6610b089e73
parent a16e562c4cb1e4cc014220ec62f1182b3928935c
author John Doe <john@example.com> 1695894078 +0900
committer John Doe <john@example.com> 1695894078 +0900

Set up the repository base documentation
```

> **Important note**
>
> When dealing with hashes in Git commands, it is not necessary to pass the 40 characters as they are; they can be omitted. In this sample case, the first seven letters are passed as an argument, but a minimum requirement is four letters. Although it depends on the size of the project, it is relatively safe to specify at least seven characters to avoid key collisions.

In Git, there are four main objects that are managed and used:

- `commit` object: Has a reference to the tree object

- `tree` object: Has references to blob and/or other tree objects

- `blob` object: Has the data (like file content)

- `tag` object: Has information about the annotated tag

The commit references are structured to embed the Id of the `parent` commit in the value. But where did the actual commit file go? In the output, we see a `tree` labeled Id as well as `parent`. It seems that this tree also has a SHA-1 hash, so let's examine its value using the `git cat-file` command:

```
# Passing the first seven letters of the Tree Id as an argument
$ git cat-file -p af4fca9
100644 blob b1b003a2...a277 CONTRIBUTING.md
100644 blob ea90ab4d...79ca README.md
100644 blob e69de29b...5391 main.py
```

Upon invoking the `git cat-file` command for the Id tagged with `tree`, we get a result showcasing a file type named `blob`. Let's reference the blob ID for README.md using the `git cat-file` command. This reveals the file content, indicating that data stored as the blob type within the key-value store represents the actual file. These observations give us a clearer picture of Git's architecture:

```
$ git cat-file -p ea90ab4
# README

Welcome to the project
```

Now you know how Git stores value in the key-value store. You should understand that Git is not a black box; it is a system that manages history as value, keyed by a SHA-1 hash.

git show – Easier to use in your daily activities

Previously, we used the `git cat-file` command to learn how Git works, but there is a similar command, `git show`. Both are powerful Git commands, but they serve somewhat different purposes and provide different outputs. `git cat-file` is a low-level utility that is primarily designed to inspect Git objects, such as blobs, trees, commits, and tags. It can display the object's type, its size, and even its raw content. On the other hand, `git show` is more user-friendly in nature; this command provides a readable view of various types of Git objects. By default, it showcases the log message and textual difference for a commit. However, it is versatile enough to display other object types, such as blobs, trees, and tags, in an easy-to-read format:

```
$ git show b641640
commit b641640413035d84b272600d3419cad3b0352d70
Author: John Doe <john@example.com>
```

```
Date:    Thu Sep 28 18:41:18 2023 +0900

    Set up the repository base documentation

diff --git a/CONTRIBUTING.md b/CONTRIBUTING.md
new file mode 100644
index 0000000..b1b003a
--- /dev/null
+++ b/CONTRIBUTING.md
@@ -0,0 +1 @@
+"# CONTRIBUTING"
diff --git a/README.md b/README.md
index 7e59600..ea90ab4 100644
--- a/README.md
+++ b/README.md
@@ -1 +1,3 @@
 # README
+
+Welcome to the project
diff --git a/main.py b/main.py
new file mode 100644
```

If you are a developer or a Git user wanting to see the changes introduced by a commit or view the content of a file at a particular revision, `git show` is the more intuitive choice. In contrast, `git cat-file` dives deeper into the internal structure of Git, allowing users to directly interact with and inspect the raw Git objects. For someone deeply involved in the inner workings of Git or developing tools that interface with Git's core system, `git cat-file` provides a granular level of detail. However, for the majority of everyday tasks and for those who are just starting their journey with Git and GitHub, `git show` offers a more user-friendly way to view changes and content without the need to delve into the intricacies of Git's object database.

Git tree structure

Now, we know that Git is essentially a key-value store. Next, let's look at how each object is connected and managed in a consistent manner as historical data. In the previous section, we saw the keywords `tree` and `parent`, but what are they really? We will now explore the relationship between commits and objects to which those keywords link to.

Commit, tree, and blob

In Git, the concept of a tree structure plays a vital role in maintaining the state of the repository. Each commit is not just a set of changes.

Explanation of each keyword:

- **Commit**: Every commit in Git is uniquely identified by an SHA-1 hash. It carries with it a snapshot of the repository's state by referencing a tree object.

- **Tree**: Trees in Git act like directories. They can reference other trees (subdirectories) and blobs (files). Each tree has its distinct SHA-1 hash. The primary tree, representing the repository's top-tier directory, is the root tree.

- **Blob**: A blob represents the content of a file in the repository. Like commits and trees, each blob has its unique SHA-1 hash.

Parent and child

The lineage and progression of a repository's history are captured through the parent-child relationships between commits.

Most commits in Git reference a single parent commit, representing the direct predecessor in the repository's timeline.

As explained in the previous page, a commit holds the ID of its parent commit, establishing a referential relationship. In many visual representations of commits, arrows often depict this relationship. It is worth noting that the direction of these arrows often appears inverse to the sequence of commits. Each commit has the relationship shown in the figure.

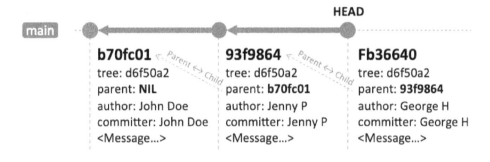

Figure 2.10 – Git commit relation

> **Important note**
> Commits can sometimes have multiple parents, especially when two branches merge. This dual parentage signifies the joining of two separate lines of development.

How does Git store trees and blobs?

The marvel of Git's efficiency is deeply rooted in how it stores its trees and blobs.

Let's illustrate the relationship between each of these:

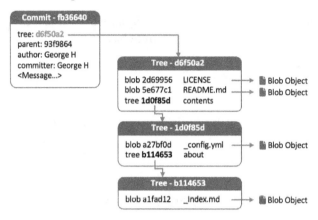

Figure 2.11 – Git tree structure

Every commit in Git corresponds to a tree, representing the state of the repository's files and directories at that specific moment. For a deeper dive, consider the diagram presented. The commit labeled fb36640 holds a reference to the tree d6f50a2. This tree mirrors the repository's root directory during that commit.

As we traverse this tree (d6f50a2), we encounter various pointers. Some of these lead us to blobs, while others to trees. A blob, such as 2d69956, corresponds to a file—in this case, LICENSE. Meanwhile, a tree, such as 1d0f85d, stands for a subdirectory named contents. This subdirectory tree can further point to its own set of blobs and trees.

This intricate linkage crafts a hierarchy reminiscent of a traditional filesystem. Each layer of this hierarchy denotes different files and directories in your repository. Central to Git's design philosophy is efficiency. By structuring its data in this hierarchical manner, Git can swiftly track changes across files and directories without redundant storage. For instance, unchanged files across commits point to the same blob, optimizing storage and retrieval:

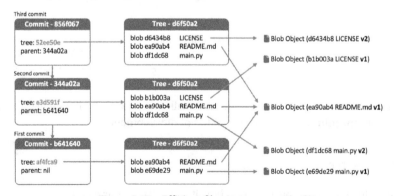

Figure 2.12 – Efficient file management in Git

Understanding Git's tree structure and how it relates to blobs and commits is fundamental for any developer. It is not just about using Git commands; it is about appreciating the ingenious architecture beneath, ensuring that your code's history is efficiently and accurately preserved. As you progress in your Git journey, this knowledge will empower you to utilize Git's capabilities to their fullest.

Up to this point, you have learned that Git recognizes the state of each file and registers it in a key-value store. You also learned that this key-value store has a tree structure with parent-child relationships. If you peek into the `.git/` directory, you will see that it has a very simple structure, and it is thanks to this simplicity that Git can manage complex projects.

If you have understood all this, then you are well-prepared for your journey to mastering Git. While this book cannot cover every Git command, understanding these basics will ensure you will be okay even if you encounter unfamiliar Git commands in the future. You have the technical foundation to understand them.

Now, let's learn one more thing to conclude your preparation for your Git journey in this chapter. That is the mindset for the journey with Git. This mindset is not only for using Git but is directly related to collaboration in DevOps as well.

Becoming a guru of Git communication

Let's hit the pause button for a moment. While most resources might hurry you along to cover essential Git commands, conflict resolutions, merge types, and Git workflows, we are taking a breather to focus on the core of the matter.

So, why was Git even developed in the first place? At its essence, Git was created to streamline communication in complex development projects. Since this book aims to elevate your role within a DevOps team, understanding the communicative power of Git is key. After all, DevOps is not just about technology; it is about improving collaboration, breaking down silos, and facilitating smoother workflows.

As you navigate through Git commands and repositories, bear in mind that you are not just sharing code; you are also communicating with your team. Your commits, pull requests, and merges should be thought of as dialogues in a broader conversation aimed at creating something magnificent.

So, as you proceed with learning Git, focus on honing your mindset. A well-tuned approach to Git goes beyond mere commands; it makes you an invaluable team player, aligned with the overarching objectives of your DevOps environment.

Remember: haste makes waste. Take the time to understand the Git essentials deeply, and you will not only be a proficient coder but also an exceptional collaborator in your DevOps team.

git commit – Revisiting the most important command

If you ask me, the most important command in Git is git commit. If it is perfect, everything else is secondary. This command delineates the scope of all your coding activities and solidifies your output, determining the quality of your work. A commit serves as a unit of communication. Getting this unit of communication wrong can confuse all subsequent communication.

Have you ever built something using LEGO bricks? The essence of LEGO is not only just about following instructions but also about sparking creativity and building something original. Sometimes, you collaborate with friends, like building a castle together. Everyone might have a role: someone makes the gate, another the foundation, and someone else the tower. Your success lies in building a magnificent castle as a team. But consider this: even if you individually craft a brilliant part, it may not be appreciated if it does not align with others' visions or does not fit with the pieces they have created. It is essential to ensure that the parts match in size and to frequently verify this compatibility. In other words, you need to continually adjust the way and parts of the build while communicating at the right times. As kids, you might have made strange creations without perfect communication, and while it might have been praised for its creativity, the situation is different now. If you are reading this book, you likely work in an organization, creating some product, possibly earning a salary, and holding responsibility. This means these considerations are not just nice to have; they are a must.

Let's transition back to coding. When you code within a team, not only you but all team members, past and present, will review your code and actions in Git. Even when you code alone, your future self and past self are your collaborators. Many times, I have struggled to understand my old code or recall what I was trying to accomplish by running git log command and still have no idea. How well Git operations are managed will be reflected in the code management and production process. It would be better to have a principle that you can remember when using Git.

Control quality and quantity to be a good communicator

There are plenty of good practices out there on how to use Git. However, many things can be categorized somewhere in the four boxes of the following diagram:

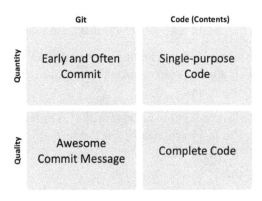

Figure 2.13 – Excellence in git commit

Early and often commit – Embracing a core principle for DevOps success

The modern software development landscape has changed drastically over the past few decades. Traditional Waterfall have made way for Agile methodologies, and this has further evolved into the DevOps culture that many organizations now embrace. Central to this evolution is the notion of **Continuous Integration and Continuous Delivery (CI/CD)**. One of the foundational practices supporting this methodology is the idea of committing code early and often. In this section, we will delve into the importance of this practice, especially in the context of Git and GitHub for DevOps.

The traditional paradigm

In the days of yore, developers would often spend days or even weeks working on a feature or a fix, only to merge their changes into the main branch at the end. This would often lead to merge conflicts, bugs, and a lot of manual intervention to rectify issues. This model was not scalable and was antithetical to the fast-paced, customer-centric demands of today's tech environment.

The shift to early commits

Committing early means that as soon as you have a logical chunk of work completed, you commit it. This does not necessarily mean the entire feature is done, but maybe just a function or a class. Why is this beneficial?

- **Smaller changes**: Smaller changes are easier to review. They are more digestible, making the code review process more efficient and effective.

- **Reduced merge conflicts**: By committing and pushing your changes early, you reduce the chances of running into a merge conflict since you are frequently syncing your branch with the main branch.

- **Faster feedback loop**: The sooner you commit and push your changes, the sooner automated tests can run, and the sooner you can get feedback on your code. This allows for quicker iterations and faster delivery of features and fixes.

The benefit of often commits

Committing often goes hand-in-hand with committing early. The more frequently you commit, the more the following points are kept to:

- **Easier to pinpoint issues**: If a bug arises, it is much simpler to identify the cause when you are sifting through a small commit rather than a massive one.

- **Easier to roll back**: If a commit causes an unforeseen issue, rolling back to a previous stable state is straightforward. This safety net can be a lifesaver in production environments.

Awesome commit message – Crafting clear, informative, and concise narratives for your code

In the realm of software development, the code we write is not merely a set of instructions for machines; it is also a form of communication with our peers. However, while code shows the *how*, it is the commit message that illuminates the *why*. A well-crafted commit message is a beacon for fellow developers, providing context, clarity, and a historical record of code changes.

The purpose of commit messages

At its core, a commit message serves several key functions:

- **Historical record**: It offers a chronological account of changes, allowing developers to understand the evolution of a codebase.

- **Context**: It provides reasoning for changes, granting insights that the code alone might not convey.

- **Documentation**: Beyond inline comments and external documentation, commit messages act as a form of documentation that can explain decisions and trade-offs.

Characteristics of an awesome commit message

What differentiates a good commit message from an awesome one? Here are the hallmarks of an exceptional commit message:

- **Concise subject line**: Begin with a brief and direct subject line, ideally under 50 characters, capturing the essence of the commit.

- **Detailed body**: If the change warrants further explanation, use the body to provide context, describe the problem the commit solves, or explain the chosen solution. Keep lines to 72 characters or fewer to maintain readability. You can write this by using the `git commit -m "subject-line" -m "description-body"` command.

- **Use the active voice**: Phrases such as "*Add feature*" or "*Fix bug*" are clearer and more direct than "*Added feature*" or "*Fixed bug.*"

- **Reference issues**: If the commit relates to a specific issue or task in a tracking system, reference its ID or link, aiding in traceability.

The DevOps connection

For the contemporary DevOps engineer, commit messages are not just an afterthought; they are a core component of the DevOps philosophy.

In today's software landscape, the line between application development and infrastructure has become increasingly blurred. Engineers skilled in infrastructure might find themselves reading application code and vice versa. More importantly, tools across both domains are now integrating with Git, enabling professionals to view commit messages alongside Git hashes on various platforms.

Given this integration, a commit message no longer remains confined to its repository or team. It embarks on a journey across different organizational boundaries and platforms. This transition highlights the value of a well-crafted commit message as a universal language that can be understood and appreciated by diverse stakeholders in the software development and delivery pipeline. In the quest to break organizational silos and improve developer experience, your awesome commit message will help your journey.

Here are some tips for a great commit message:

- **Transparency is key**: Clear commit messages allow teams, from development to operations, to understand code changes, reducing friction and enhancing collaboration.

- **Continuous delivery relies on history**: As organizations push towards more frequent releases, the ability to quickly understand and verify changes becomes paramount. An informative commit message is a critical tool in this process.

Commit message examples

Here is an example of a commit message. This is basic, and you can use it as a starting point to add your own context from here, but it should not be too long:

Category	Example commit messages
Simple changes	Add README.md
	Update license expiration date
	Remove deprecated method XYZ
Feature additions/updates	Implement user authentication flow
	Add search functionality to the homepage
	Extend API to support versioning
Bug fixes	Fix login bug causing session timeouts
	Resolve memory leak in the data processing module
	Correct the typo in the user registration form
Refactoring and code quality improvements	Refactor database connection logic for pooling
	Optimize image loading for faster page rendering
	Improve error handling in the payment gateway
Documentation and comments	Document main algorithms in XYZ module
	Update comments for clarity in the X function
	Revise API documentation for new endpoints
Reverting changes	Revert "Add experimental feature X"
	Rollback to a stable state before the caching layer update

Dependency and external integrations	Upgrade to v2.1.3 of ABC library
	Integrate the latest security patches for the XYZ framework
With issue/task tracking references	Fix #1234: Address edge case in order checkout
	Feature #5678: Add multi-language support
Merges operations	Merge branch 'feature/user-profiles'
	Resolve merge conflict in main.css
Test-related changes	Add unit tests for utility functions
	Refactor integration tests to use mock data
	Fix flaky test in user registration flow

Table 2.1 – Commit message example

Single-purpose code

In the evolving landscape of software development, where Agile and DevOps practices champion swift iteration and robust collaboration, the principle of single-purpose code gains heightened importance. Its influence transcends the realm of code structure, weaving itself into the very fabric of developer experience and Git communication. Let's delve into the profound connections that intertwine these concepts.

Aligning with Agile principles

Agile methodologies, at their core, promote adaptability, continuous improvement, and delivering value in small, manageable increments. Single-purpose code seamlessly aligns with these tenets:

- **Incremental development**: Just as Agile breaks down features into smaller user stories or tasks, single-purpose code encourages breaking down software components into focused, manageable chunks.
- **Adaptability**: Single-purpose components are easier to modify or replace, aligning with Agile's embrace of change.

Enhancing the DevOps pipeline

DevOps emphasizes the continuous integration and delivery of software, bridging the worlds of development and operations. Here's where single-purpose code shines:

- **Streamlined CI/CD**: With code components being focused and independent, the chances of one module unexpectedly affecting another during integrations are reduced, leading to smoother CI/CD pipelines.
- **Better monitoring and logging**: When components have a single responsibility, it is easier to monitor their behavior and log relevant events. Any anomalies can be traced directly to a specific functionality.

Elevating the developer experience

The concept of **Developer Experience (DX)** revolves around making developers' lives easier, promoting productivity, and reducing friction. Single-purpose code plays a pivotal role in this:

- **Intuitive onboarding**: New team members can understand and contribute faster when the codebase consists of clear, focused components
- **Efficient debugging**: With each component doing one thing, identifying and resolving issues becomes a more streamlined process

The deep-rooted connection with Git communication

As previously noted, there is a profound synergy between single-purpose code and Git:

- **Clear commit messages**: Writing single-purpose code results in precise commit messages. A change to a singularly focused function or module can be succinctly described in Git, promoting transparency and clarity in communication.
- **Simplified code reviews**: Pull requests on platforms such as GitHub become more straightforward when they revolve around focused changes. It is easier for reviewers to understand the intent and verify the implementation, leading to more meaningful feedback and collaboration.

Complete code: Striking a balance between precision and progress

In the realm of software development, there is an age-old tension between the need for perfection and the demands of progress. Developers often grapple with the question, When is my code ready? In this discourse, we aim to elucidate the concept of complete code, a philosophy that emphasizes producing robust, fully realized solutions without getting mired in the unattainable pursuit of perfection.

The essence of complete code

The ethos behind **complete code** is simple yet profound: any code written should be whole in its intent and execution. This means the following:

- **No half-measures**: If you are implementing a feature or fixing a bug, the code should accomplish its goal fully, not just partially or superficially.
- **Review-ready**: The code should be of a quality that it is ready for peer review. This means not only being functional but also adhering to coding standards and best practices of the team or organization.
- **Accompanied with tests**: Wherever applicable, the code should come with tests, ensuring that it not only works as intended now but continues to do so as the software evolves.

Done is better than perfect

While the emphasis is on completeness, it is crucial to recognize that chasing perfection can be a counterproductive endeavor. Software is inherently iterative, and waiting for the perfect solution can stall progress. The mantra "done is better than perfect" serves as a reminder of the following:

- **Iterative improvement is key**: It is okay if the solution is not the most optimal out of the gate. It needs to work, and improvements can be made over time.

- **Feedback fuels perfection**: Often, getting the code out and gathering feedback leads to better solutions than endless internal iterations.

The role of testing in complete code

Testing is a linchpin in the complete code philosophy:

- **Validation**: Tests validate that the code does what it is supposed to do, offering a safety net against regressions.

- **Documentation**: Well-crafted tests also act as documentation, providing insights into the expected behavior of the code.

- **Confidence**: Tests instill confidence. When developers write complete code backed by tests, they can make changes or add features with the assurance that they will know if something breaks.

The importance of modern development practices

In an era where Agile and DevOps dominate and CI/CD pipelines automate software delivery, the importance of complete code becomes even more pronounced:

- **Streamlined pipelines**: The CI/CD pipeline is executed with the consideration that the integrated code may be incomplete. That does not mean it can be incomplete at any time, and your team's testing statistics will turn red if there are too many failures. Incomplete code disrupts the pipeline, causes bottlenecks and inefficiencies, and is indicative of the quality of your team's code.

- **Collaborative efficiency**: In team settings, when a developer commits complete, review-ready code, it fosters a smoother collaboration. Reviewers spend less time pointing out basic issues and more time delving into architectural or logical discussions.

Now you understand how to preserve history in Git. Commit messages are a pain to write. You have to describe your work in just a few dozen characters. However, it is important to pay attention to these details in Git collaboration.

Because you are spending a few hours to make the commit (maybe dozens of hours), it would be a shame to ruin it when you could make the collaboration great with just a few more seconds or a few more minutes of attention.

The excellence is in the details. Let's practice and become a real guru!

Summary

As you wrap up this chapter, you should feel more acquainted with Git's essential features, underlying mechanics, and, most importantly, the philosophy of collaboration it champions. Understanding these fundamentals is often far more crucial than memorizing a litany of Git commands or stashing away snippets for quick use.

If you have internalized the insights from this chapter, rest assured you have obtained a solid grasp of Git's basics. You are not just prepared to commit code; you are ready to be a collaborative force within your team.

When you first join a project managed by Git, the initial challenges are usually not resolving intricate conflicts or juggling chaotic branches; rather, the challenge lies in crafting meaningful commits and proving yourself to be an invaluable team player. Each well-considered commit you make not only contributes to the project but also fortifies your standing within the team.

Now, let's move on to more advanced Git usage to help you shine as a team player.

3

Advanced Git Usage for Team Collaboration

Now, we move on to the aspect of actual collaboration. In this chapter, we will delve into various collaboration practices that you will want to adopt. You will learn how to organize your commit history, manage complex branches, and resolve conflicts during merges. The goal of this chapter is to help you become wonderfully in control of this branch flow team collaboration.

Here, the focus is not just on getting the job done but also on doing it in a way that enhances teamwork. Recognize that there is a thoughtful strategy behind managing an entire code base to maximize the teams' productivity and impact. Different strategies are employed based on the type of products or projects, the team size, and its maturity. Before we plunge into the Git commands, it is crucial to comprehend this underlying strategy—branching strategies.

So, let's get started on making your collaboration seamless and efficient.

We will cover the following topics in this chapter:

- Branching strategy for team collaboration
- Ways to apply your changes on a branch
- Navigating conflicts
- Mastering better collaboration

Technical requirements

Configuration instructions for proceeding with this section can be found in the following GitHub repository link. Please make sure Git and SSH tools are installed. For Windows users, it is recommended to use PowerShell. I also encourage you to get the most up-to-date information written about the different commands and environments.

```
https://github.com/PacktPublishing/DevOps-Unleashed-with-Git-and-GitHub
```

Branching strategies for team collaboration

In the realm of team collaboration, commits act as the essential building blocks. These commits link together to form a chronological history, a record of your project's evolution. This history is organized and maintained through branches.

So, how can engineers and teams knit this history into a cohesive meaningful narrative? The branching strategy is the answer to this question. The branching strategy is a development strategy for effectively managing branches in Git to enable smooth collaboration and service delivery.

Why a branching strategy is important

A well-crafted branching strategy is not just nice to have; it is crucial in a team development environment. Your branching strategy has a ripple effect on your DevOps processes, affecting deployment units and workflow efficiency. The ability to collaborate smoothly depends not only on good communication within the team but also impacts the speed at which your product evolves. This ties back into all the elements we have covered in the previous chapters, such as the frequency and methodology of your CI/CD tests. In essence, your branching strategy is pivotal in removing organizational friction, which is the ultimate aim of DevOps.

Here are some reasons why a well-thought-out branching strategy is non-negotiable:

- **Isolation of changes**: It allows individual team members to work on distinct features or bugs without interfering with each other's work.

- **Risk mitigation**: A branching strategy safeguards the main (often called master) branch from being destabilized by untested or volatile code.

- **Facilitates collaboration**: With a good branching strategy, multiple team members can work on different branches in parallel, thereby increasing overall team efficiency.

In the context of DevOps, a branching strategy also does the following:

- **Automated testing integration**: A branching strategy can be designed to trigger automated tests at various stages. This ensures that only well-tested code is merged back into the main branch, aiding in continuous integration.

- **Simplifies deployment**: A well-organized branch structure can streamline the deployment process, making it easier to move code from development environments to staging and finally to production.

- **Enhances developer experience**: It improves the overall **Developer Experience** (**DX**) by making collaboration more transparent and efficient, a key strategy for successful DevOps.

- **Environment-specific branches**: Having branches dedicated to particular environments (development, staging, production, etc.) allows for smoother and more controlled deployments.

- **Enhances security**: By establishing clear boundaries between branches, a branching strategy can enhance security by controlling access to sensitive code and ensuring that changes undergo proper review and approval processes before being merged into critical environments.

Branch strategy and branch policy

In the landscape of software development and DevOps, the terms **branching strategy** and **branching policy** might appear synonymous. While they are frequently mistaken for one another, it is vital to recognize that a branching strategy is a more expansive concept that encompasses a branching policy.

A branching strategy is a comprehensive plan that outlines how branches are managed, created, and integrated within your development workflow. It encapsulates more than just the technical aspects of handling branches. It also involves contextual variables such as the size of your organization, the culture within your team, and the specific requirements of your project or product.

Branching policies, on the other hand, are more specific sets of rules or guidelines for branch management. These often form the backbone of a branching strategy, serving as templates to be customized according to your specific needs. Sometimes, policies such as **Git Flow** or **GitHub Flow**, which we will discover in this chapter, are used as the names of strategies for development. They should be considered as types of branching policies. Renowned software thought leader Martin Fowler discusses these items not as strategies themselves but rather under the *Looking at some branching policies* section in his article *Patterns for Managing Source Code Branches* (`https://martinfowler.com/articles/branching-patterns.html`).

Therefore, when establishing a branching approach, it is crucial to choose a branching policy that serves as a foundation. This policy should then be customized to align with your organization's unique needs and objectives to effectively mitigate friction in development processes and accelerate software releases. This tailored approach ensures that your branching strategy not only optimizes workflow but also integrates seamlessly with the cultural and organizational aspects of your team.

Smaller and frequent versus larger and less frequent

There are many branching policies in existence. Companies often coin specific branching policy names and publish them as best practices, such as **GitHub Flow**. Fundamentally, all branching strategies map to one of two principles: make smaller changes frequently or make larger changes occasionally.

For smaller teams, naturally, the friction in integrating changes and pushing releases quickly is less. But in larger organizations, with larger products or a lengthy approval process, the friction inevitably increases. More conflicts arise, and more checks are needed to prevent them.

However, allowing these challenges to slow down your development process can adversely affect the timeliness of your product or project releases, ultimately impacting business success.

Over time, various companies have devised a multitude of branching strategies to mitigate these issues. Most of them are extensions of existing practices, designed to reduce friction within the constraints of an organization or product, aiming for faster releases.

It is crucial to understand that no branching strategy serves as a one-size-fits-all solution. The base strategy often gets selected depending on the team's composition and culture, and from there, customizations are made to fit specific needs.

This section introduces the branch policies trunk-based development, Git Flow, and GitHub Flow, each mapped as follows:

Figure 3.1 – Branching policies mapping

Trunk-based development is renowned for integrating smaller, frequent changes directly into the main branch. In contrast, Git Flow is known for a strategy that integrates larger changes less frequently. Both have their pros and cons, and your choice between them often boils down to your team's specific requirements and workflows.

For larger organizations aiming to release a higher volume of changes more frequently with reduced friction, GitHub Flow serves as an excellent representative. These strategies are essentially designed to adapt the core principles of frequent, small changes to fit the complexity and scale of larger enterprises.

Policies such as GitHub Flow are built under the influence of Git Flow, but many companies nowadays use GitHub Flow as a template upon which they build their own customized branching policies.

Types of branch policies branch policies

Now then, let's look at a typical branch policy.

This section introduces three typical branching policies:

- Trunk-based development
- Git Flow
- GitHub Flow

Consider each in terms of how frequently your team or organization needs to release and how large your product and project are.

Trunk-based development

Trunk-based development (**TBD**) is a software development approach where developers work in short-lived branches, typically less than a day, or directly off a single branch called the **trunk** or the mainline. The key principle is to minimize the lifespan of branches to promote frequent integrations and to avoid the pitfalls of long-lived feature branches, such as merge conflicts and diverging codebases.

In TBD, the trunk is always in working and healthy condition, and it should always be in a deployable state. Developers take a small chunk of a feature or task and work on it, aiming to merge it back into the trunk as soon as possible. If a feature is not yet ready for production, **feature flags** can be used to hide these functionalities until they are complete, allowing the code to be merged without affecting the end users. Release practices such as feature flags are covered in *Chapter 5*.

As shown in the figure, in the TBD, many short-lived branches are created, and they are merged into the mainline.

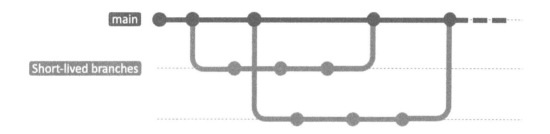

Figure 3.2 – Trunk-based development

Since integration happens frequently, it is crucial to have a robust suite of automated tests to run every time code is merged into the trunk. This ensures that the code base remains stable and deployable at all times. **Continuous Integration** (**CI**) tools are commonly used in conjunction with TBD to automate the testing and build processes, ensuring that the trunk is always in a good state.

To accommodate hotfixes that provide urgent fixes, developers may create short-lived branches that are immediately merged back into the trunk upon completion. This ensures that critical issues can be addressed quickly without jeopardizing the stability of the mainline.

One of the main advantages of TBD is its simplicity and focus on producing a clean, deployable code base. Encouraging frequent merges reduces the likelihood of merge conflicts and keeps all developers aligned with the latest version of the code. This is particularly beneficial in a DevOps culture that prioritizes quick iterations and rapid delivery.

Here are the pros and cons of trunk-based development.

Pros:

- **Frequent integration**: Because code is merged frequently, merge conflicts are less likely and easier to resolve
- **Fast feedback loop**: Integrating changes often helps in identifying issues earlier in the development process
- **Simplified workflow**: Without a proliferation of long-lived feature branches, the development workflow is simplified, making it easier to manage

Cons:

- **Risk of instability**: If not properly tested, frequent merges can lead to unstable code getting into the mainline
- **Not ideal for large features**: For very large or disruptive changes, this approach can cause problems, as those changes might destabilize the mainline for an extended period

In summary, TBD is all about rapid integrations, keeping the trunk always deployable, and employing automated testing to maintain code quality. It aligns well with Agile and DevOps methodologies, aiming to remove friction and improve developer experience by streamlining the development process.

Git Flow

Git Flow is a branching policy mainly aimed at robust project versioning and is particularly well-suited for projects that have a scheduled release cycle. It introduces a structured approach involving multiple types of branches, including `feature`, `release`, `develop`, and `hotfix`, alongside the `main` (or `master`) branch.

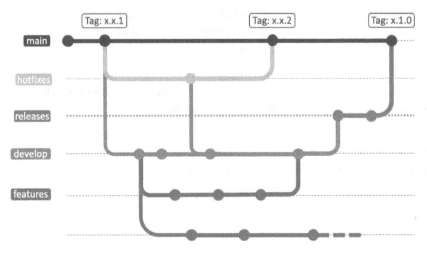

Figure 3.3 – Git Flow

In Git Flow, development begins by branching off a `develop` branch from `main`. The `develop` branch serves as the integration branch for features and is where all developers' branches get merged. When you are set to work on a new feature or a bug, you branch off a `feature` branch from `develop`. This isolated environment allows you to work without affecting the broader code base.

As the feature progresses, incremental changes are committed to this `feature` branch. Once the feature is complete and tested, it gets merged back into the `develop` branch. For release preparation, a `release` branch is created from the `develop` branch. This branch is where any final minor bug fixes or documentation updates occur. Once everything is ready, the `release` branch is merged into `main` and tagged with a version number. Simultaneously, it should also be merged back into `develop` to ensure that future releases also have these changes. For immediate, critical fixes, a `hotfix` branch may be created directly off the main branch.

Git Flow provides a rigid structure that can be beneficial for large projects with multiple developers, requiring a balance of stability and new features. It ensures that development processes are separate but parallel, allowing for project history to be more legible and revertible.

Here are the pros and cons of the Git Flow.

Pros:

- **Structured workflow**: It's suitable for projects that have scheduled release cycles
- **Isolation**: Feature branches allow developers to work in isolation, making it easier to manage complex features
- **Hotfix support**: The dedicated hotfix branches make it easy to quickly patch production releases

Cons:

- **Complexity**: For smaller teams or projects, Git Flow may introduce unnecessary complexity
- **Delayed Integration**: As feature branches are long-lived, this could lead to merge conflicts or bugs that are discovered late in the development process

In summary, Git Flow provides a model for more complex projects, ensuring that the code base remains organized and that releases are well managed. It is especially useful for larger teams where coordination and release planning are critical.

GitHub Flow

GitHub Flow is a simplified workflow that encourages continuous delivery practices. It consists of just the mainline and short-lived feature branches. The main principle is to branch off, develop a new feature, submit a pull request, and review the code before deploying. Pull request is an invention by GitHub and is a method for developers to notify team members that they have completed a feature or fix, which is then reviewed and discussed before being merged into the main branch of a code base. It will be covered in *Chapter 4*.

The GitHub Flow is simple, but the context is not confined to Git alone. Note the inclusion of GitHub processes such as pull requests and approvals, as shown in the figure:

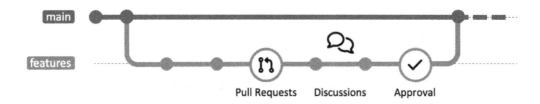

Figure 3.4 – GitHub Flow

It begins with creating a new, descriptive branch off the default repository branch, serving as a safe environment for making changes without affecting the main code base. Changes are committed and pushed to this remote branch. When ready, a detailed pull request is created for team reviews, often linked to related issues for context. Reviews might include questions, suggestions, or line-specific comments. Subsequent commits addressing feedback are automatically added to the pull request. After approval, the pull request is merged into the default branch, making your contributions part of the main code base. Depending on settings, resolving merge conflicts or meeting approval criteria may be required. Post-merge, the working branch is deleted but the commit history and discussions remain accessible for future reference.

In essence, GitHub Flow fosters collaboration, transparency, and incremental development, offering a flexible yet structured approach for team projects.

Here are the pros and cons of the GitHub Flow.

Pros:

- **Simplicity**: GitHub Flow offers a straightforward approach with a single mainline and short-lived feature branches, making it accessible and easy to manage, even for newcomers. This simplicity streamlines development, allowing for a focus on productivity rather than complex branching strategies.

- **Faster deployment**: By encouraging continuous integration and delivery, GitHub Flow enables teams to release updates more frequently. This rapid deployment cycle allows for immediate feedback and quicker iteration, reducing the time from development to market.

- **Enhanced collaboration**: The pull request mechanism central to GitHub Flow fosters transparent code reviews and collaboration. It allows every team member to contribute to discussions, ensuring code quality and collective ownership of the project.

Cons:

- **Platform compatibility considerations**: Adopting GitHub Flow enhances collaboration and efficiency, particularly on GitHub where it is fully supported. However, when integrating with different platforms, it might necessitate supplementary tools or adjustments to harness its full potential, ensuring seamless project management across diverse environments.

- **Adaptability for complex projects:** While GitHub Flow offers a streamlined, straightforward approach conducive to rapid deployment and continuous delivery, larger teams working on multifaceted projects may encounter challenges. This workflow's emphasis on simplicity and single mainline development can sometimes limit the granularity of control over multiple simultaneous developments or the nuanced handling of various project timelines. For instance, in projects requiring extensive integration testing or coordination across multiple sub-teams, the need for additional branch management strategies or more robust release planning mechanisms becomes apparent.

Branch naming conventions – Discover the best practices for naming branches in Git

In the realm of Git and DevOps, naming is a crucial aspect of effective team collaboration and code management. A clear, descriptive name can make a world of difference when you are navigating through a sea of branches, trying to understand their specific functions, ownership, and lifecycle status. Establishing a coherent branching naming convention is an integral part of an effective branching strategy.

Let's delve into the best practices for naming branches in Git, aiming to remove organizational friction and accelerate releases. A well-defined naming convention allows engineers to instantly understand the purpose of a branch, whether it is for a feature, a bug fix, a hotfix, or an experimental endeavor. This clarity is vital when a team is sifting through dozens, or even hundreds, of branches. Naming conventions set the stage for a more transparent, efficient, and streamlined workflow, making it easier for everyone on the DevOps team to collaborate.

Branch naming guidelines and examples

The following are the main guidelines and examples for naming each topic. Please note that these are only examples, and each team can have very different naming conventions.

Here's some general guidance:

- **Use hyphens, underscores, or slashes**: Using spaces in branch names can lead to errors and complications when interacting with the Git command line. Instead, use hyphens (-), underscores (_), or slashes (/) to separate words. Slashes are especially used as a separator when dealing with topics such as hotfixes and features.

- **Lowercase names**: While Git is case-sensitive, sticking to lowercase letters helps maintain consistency and avoids confusion.

- **Make it descriptive but short**: The name should give an instant idea of what the branch is about while remaining as succinct as possible.

Here are examples of names for each branch:

- **Feature branches**: A feature branch is typically where new functionalities are developed. Names for feature branches should start with `feature/`, followed by a brief description. An example would be `feature/user authentication`.

- **Bugfix branches**: If a branch is specifically for fixing a bug, name it starting with `bugfix/`, followed by a short descriptor. For example, `bugfix/login-error`.

- **Hotfix branches**: A hotfix branch is for urgent fixes that need to be pushed to production as quickly as possible. Begin these with `hotfix/`. For example, `hotfix/xyz-security-vulnerability`.

- **Release branches**: For branches that are in preparation for a release, use `release/` as a prefix. An example would be `release/v1.2`.

Contextual naming

While these categories offer a good starting point, you may also consider adding more contextual information to the branch name. For example, you could append the issue number at the end (`feature/123-user-authentication`) or include the name of the person responsible for the branch (`feature/teamxyz-authentication`).

In this section, we recognized that a solid branching strategy stands as the backbone of any collaborative development project. We have explored the significance of branch strategies in maintaining a stable code base while facilitating continuous integration and delivery. Whether it is adopting the small and frequent commits of TBD, the structured roles of Git Flow, or the simplicity of GitHub Flow, the right strategy is paramount to a team's success.

Remember, these conventions should align with your broader branching strategy and policy and be adapted to the size of your team and the project and your organization's unique constraints and goals. A well-chosen naming convention will reinforce the effectiveness of your branching policy, aiding in the quest to mitigate friction and accelerate releases. By adhering to a well-defined naming convention, you empower your team to work more efficiently and foster a culture of clarity and accountability.

In the upcoming section, you will learn how to bring together disparate lines of development while maintaining the integrity and history of your code. Let's move forward with confidence, ready to merge our knowledge of branching into the practical skills of Git merging.

Ways to apply your changes on a branch

Now that you have delved into the intricacies of branch management and workflows in DevOps, you are likely starting to see the big picture. You have come to understand how your individual commits contribute to the overall development stream. The next step in this journey is *to connect the dots*—more specifically, consider how the code you have written gets merged into the mainline.

The code base is a living, collaborative environment; it holds a history of contributions from various team members. In a fast-paced environment, it may be tempting to rush through commits or push large chunks of changes all at once to meet deadlines. However, when merging, it is crucial to consider how your changes contribute to a consistent, understandable, and stable shared environment. This consideration becomes particularly vital in a DevOps culture, where the objective is not just rapid deployment but also frictionless collaboration.

In the upcoming sections, we will explore various tactics and best practices for executing successful merges in Git, particularly tailored to the needs and challenges that arise in a DevOps setting.

Merging vs rebasing

Git offers two main techniques for integrating these changes: merging and rebasing. While they serve the same ultimate purpose—bringing different strands of code together—they have distinct operational nuances. Before diving into various actual commands, let's distinguish between merging and rebasing.

Merging

Merging takes the content of a source branch and integrates it with a target branch. This new commit will have two parent commits, preserving the independent histories of the branches being merged. Merging can be cumbersome because it keeps the history from the various branches as it is, but it is also good in terms of flexibility during integration when various people are working on a project at the same time. Mainly, there are two types of merge options: **non-fast-forward merge**, which creates a new merge commit to log the merge, and **fast-forward merge**, which does not create a merge commit. There is also the squash function—an option that compresses multiple commits into a single commit for merging.

On platforms such as GitHub, the default setting is for merge commits to be made like in the following figure:

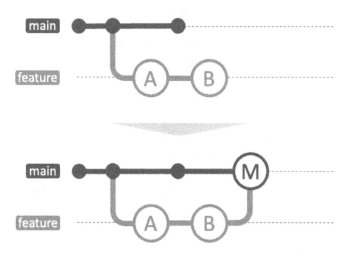

Figure 3.5 – Merging example (non-fast-forward)

Here are the pros and cons of merging.

Pros:

- **History preservation**: Merging keeps the history of both branches, offering a detailed log
- **Simplicity**: It is usually easier for beginners to understand
- **Branch isolation**: Individual branches can continue to make separate changes without affecting the merge

Cons:

- **Complex log**: While preserving history, merges can lead to a complicated and cluttered log history
- **Lack of linearity**: The project history becomes non-linear, making it challenging to navigate the commit history

Rebasing

Rebasing is the process of moving or combining a sequence of commits to a new base commit. It essentially takes the changes made in a feature branch and replays them on top of another branch. Instead of creating a new commit, as is the case with merging, rebasing rewrites the commit history to produce a linear succession of commits. The great thing about rebasing is the linearity of its history. When looking back in time, it is easy to follow the flow of what happened in the mainline branch, which is very good in terms of bug fixes.

Once you master rebasing, you can contribute to a noise-free history:

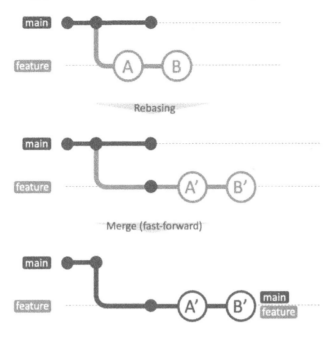

Figure 3.6 – Rebasing

Here are the pros and cons of rebasing.

Pros:

- **Cleaner history**: Rebasing results in a much cleaner, linear project history
- **Eliminates Noise**: It removes unnecessary merge commits that appear when performing the git merge
- **Simpler Debugging**: With a cleaner history, debugging becomes easier

Cons:

- **Shared Branch Risk**: Rebasing can be destructive; it can be risky on shared branches because it rewrites commit history
- **Complexity**: Rebasing can be more complicated to understand and execute correctly

Both techniques have their pros and cons. Merging preserves the original branch history but can lead to a complicated log. Rebasing offers a cleaner, more linear project history but carries risks, especially when working on a shared branch.

Exploring different ways to merge in Git

Now let's dive into the practical steps. We will explore the process of merging two branches, offering hands-on experience to help you better understand each method. In this section, we will cover some of the most commonly used methods to merge branches, enabling you to make informed decisions based on your project needs.

git merge --ff – Keeping it straight

Let's dig into the practical aspects now. This section focuses on a common default behavior in Git merging called **fast-forward**, which is - - f f as a command option. We will go through the process, ensuring you understand how it works and when to use it.

Fast-forward merging is one of the simplest ways to integrate branches in Git. In essence, a fast-forward merge moves the tip of the targeted branch to the latest commit on the source branch.

With fast-forward merges, when looking at the history, nothing actually appears to have changed, as shown in the following figure. That is the benefit of fast-forward merging. HEAD is moving without fail and merging can be done smoothly:

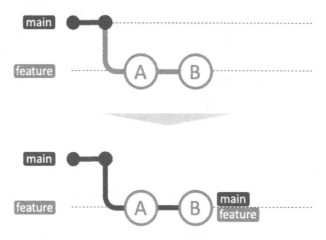

Figure 3.7 – Fast-forward merging

In Git, a fast-forward merge is possible when there are no new commits on the base (or target) branch that occurred after the feature branch was created. Essentially, it eliminates the need for a new commit to join the branches, keeping your project history linear.

Practical steps for fast-forward merging

For the context of this guide, assume you have a main branch and an add-description branch. The add-description branch has derived from the main and you are planning to merge the feature back into master:

```
# Initialize a new repository
$ mkdir try-fast-forward-merge
$ cd try-fast-forward-merge
$ git init


# Add and commit initial README.md to master
$ echo "# My Project" > README.md
$ git add README.md
$ git commit -m "Initial commit on master"


# Create and switch to a new branch 'add-description'
$ git checkout -b add-description


# Make changes to add a description, add and commit changes
$ echo "This project is an example of how to use Git." >> README.md
$ git add README.md
$ git commit -m "Add project description to README.md"
```

At this point, your repository structure would resemble the following diagram:

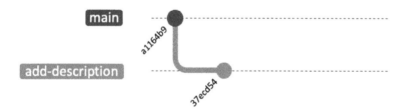

Figure 3.8 – git merge –ff (1)

Now, let's proceed to merge these branches by switching back to the main branch:

```
# Switch back to 'main' and perform a Fast-Forward merge
$ git checkout main
$ git merge add-description
# View the linear history
$ git log --graph --oneline
* 26d90bf (HEAD -> main, add-description) Add project description to
README.md
```

```
* 37ecd54 Add project description to README.md
* a1164b9 Initial commit on master
```

Now, your repository history would look like this:

Figure 3.9 – git merge –ff (2)

Why fast-forward merges are preferred in DevOps and team collaboration

Behind the scenes, a fast-forward merge merely moves HEAD, the pointer, to the latest commit. Moreover, fast-forward merges do not create a new merge commit, keeping the Git history clean and linear. This makes it a simple and efficient operation.

Fast-forward merges are often preferred in team collaboration for a few reasons:

- **Simplicity**: They keep the git history linear, which makes it easier to follow
- **Transparency**: With a straightforward history, it is easier to track changes, debug issues, and understand the sequence of feature integrations
- **Efficiency**: Fast-forward merges eliminate the need for an extra merge commit, simplifying code reviews

However, keep in mind that fast-forward merges are not always possible. You can use this way when you are developing with just yourself or when doing simple development, but in most development, there are many things going on in parallel. When simultaneous changes occur in the master and feature branches, a non-fast-forward merge, which is sometimes called a three-way merge, may be necessary.

git merge --no-ff – Preserving branch history

Non-fast-forward merges, commonly invoked with the --no-ff flag, offer an alternative merging strategy that differs from the fast-forward merges we discussed earlier. Unlike fast-forward merges, which move the tip of the targeted branch to the latest commit of the source branch, non-fast-forward merges generate a new merge commit. This new commit has two parent commits: one from the source branch and one from the target branch.

Non-fast-forward merges can embed context into the merge commit so that it is possible to look back later to see why this merge was performed.

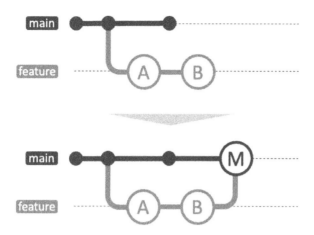

Figure 3.10 – Non-fast-forward merging

This approach keeps track of the fact that a feature branch was merged into the main branch, preserving the context in which past commits were made.

Practical steps for non-fast-forward merging

Let's assume you are working with a main branch and add-feature branch. The following are the steps to perform a non-fast-forward merge:

```
# Initialize a new repository
$ mkdir try-no-fast-forward-merge
$ cd try-no-fast-forward-merge
$ git init

# Add and commit initial README.md to master
$ echo "# My Project" > README.md
$ git add README.md
$ git commit -m "Initial commit on main"

# Create and switch to a new branch 'add-feature'
$ git checkout -b add-feature

# Make changes, add and commit them
$ echo "Adding a new feature..." >> README.md
$ git add README.md
$ git commit -m "Implement a new feature"
```

Now the `commit` log is as shown in *Figure 3.11*. What you did so far is the same as what you did in the `git merge --ff` section.

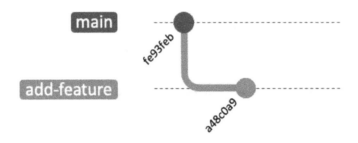

Figure 3.11 – git merge --no-ff (1)

Then, let's switch back to `main` and perform a **non-fast-forward** merge:

```
$ git checkout main
$ git merge --no-ff add-feature
```

The following edit message will appear in the terminal. Edit the commit message and save it:

```
git merge branch 'add-feature'
```

After the edit, let's see the log now:

```
# View the history
$ git log --graph --oneline
*   f58977f (HEAD -> main) Merge branch 'add-feature'
|\
| * a48c0a9 (add-feature) Implement new feature
|/
* fe93feb Initial commit on main
```

Your repository history will show a new merge commit indicating where the `add-feature` branch was integrated into the `main` branch.

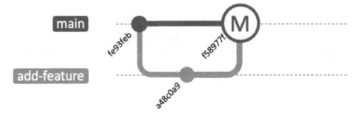

Figure 3.12 – git merge --no-ff (2)

Why use non-fast-forward merges in DevOps and team collaboration?

Non-fast-forward merges offer benefits that can be valuable in various DevOps and team collaboration scenarios:

- **Context preservation**: Generating a new commit during the merging process preserves not just the code but the history and context as well. This clear record of integration makes it much easier to understand when and how changes from different branches were combined.

- **Traceability**: Using `--no-ff` offers invaluable transparency, providing a clear record of who made what changes, when they made them, and why. This is particularly beneficial in larger teams and complex projects where it is crucial to understand the flow of contributions.

While merge commits can provide rich context and history, they can also clutter the Git history if overused or poorly documented. It is important for teams to consider their merging strategy carefully and make concerted efforts to maintain a clean shared repository.

git merge --squash – Squashing complexity

The `git merge --squash` option provides a different merging technique that offers both clarity and tidiness. While fast-forward and non-fast-forward merges are excellent for tracking branch histories, there might be cases where you want to condense your `feature` branch changes into a single commit before merging. That's where `git merge --squash` shines.

In a squashed merge, all changes from the source (or feature) branch are combined into a single commit on the target (or main) branch. This action effectively condenses the feature branch history into one commit while merging, offering a clean, easy-to-follow Git history. This leaves the changes in an uncommitted state, allowing you to modify the differences before finalizing the commit.

While teams are committed to maintaining a clean shared repository, individual development branches often become cluttered with various trial-and-error attempts. Squash merges contribute to preserving the cleanliness of the main code base by preventing these messy, experimental logs from infiltrating the production history.

The squash merge, as shown in the following figure, is in some ways the cleanest merge, and it has a lot of benefits. However, keep in mind that it is a way of incorporating changes that lose the previous change history and the commit history of other companies. This will be mentioned later in this section.

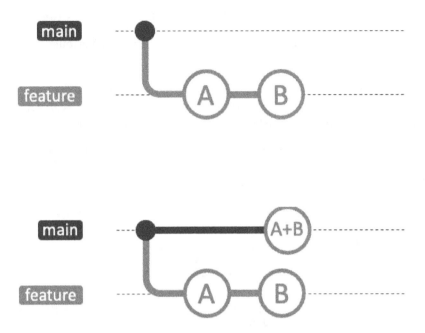

Figure 3.13 – Squash merging

Practical steps for squash merging

Let's say you have a main branch and an add-multiple-features branch. To perform a squash merge, do the following:

```
# Initialize a new repository
$ mkdir try-squash-merge
$ cd try-squash-merge
$ git init

# Add and commit initial README.md to main
$ echo "# My Project" > README.md
$ git add README.md
$ git commit -m "Initial commit on main"

# Create and switch to a new branch 'add-multiple-files
$ git checkout -b add-basic-files

# Make some changes, add and commit them
$ echo "# HOW TO CONTRIBUTE" >> CONTRIBUTING.md
$ git add CONTRIBUTING.md
```

```
$ git commit -m "Add CONTRIBUTING.md"
$ echo "# LICENSE" >> LICENSE.txt
$ git add LICENSE.txt
$ git commit -m "Add LICENSE.txt"
```

Now the branches should look like those in the following figure:

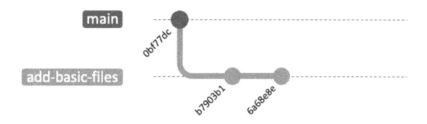

Figure 3.14 – git merge --squash (1)

Let's switch back to the mainline and perform a `squash` merge:

```
# Switch back to 'main' and perform a squash merge
$ git checkout main
$ git merge --squash add-basic-files
```

The commits are then squashed and become a single commit:

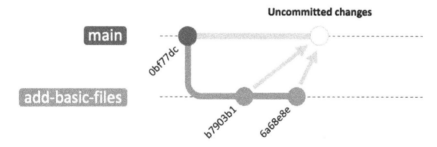

Figure 3.15 – git merge --squash (2)

Then, Git will add uncommitted changes to the main branch. It is time to complete the merge process. To complete the merge, you need to commit those uncommitted changes:

```
$ git add .
$ git commit -m "Add repository standard docs"
$ git log --graph --oneline
* 6eb6df3 (HEAD -> main) Add repository standard docs
```

```
* ffc2ed5 Add CONTRIBUTING.md
* 2c5ad11 Initial commit on main
```

This will combine all the changes from the `add-multiple-features` branch into a single new commit on the `main` branch:

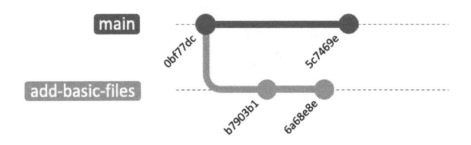

Figure 3.16 – git merge --squash (3)

Why use squash merges in DevOps and team collaboration?

Squash merges offer a unique set of benefits for DevOps and collaborative development:

- **Atomic changes**: A squashed merge creates a single commit that contains all the feature changes, making it easier to roll back if needed.

- **Reduced noise**: Squash merges eliminate the clutter of many small, perhaps experimental, commits from the main branch. This makes for a cleaner log history that's easier to read and understand.

- **Strategic commit messages**: Squashing allows you to create a comprehensive commit message that can encapsulate the purpose and impact of a feature more effectively than a series of smaller commits.

However, it is worth noting that while squash merges can simplify history, they can also obfuscate it. Individual commits from the feature branch are lost in the main branch, making it hard to understand the development context of each separate change. Use this merge strategy judiciously and understand its impact on your development history.

The ethics and pitfalls of squash merging

Squashing someone else's commits can sometimes be problematic.

The `git merge --squash` command is a powerful tool for consolidating multiple commits into a single one. While this function keeps your commit history clean and manageable, it raises ethical and practical issues when used on commits made by others.

It is important to be aware of the following concerns in team collaboration:

- **Authorship misattribution**: By default, the person who performs the squash becomes the author of the consolidated commit, effectively erasing the original contributors' history. This could demotivate team members by not recognizing their contributions.

- **History alteration**: The command alters the commit history, which could be considered disrespectful to the original author's work.

If maintaining the integrity of individual commits is important, consider using a standard merge. This may result in a messier history, but it preserves the work and recognition of all contributors.

Additionally, the `git rebase` command offers more control over the commit history, which is useful for cleaning up or rearranging your own work without affecting others.

Let's explore this command next.

git rebase – Rewriting for clarity

Rebasing is another powerful technique in Git that differs significantly from merging. The primary difference between merging and rebasing is how they integrate changes. While `git merge` integrates changes from one branch into another, `git rebase` moves or combines a sequence of commits to a new base commit.

In the team collaboration context, rebasing is used to maintain a linear project history, which simplifies debugging and makes code reviews easier. However, rebase comes with its share of complexities and pitfalls and is generally best used in specific circumstances.

Before delving into the hands-on tutorial, let's understand how `git rebase` works at a high level. The primary utility of rebasing is to place the changes from the `feature` branch on top of another branch.

For example, consider the following branches:

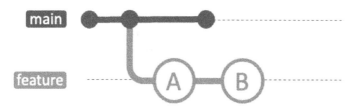

Figure 3.17 – Rebasing (1)

After rebasing `feature` onto `main`, your branch might look like this:

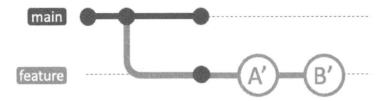

Figure 3.18 – Rebasing (2)

Finally, you can merge back to main, at which point a fast-forward merge can be performed:

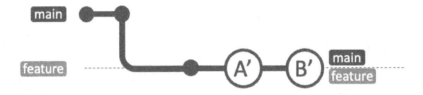

Figure 3.19 – Rebasing (3)

Practical steps for git rebase

Let's take a practical example with a `main` branch and a `new-feature` branch. Here's how to perform rebase:

```
# Initialize a new repository
$ mkdir try-git-rebase
$ cd try-git-rebase
$ git init

# Add and commit initial README.md to main
$ echo "# My Rebase Project" > README.md
$ git add README.md
$ git commit -m "Initial commit on main"

# Create and switch to a new branch 'new-feature'
$ git checkout -b new-feature

# Make some changes, add and commit them
$ echo "This is a new feature." >> NewFeature.md
$ git add NewFeature.md
$ git commit -m "Add new feature"
```

At this point, your branch history may look something like this:

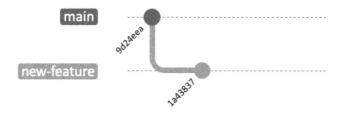

Figure 3.20 – git rebase (1)

Now, let's say new commits have been added to `main` while you were working on `new-feature`:

```
# Switch back to 'main' and add new commits
$ git checkout main
$ echo "Updates to the project." >> Updates.md
$ git add Updates.md
$ git commit -m "Update main"
```

Your commit graph now diverges:

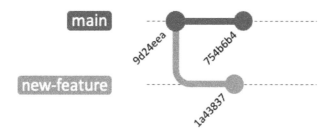

Figure 3.21 – git rebase (2)

Now, rebase `new-feature` onto `main`:

```
# Switch to 'new-feature' and rebase onto main
git checkout new-feature
git rebase main
```

Let's check what it looks like now:

```
$ git log --graph --online
* 43ea59e (HEAD -> new-feature) Add new feature
* 16e1878 (main) Update main
* 3021494 Initial commit on main
```

After this, your branches will look as follows:

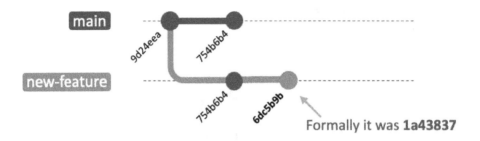

Figure 3.22 – git rebase (3)

Now it is time to merge and complete the git rebase process:

```
# Switch to 'main' and perform fast-forward-merge
$ git checkout main
$ git merge new-feature
```

When a fast-forward merge is performed, the HEADs of the main and new-feature branches will be the corresponding commits, as shown:

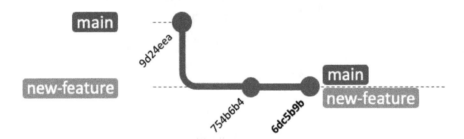

Figure 3.23 – git rebase (4)

Why rebasing is powerful in DevOps and team collaboration

The primary advantage of rebasing in a DevOps culture is that it results in a much cleaner project history than merging. Cleaner histories are easier to debug and simpler to understand, and they make more logical sense to developers who join the project at a later time.

Here are some benefits:

- **Linear history**: It is easier to understand than the non-linear history created by git merge

- **Simplified debugging**: With a cleaner history, tracking down when a particular bug was introduced becomes easier

- **Code hygiene**: Rebasing encourages you to squash fixup commits or split larger commits, making your changes more understandable compared to the other developers'

The cautions and pitfalls of git rebase

There are golden rules to follow: *do not rebase public (team) branches*. One such cardinal rule is to avoid rebasing public branches. Rebasing can be a great tool for cleaning up a feature branch, but when done on branches that are publicly available, it can become a disaster.

Here are the things to consider when you use `git rebase`:

- **Conflicts for collaborators**: Imagine that you have rebased a public branch and pushed the changes. Other developers who have already pulled the old version of the branch now have a divergent history. When they try to push their changes, Git will reject the push, forcing them to reconcile the histories. This creates extra work and increases the chance of merge conflicts.

- **Complex merges**: After a public branch has been rebased and the history altered, merging it with other branches can become a real challenge. Because Git uses the commit history to determine how to integrate changes, modifying that history can make merging far more complicated than it needs to be.

- **Loss of context**: Rebasing can squash commits together or change their order, which may result in a loss of context for those changes. This makes debugging more difficult and can complicate the task of understanding the development process that led to the current code base.

Rebasing can be complex and risky, especially for inexperienced developers. In worst-case scenarios, you may have to resolve many conflicts, leading to errors and bugs if not done carefully.

By understanding and using `git merge` and `git rebase`, you can handle pretty much any situation that requires combining different lines of development. Each has its place in a Git command, and understanding when to use each one is the key to maintaining a clean and understandable code base—something that is highly valuable in the world of DevOps.

git cherry-pick – Picking specific commits

One of the most flexible tools in the Git commands is the `git cherry-pick` command. While the previous merge methods were mainly used for integrating entire branches, `git cherry-pick` allows you to select specific commits from one branch and apply them to another branch. This method can be incredibly useful when you need to apply just a few specific changes without taking all the modifications from a different branch.

Imagine you have two branches, main and feature. You realize that one or two commits from the feature branch should be moved to main, but you are not ready to merge the entire branch. The git cherry-pick command allows you to do just that:

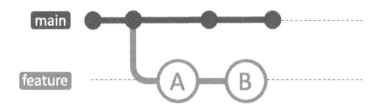

Figure 3.24 – Cherry-picking (1)

You can cherry-pick the changes from a specific commit in the feature branch and apply them to main. This action will create a new commit on the main branch:

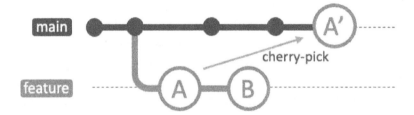

Figure 3.25 – Cherry-picking (2)

Practical steps for cherry-picking

Now let's go over the practical steps for cherry-picking changes and merging them into a branch. Each commit adds a file to each of them. Let's take some of those commits and merge them into main. First, we add the files:

```
# Initialize a new repository
$ mkdir try-cherry-pick
$ cd try-cherry-pick
$ git init

# Add and commit initial README.md to main
$ echo "# My Project" > README.md
$ git add README.md
$ git commit -m "Initial commit"

# Create and switch to a new branch 'add-base-documents'
```

```
$ git checkout -b add-base-documents

# Make changes and commit
# Add CONTRIBUTING.md
$ echo "# CONTRIBUTING" >> CONTRIBUTING.md
$ git add CONTRIBUTING.md
$ git commit -m "Add CONTRIBUTING.md"

# Add LICENSE.txt
$ echo "LICENSE" >> LICENSE.txt
$ git add LICENSE.txt
$ git commit -m "Add LICENSE.txt"

# Take a look at the 'add-base-documents' branch log
$ git log add-base-documents --graph --oneline
* 02ee2b4 (HEAD -> add-base-documents) Add LICENSE.txt
* a80e8ad Add CONTRIBUTING.md
* cfb060a (main) Initial commit
```

Now the branches look like those in the following diagram:

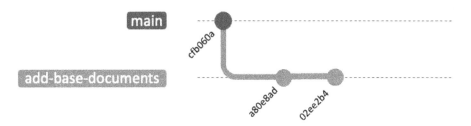

Figure 3.26 – git cherry-pick (1)

Now, let's only pick the a80e8ad commit and put it on the main branch. Please replace the hash value in your environment:

```
# Now switch back to the 'main' branch and cherry-pick the commit
$ git checkout main
$ git cherry-pick a80e8ad
[main 9a36741] Add CONTRIBUTING.md
Date: Sun Oct 29 16:04:56 2023 +0900
1 file changed, 1 insertion(+)
create mode 100644 CONTRIBUTING.md

# Let's check the 'main' branch log
$ git log --graph --oneline
```

```
* 9a36741 (HEAD -> main) Add CONTRIBUTING.md
* cfb060a Initial commit
```

After you have successfully cherry-picked the commit, a new commit will be added to your current branch (`main` in this example) and it will include the changes from the cherry-picked commit. Note that the new commit has the same changes but a different commit hash value:

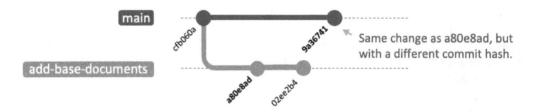

Figure 3.27 – git cherry-pick (2)

Why cherry-pick is useful in DevOps and team collaboration

Team development requires flexible development. `git cherry-pick` is a useful command in collaborative coding environments, allowing teams to selectively integrate changes and maintain code integrity.

Let's see what value `cherry-pick` can offer:

- **Selective integration**: It allows specific bug fixes or features to be moved into production without having to move all changes from a development branch

- **Easy reversion**: If something goes wrong, you only need to revert a small change rather than an entire branch merge

- **Clean history**: Keeps your Git history tidy by only including relevant commits, making it easier to read and understand

`git cherry-pick` offers a high level of precision for integrating changes between branches. It allows you to select exactly which commits to include, providing granular control over your project history. This makes it an invaluable tool for any DevOps engineer aiming for a flexible and efficient version control workflow.

After exploring the various merging strategies in Git, you might be asking yourself, "*Which method should I use?*" The answer, as with most things in engineering, is, "*It depends.*" Several factors come into play when determining which Git merge strategy best suits your needs. Additionally, it is worth noting that you do not have to stick to a single method; you can vary your approach depending on the situation. Understanding these factors can help you make an informed decision.

Let's check the following factors to see how you should choose:

- **Project complexity**: Complex projects with multiple contributors and parallel development lines may require a more consistent merging approach to minimize conflicts. Platforms such as GitHub allow you to set merge strategies for your projects.

- **Team preferences and skill level**: The merging strategy you choose should be one that your team is comfortable with. This could depend on the experience level of the team members and their familiarity with Git commands and practices. When a development team consists of members with varying skill levels, sticking to simpler methods such as `git merge` can reduce the chances of mistakes. However, if the majority of the team is experienced, you may want to leverage the benefits of `rebase` to maintain a cleaner Git history while also facilitating smoother communication.

- **Desired cleanliness of Git history**: If a clean, linear Git history is of utmost importance to you, then opting for fast-forward merges or rebasing might be the best route. On the other hand, if you value detailed documentation of your project's development process, a non-fast-forward merge would be a better choice for maintaining a comprehensive record of changes.

As you move forward, let the knowledge from this section guide you in choosing the appropriate merge approach for your projects. Practice with real-world scenarios to gain confidence. Remember, there is no one-size-fits-all answer in Git—flexibility and adaptability are your allies

Navigating conflicts

In a collaborative development environment, conflicts are not just possible—they are inevitable. When multiple developers are working on the same code base, or even the same files, there is a good chance that changes will overlap, leading to conflicts. Navigating and resolving these conflicts is crucial for maintaining a smooth and efficient DevOps workflow.

Why conflict happens

Conflicts generally occur when two branches have changes in the same line or section of a file and are then attempted to be merged. Git, as sophisticated as it is, can not decide which change to take precedence. The key to efficiently resolving these conflicts is understanding why they occur and being proactive in preventing them when possible.

How to merge conflicts in Git

Let's start with the basics. Conflict resolution in Git usually involves manual intervention. Here is how to go about it:

1. Identify conflicts. Use `git status` to see which files are conflicted.

2. Examine the conflicted files. Open them up and look for the conflict markers (<<<<<<<, =======, and >>>>>>>). These markers delineate the changes from the different branches:

```
<<<<<<< HEAD
Someone's change is here
=======
Your change is here
>>>>>>> branch-you-want-to-merge
```

3. Resolve the conflicts. Choose which changes to keep. You can keep the changes from one branch, mix both, or even add something entirely new.

4. Commit the resolved files. After resolving, you need to add the files to the staging area and commit them.

How to resolve merge conflicts

Merge conflicts are inevitable in a collaborative development environment. The key is knowing how to resolve them efficiently. There are several patterns you can follow, depending on the nature of the conflict.

When there is a definitive version to retain

If you have merged two branches and want to fully accept one version over the other, you can opt to use `git checkout --ours` or `git checkout --theirs`:

*   `checkout --ours`: Use this command to keep the files from your branch when a merge conflict arises:

    ```
    $ git checkout --ours -- <file-path>
    ```

*   `checkout --theirs`: This command will retain the files from the merged branch, discarding the ones in your current branch:

    ```
    $ git checkout --theirs -- <file-path>
    ```

After running one of these commands, you will need to add the updated files to the staging area and then commit them.

When you need to evaluate both versions

In cases where it is not clear which version should take precedence, a more nuanced approach is required.

*   **Review the code**: Open the conflicting files in a text editor to manually inspect the clashing lines of code. Decide which parts to keep and edit the files accordingly.

- **Communication**: If necessary, consult with your teammates to decide which changes should be kept. This can be done through in-person discussions, virtual meetings, or code review tools.

- **Run tests**: Once you have resolved the conflicts manually, it is crucial to run tests to ensure that the code base is still stable.

- **Commit the changes**: After successful testing, stage the resolved files and commit them to your repository.

By carefully handling merge conflicts, you can help maintain a clean code base and foster better communication within your team.

Useful commands for supporting merge activities

Merging is an activity that comes with its own set of challenges. Having the right set of tools and commands at your disposal can make the process smoother and less error-prone. In this section, there are some useful Git commands that can help you effectively manage your merges.

git diff – Spot the difference

The `git diff` command is an essential tool for identifying the differences between two sets of code. It helps you see what exactly has changed between two branches or two commits, making it much easier to resolve conflicts when they arise.

You can compare the current branch to a target branch like so:

```
$ git diff feature-branch..main
```

This command displays a line-by-line comparison of the changes between `feature-branch` and `main`. You can also focus on specific files or even specific lines of code, which makes it a flexible tool for spotting differences at various granularities.

Although Git does not have a built-in dry-run option for `git merge`, you can simulate a merge to see what will happen:

```
$ git merge --no-commit --no-ff feature-branch
$ git diff --cached
```

This command sequence attempts to merge changes from develop into your current branch but stops just before committing them. You can then use `git diff --cached` to view the staged changes. If the merge is not what you expected, you can simply abort:

```
$ git merge --abort
```

git mergetool – A simplified guide tooling to visual conflict resolution

When you run into a merge conflict that's challenging to resolve manually, or if you are more comfortable with a graphical interface, Git's built-in `git mergetool` can come to your rescue.

The following items can be set:

- **Choose your merge tool**: First, decide which merge tool you'd like to use. Common options include `kdiff3`, `meld`, and `vimdiff`.

- **Global configuration**: Set your chosen tool as the default for all your Git repositories with the following command:

  ```
  # For example, if you chose vimdiff, you would run:
  $ git config --global merge.tool vimdiff
  ```

  Once configured, you can activate `git mergetool` whenever you face a merge conflict:

  ```
  $ git mergetool
  ```

  This command opens your chosen graphical tool and displays the conflicting changes side by side. This interface simplifies the process of understanding conflicts and deciding which changes to keep. This setting allows you to specify not only command line tools but also modern tools such as Visual Studio Code to resolve merges graphically.

By following these straightforward steps, you can resolve complex merge conflicts in a more intuitive way, making the process accessible for team members of all skill levels.

In a nutshell, conflict resolution is an essential skill for any engineer. While conflicts can be complex and challenging, knowing how to navigate them efficiently can make your development workflow much smoother. It is not just about resolving the conflicts themselves but understanding the underlying issues that lead to them. This nuanced approach is crucial for fostering better communication and collaboration within your development team.

As team development progresses, projects become more complex. Conflicts are inevitable. Conflict is a great opportunity to help your team to improve its collaboration skills. You should not be afraid of conflicts, and you should also learn how to communicate best for your team by solving them one by one.

Mastering better collaboration

Up until now, we have discussed how to handle merges and resolve conflicts in Git. We have seen that you can clean up your local changes with `git merge --squash` or adjust commit history with `git rebase`. While it is great to keep your workspace neat, the ideal scenario is to maintain a clean code base, especially when you push to a shared environment. Next, let's talk about the commands that enable you to be an excellent collaborator, whether you are an individual contributor or a team leader managing the main shared branch.

Rolling back time

In any collaborative project, mistakes are inevitable. Even if it was not a mistake, there will be many times you will want to rewind and go back in time. Whether it is a bad commit that breaks the build or a feature that did not pan out as expected, the ability to roll back changes is crucial. Two commands that are indispensable for this are `git reset` and `git revert`.

git reset – Rolling back changes

The `git reset` command allows you to *rewind* your Git history, essentially moving HEAD and, optionally, the working directory to a specific commit. This is incredibly powerful but should be used cautiously. There are several different ways to use `git reset`. Know them so that you can organize your environment efficiently:

- **Soft reset**: This keeps your working directory and index intact but moves HEAD. This command is used when you want to leave the index working tree untouched and only undo the commit:

    ```
    $ git reset --soft <commit hash>
    ```

    The following is the area of impact of the `git reset --soft` command:

Figure 3.28 – git reset --soft

- **Mixed reset**: This resets the index but keeps the working directory unchanged. This command is used when you want to undo only what you `git add` and `git commit`. File changes will remain; this is the default when no options are specified with `git reset`:

    ```
    $ git reset --mixed <commit hash>
    ```

    The following is the area of impact of the `git reset --mixed` command:

Figure 3.29 – git reset --mixed

- **Hard reset**: This resets the index and working directory, permanently deleting uncommitted changes. It deletes all changes to commits, indexes, and files, so all the changes themselves do not remain with you. If you want to delete everything, this is the way to do it:

```
$ git reset --hard <commit hash>
```

The following is the area of impact of the `git reset --hard` command:

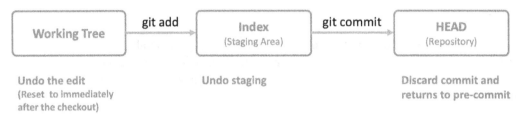

Figure 3.30 – git reset --hard

git revert – Undoing without rewriting history

Unlike `git reset`, which alters commit history, `git revert` creates a new commit that undoes the changes made by a previous commit. This is extremely useful in a shared environment where rewriting history is highly discouraged.

`git revert` creates a reverse commit as follows:

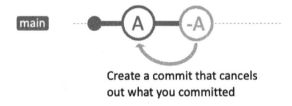

Figure 3.31 – git-revert creates a commit to cancel the commit

This command will undo the changes made by the commit with the specified hash and create a new commit to record this action:

```
$ git revert <commit_hash>
```

The following are cases when you can use `git revert`:

- **Shared branches**: Since `git revert` does not rewrite history, it is safe to use on shared branches
- **Rolling back features**: If a feature turns out to be buggy or unwanted, `git revert` is a clean way to remove it

- **Automated deployments**: In a CI/CD pipeline, you can automate the `git revert` operation as part of your rollback strategy

Let's learn about some additional advanced `git revert` options:

- **Reverting multiple commits**: You can revert a range of commits by specifying a commit range:

```
git revert OLDEST_COMMIT^..NEWEST_COMMIT
```

- **Revert with manual edit**: If you want to manually edit the changes before committing them, you can use the `-n` or `--no-commit` flags:

```
git revert -n <commit_hash>
```

  This will apply the revert changes to your working directory but will not commit them. You can then make further changes and commit manually.

> **Note**
>
> Note the caret (`^`) symbol. This means the oldest commit in the range of commits to revert is included.

Mastering `git revert` is crucial for any developer or DevOps professional. It provides a safe mechanism for undoing changes, enabling better collaboration and more reliable code.

git checkout – More than just branch hopping

In previous discussions, we have touched on the `git checkout` command mainly in the context of switching between branches. While this is certainly one of its primary functions, it is crucial to understand that `git checkout` is a multi-purpose tool that can operate at the granularity of individual files or directories as well. In this section, let's expand our understanding of `git checkout` and see how it plays a vital role in efficient collaboration and error correction.

Here's a refresher on the basic command for switching branches:

```
$ git checkout <branch_name>
```

But what if you only need to restore a single file to a previous state? `git checkout` has got you covered. If you have made changes to a file but have not committed yet and you decide you want to undo those changes, you can do this:

```
$ git checkout -- <file_name>
```

This will discard changes in your working directory and revert the file back to the state of the last commit. Sometimes, you might want to partially apply changes from another branch to your current working branch. git checkout can also do this:

```
$ git checkout <branch_name> -- <file_name>
```

This command will check out a specific file from another branch into your current working branch, allowing you to mix and match code as needed.

It offers versatility in team collaboration:

- **Quick rollbacks**: If something goes wrong in the production, you can quickly check out the specific files from a stable branch.

- **Selective feature testing**: Before merging a new feature, you can check out only the files relevant to that feature for testing.

- **Easy error correction**: Mistakes happen all the time. The ability to check out individual files makes it easier to correct them without affecting other parts of the code base.

> **Note**
>
> Using `git checkout` on files will discard changes. Make sure this is what you intend to do. If you are experimenting, it is a good idea to commit your changes often. That way, you can easily revert back to a specific commit if needed.

Understanding the full range of `git checkout` capabilities can significantly enhance your workflow and collaboration efficiency. Whether you are working alone or as part of a team, the ability to manipulate not just branches but also individual files grants you a higher degree of control and adaptability in your team collaboration.

Organizing your working environment

In the realm of team development, your individual workspace is your personal lab—a space where you can innovate, debug, and test freely without affecting the broader project. Managing this space efficiently is crucial, and Git offers a set of powerful commands to help you do just that. In this section, we will explore three essential Git commands—`git clean`, `git stash`, and `.gitignore`—that can easily keep your workspace clean.

git clean – A fresh start

The `git clean` command offers a quick way to clear your working directory of untracked files and directories, essentially providing a clean slate. This can be especially useful before or after executing a merge, or when you want to remove any clutter that does not need to be version-controlled:

```
# Remove untracked files and directories
$ git clean -fd
```

git stash – Pause and resume work effortlessly

`git stash` is an invaluable tool for temporarily stashing away changes that you have made but are not yet ready to commit.

As a developer, multitasking is often the name of the game. Whether you are interrupted by an urgent bug fix or need to switch context temporarily, `git stash` comes to the rescue. This command allows you to save your current changes without making a formal commit, giving you the freedom to switch tasks and then return to where you left off:

```
# Stash changes with a description
$ git stash save "WIP: New Feature"
# Reapply the stashed changes
$ git stash apply stash@{0}
```

In addition, here is a rundown of common `git stash` commands that can significantly enhance your workspace management:

- `git stash`: This stashes your changes, leaving your working directory clean. Untracked files are not stashed.

- `git stash save "Your Comment"`: This stashes your changes and allows you to attach a comment. This is useful for identifying stashes later with `git stash list`.

- `git stash list`: This displays a list of all your stashed changes. If you used `git stash save`, you will see your comments here, making it easier to identify each stash.

- `git stash apply`: This restores the most recently stashed changes to your working directory. The stash remains in the `git stash list`.

- `git stash apply [stash@{n}]`: This restores a specific stash based on its index number, which you can find using `git stash list`.

- `git stash drop`: This deletes a specific stash from the stash list.

- `git stash drop [stash@{n}]`: This deletes a specific stash based on its index number.

- `git stash clear`: This deletes all stashes, clearing your `stash list`.

.gitignore – Personalize what gets shared

When working on complex projects, your local environment may generate files such as logs or contain personal configuration settings—things you do not want to share with the rest of the team. The `.gitignore` file enables you to specify which files and folders should be ignored during a `git add`, ensuring they remain exclusive to your local environment.

This is an example of a `.gitignore` file:

```
# Ignore all log files
*.log

# Ignore personal config files
config/personal/
```

Who did what? Great ways to help you debug

Git has a couple of typical ways to analyze the past. `git blame` and `git bisect` are useful to remember because they are easy to use to go back and debug who made what changes.

git blame – Who did what?

When working in a shared code base, there may be instances where you need to understand the history of specific lines of code. The `git blame` command provides a breakdown of a file, annotating each line to show the last person who modified it and what commit it belongs to. This helps in identifying the responsible parties for particular changes, which is useful for debugging, refactoring, or simply understanding why a particular piece of code exists.

```
$ git blame file.txt
```

The `-L` option allows you to specify the lines of output:

```
$ git blame -L 5,10 README.md
$ git blame -L 5,+5 README.md
```

It is essential to highlight that the aim of `git blame` is not to single out individuals for errors or questionable decisions. In any collaborative setting—especially in DevOps where teamwork is paramount—it is crucial to remember that mistakes are a collective responsibility. Everyone can err; what is important is how the team collaborates to fix those errors. From a psychosocial safety perspective, using `git blame` should be approached as a way to enhance team communication and identify areas for improvement rather than as a mechanism for casting blame.

git bisect – Efficient bug hunting in commit ranges

Debugging can often feel like looking for a needle in a haystack, especially in large codebases with a long history of commits. In the realm of DevOps, where rapid deployment cycles are the norm, a bug introduced in any of the numerous changes can wreak havoc. This is where `git bisect` comes into play, serving as a powerful tool for isolating the specific commit that introduced a bug.

The `git bisect` command performs a binary search through your commit history to find the commit that introduced the bug. The process begins by marking a known good commit and a known bad commit:

```
$ git bisect start
$ git bisect bad   # If the current version is bad
$ git bisect good <Last known good version commit hash>
```

Git will then automatically check out a commit halfway between the good and bad commits. You test this commit and then mark it as either good or bad:

```
$ git bisect good # or
$ git bisect bad
```

Git will continue this process, narrowing down the range of commits until it identifies the culprit. Once you find the problematic commit, it is easier to understand what went wrong and to devise a fix:

```
# Exit bisect mode and return to your branch
$ git bisect reset
```

In DevOps, where the speed of identifying and resolving issues is crucial for maintaining operational excellence, `git bisect` becomes an invaluable tool. It integrates well into a DevOps toolchain, allowing for automated testing and facilitating quicker rollbacks and patches. By efficiently pinpointing errors, it enhances the team's ability to collaborate on solutions, underscoring the essential DevOps principles of rapid feedback and continuous improvement.

Versioning excellence

In the DevOps ecosystem, **CI/CD** make everything incremental. Yet, it is essential to have concrete versions of your software to serve as milestones. These versions are not just markers in time; they indicate the stability, new features, and overall health of your code base. They also facilitate smoother rollbacks and make it easier to isolate issues.

What is semantic versioning

Semantic versioning is a versioning scheme designed to convey specific meanings about the underlying changes with each new release. The format consists of three numbers separated by dots (e.g., 2.4.4). Each number has a particular significance related to backward compatibility and the types of changes introduced.

Tagging in Git

Tagging becomes a cornerstone of effective version control within a DevOps environment. By marking specific points in your repository's history, you can create anchors that serve as stable release points or significant milestones. These tagged versions form the basis for your CI/CD pipelines, ensuring consistent and reliable deployments.

To make your tags more informative, consider annotating them with useful metadata and context:

```
$ git tag -a v1.0 -m "Initial stable release"
```

The commits you tag should typically represent stable release points or crucial milestones. These are the commits where all the automated tests have passed, features are complete, and the code has undergone peer review. In essence, they are your *production-ready* commits.

To tag a specific commit, use the following:

```
$ git tag v2.4.4 32de0b2
```

Git tagging and semantic versioning are not just technical procedures but strategic actions. They ensure that everyone is on the same page regarding what is being deployed and what it can do.

In this section, we have equipped ourselves with the knowledge to roll back time in our repositories, understanding when and how to use `git reset`, `git revert`, and `git checkout`. These powerful commands ensure that we can gracefully undo changes, correct course, and maintain a clean project history—all essential for a collaborative setting. Organizing your working environment with `git clean`, `git stash`, and the right `.gitignore` settings offers you a pristine workspace where focus and clarity replace clutter and chaos. This clean slate is not just about personal preference; it is about setting a standard for the team and ensuring that only intentional changes make their way into the shared repository.

Incorporating these techniques into your routine not only prepares you for better personal performance but also strengthens the whole team.

Summary

In this chapter, we delved deep into the nuances of branch strategies, the intricacies of merging and rebasing, and the art of navigating conflicts with the goal of mastering better collaboration within your teams. From understanding why a branching strategy is crucial to aligning branch naming with organizational objectives, we have laid out the groundwork for you to build a robust workflow.

We explored the various branching models, such as trunk-based development, Git Flow, and GitHub Flow, highlighting their unique benefits and scenarios where they fit best. The discussion around merge approaches provided insight into the tools at your disposal for maintaining a clean and informative project history while also addressing the sometimes daunting task of conflict resolution.

As you close this chapter, remember that the path to mastering Git is ongoing. Encourage yourself to discover more and to practice these skills through your development work with confidence. Embrace the challenges and the learning opportunities they bring and continue to grow as a developer. Git is not just a tool; it is a companion in your DevOps journey that enhances the developer's experience by removing friction and fostering a culture of collaboration.

Part 2: GitHub Excellence and CI/CD Fundamentals

This part highlights GitHub's role in DevOps, expanding its use beyond just code hosting. It discusses GitHub's features that enhance team collaboration and the transition to modern DevOps practices. Additionally, it delves into GitHub Actions, focusing on workflow optimization, advanced deployment methods such as blue-green and canary deployments, and feature release strategies. This provides an in-depth understanding of GitHub's capabilities in continuous integration and deployment.

This part has the following chapters:

- *Chapter 4, Elevating Team Collaboration with GitHub*
- *Chapter 5, Driving CI/CD with GitHub*

Elevating Team Collaboration with GitHub

Congratulations on reaching this pivotal chapter of our journey! Now, it is time to delve deeper, moving beyond the perception of GitHub as merely a code hosting platform. GitHub is where the world builds software, where development processes are streamlined, and where the spirit of DevOps truly comes to life.

In this chapter, we will dive into the practical aspects of using GitHub, transforming theory into action. Our focus will be on specific GitHub features crucial for teamwork and collaboration in a DevOps environment. Each section is crafted to enhance your understanding and skills, ensuring a smooth transition from traditional systems to modern DevOps practices. Let's embark on this exciting journey with GitHub, a powerful ally in the DevOps toolkit.

We will cover the following main headings in this chapter:

- Getting started with GitHub
- Issues – Collaboration excellence at GitHub
- Pull request excellence
- Getting the best out of GitHub
- GitHub repository excellence

We will start with a hands-on experience working with GitHub. If you want to grasp the big picture of GitHub again, please go back to *Chapter 1* to see what GitHub is all about.

Technical requirements

Configuration instructions for proceeding with this section can be found in the following repository. Please make sure the Git and SSH tools are installed. For Windows users, it is recommended to use PowerShell. I also encourage you to get the most up-to-date information written about the different commands and environments: `https://github.com/PacktPublishing/DevOps-Unleashed-with-Git-and-GitHub`.

Getting started with GitHub

Now, let's get started with the GitHub experience. This section explains how to get started with GitHub and covers basic repository operations. You will also learn how to use Git to interact with remote repositories, completing the journey of Git basics here!

Setting up your GitHub account

Embarking on your GitHub journey begins with a simple sign-up process. Navigate to the GitHub website and register by providing a username, email, and password. This step is your gateway to the realms of collaborative development, offering a suite of features for team collaboration and project management.

Once registered, you are all set to create repositories and push your code to GitHub, marking the start of your Git journey. GitHub serves not just as a tool but as a cornerstone in your DevOps journey, fostering collaboration and driving innovation. If you already have a GitHub account, feel free to move to the next steps.

To sign up, visit `https://github.com/` and click the **Sign up** button located at the top right of the page:

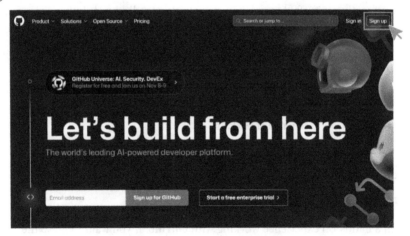

Figure 4.1 – Home page of github.com

Enter your email, choose a password, and select a unique username. After completing a few confirmation steps, you will receive a confirmation email. Use the code provided to finalize your GitHub account setup:

Figure 4.2 – Registration page on github.com and confirmation email

With these steps, your GitHub account is ready, paving the way to create your first repository. The account creation experience is current at the time of writing. It may change in the future, but it is basically a straightforward way.

Creating your first GitHub repository

When logging in to GitHub, the menu for creating a new repository varies depending on your user status. New users are directly presented with a **Create repository** button, while existing users will find the **New** button within their list of repositories:

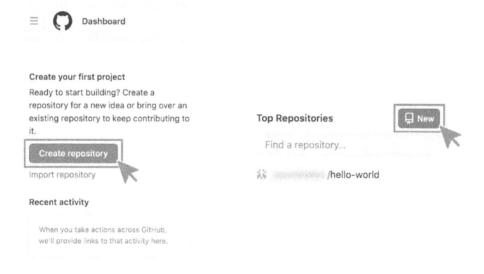

Figure 4.3 – The button to create a new repository

Then, the repository creation settings screen appears:

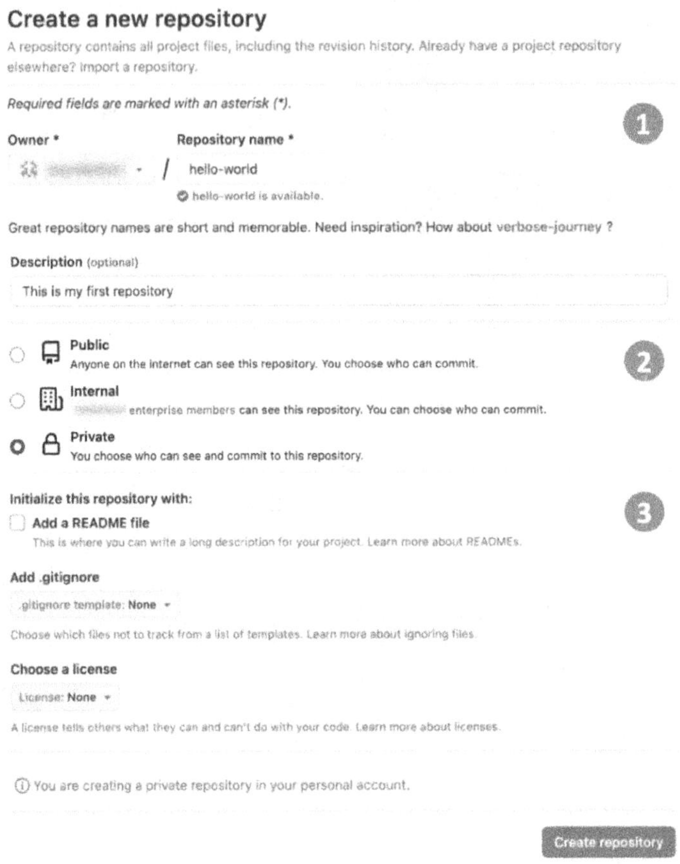

Figure 4.4 – Creating a new repository

Creating a repository involves a few key decisions:

- **Repository location**: Choose the owner (yourself or an organization you are part of) and provide a unique name for your repository under the selected owner.

- **Visibility**: Decide whether your repository will be public or private. With a **public** repository, your project is accessible to anyone around the world, making it a part of the open source community where sharing and collaboration are encouraged. On the other hand, a **private** repository is for work you want to keep to yourself or share with selected individuals, offering confidentiality. For members of organizations under a GitHub Enterprise plan, there is an option to create **internal** repositories. These repositories are perfect for InnerSource initiatives as they are only visible within your enterprise, providing a secure environment for collaborative projects.

- **Initialization**: You can initialize your repository with a `README.md`, `.gitignore`, or `LICENSE` file. Including a `README.md` file is like providing a welcoming guidebook for your project; it is where you explain what your project is about, how to use it, and any other important information a visitor should know. If your project is open source, picking the right license from the get-go is especially essential. It sets the rules for how others can use and contribute to your project. Selecting these options means GitHub will automatically run the `git init` command inside. If you are planning to push an existing project to GitHub, leave these unchecked.

For this example, leave all initialization checkboxes unchecked, resulting in a blank repository. This sets the stage for uploading your local files in the next steps. After filling in the repository details, click the **Create repository** button. This action will bring your new repository to life:

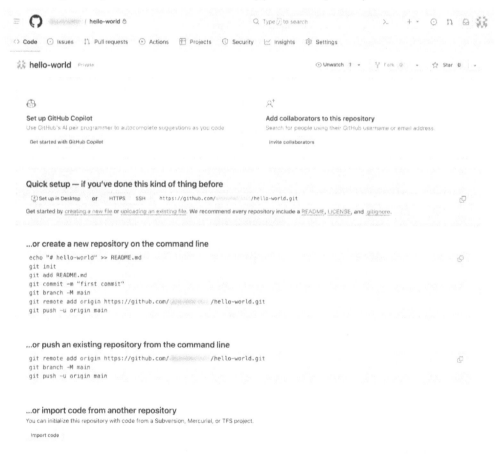

Figure 4.5 – Created repository

Congratulations on creating your new GitHub repository! This milestone marks a significant step in your journey as a developer, opening doors to collaboration, innovation, and growth in the world of DevOps and open source development.

Next, we will connect your local repository to a remote repository, which includes generating and registering an SSH key for GitHub. The details of setting up SSH connections will be crucial in upcoming sections, so make sure to take note of the SSH URL string. Click the **SSH** button and then the copy icon to copy the values as shown in the following screenshot:

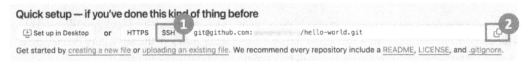

Figure 4.6 – Information on SSH connection

Registering your SSH key

Now, it is time to set up your SSH keys. To do this, navigate to the settings by clicking the top-right menu button on GitHub:

Figure 4.7 – Opening the menu

From this menu bar, you have the ability to navigate to various sections of your GitHub account. You can view your profile and manage the repositories and organizations you are a part of. Now, select **Settings** in the menu bar:

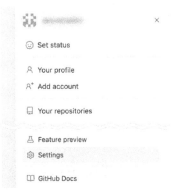

Figure 4.8 – Clicking Settings in the menu bar to open the setting

Once you are in the **Settings** section, look for **SSH and GPG keys** in the left-hand menu. Here, you will have the option to create a new SSH key:

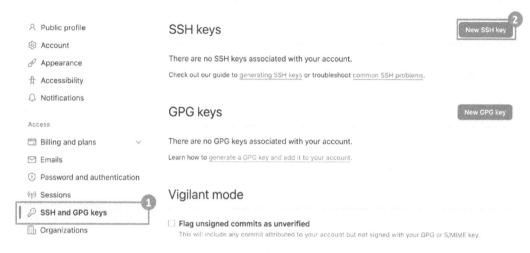

Figure 4.9 – Settings

After clicking on the **New SSH key** button, you will be prompted to input a title and select the key type. At this stage, you should choose **Authentication Key**. Then, you can input the SSH key into the given field.

Now, here you will need your SSH key to register! Let's see how to make one next. You can skip this process if you have already registered

Creating your SSH key is a crucial step in setting up a secure environment for managing your code on GitHub. This process is especially important if you are new to SSH keys or do not already have one. You can check if you have an existing key by navigating to the `~/.ssh` directory in your terminal. This directory typically holds your SSH configuration files and keys. If you find no existing keys or want to create a new one specifically for GitHub, let's create it.

First, open your terminal and navigate to the SSH directory:

```
$ cd ~/.ssh
```

Then, generate a new SSH key with the `ssh-keygen` command. You will be using an RSA key for this purpose:

```
$ ssh-keygen -t rsa
```

This command initiates the process of key generation and shows up the following message:

```
Generating public/private rsa key pair.
```

When prompted, enter the filename in which to save the key. Here's an example:

```
Enter file in which to save the key
(/Users/username/.ssh/id_rsa): [Your Key Name]
```

In this scenario, I will use `git_key` as the key name.

Next, you will be asked to enter a passphrase. This adds an extra layer of security:

```
Enter passphrase (empty for no passphrase): [Your Passphrase]
Enter same passphrase again: [Repeat Your Passphrase]
```

For further insight, adding a passphrase to your SSH key is a key security step. If someone gets your private key without permission, they still cannot use it without the passphrase. This protects against unauthorized use. You need to enter the passphrase every time you use the key, making sure only people with both the key and passphrase can get in. This extra layer of security makes your SSH connections much safer and is advised for protecting important information and access. After these steps, you will see a confirmation that your identification (private key) and your public key have been saved. A unique key fingerprint and a random art image will also be displayed.

Now, you need to check and copy your new public SSH key:

```
$ cat ~/.ssh/git_rsa.pub
```

Copy the displayed SSH key (begins with `ssh-rsa`):

```
ssh-rsa AAAAB3NzaC1yc2EAA...x4CWuT2U= a1b2@c3d4.e5f6
```

Now, let's add this SSH key to your GitHub account. Again, navigate to GitHub settings, find the **SSH and GPG keys** section, and paste and save your key there:

Add new SSH Key

Title

your-ssh-key

Key type

Authentication Key ⇕

Key

ssh-rsa

Add SSH key

Figure 4.10 – Adding a new SSH key

To set up or modify your SSH connections, let's start by creating a configuration file using the `touch` command, which creates a new file or updates the last modified time of an existing one:

```
$ touch config
```

Now, with the config file ready, it is time to add specific configurations for GitHub SSH connections. Ensure you replace `git_rsa` with the name of your private SSH key file. For those who have followed the earlier steps to create a new key, your filename should be `git_rsa`. If you are an experienced Git user, you might already have some SSH configurations in this file. In such a scenario, you should update or replace the existing configurations. For those adding new configurations, input these lines:

```
Host github github.com
   HostName github.com
   IdentityFile ~/.ssh/git_rsa # Your key file name
   User git
```

After inputting these lines, save and close the file. This configuration instructs your system on which SSH key to use for GitHub and under which user account.

It is also recommended to verify your SSH connection to GitHub to ensure everything is set up correctly. You can do this by running the `ssh -T git@github.com` command. This step helps confirm that your system can successfully communicate with GitHub using the SSH key specified in your configuration.

git remote – Connecting local and remote repositories

It is time to bridge your local development with the world of GitHub. If you are continuing from an existing repository in an earlier section, simply move into that directory with the cd command, like so:

```
$ cd path/to/your/repository
```

For those who want to create a new project, setting up a fresh repository is a straightforward affair. Begin by creating a new directory, initializing a Git repository, and preparing a README file—the hallmark of any new project:

```
$ mkdir new-project
$ cd new-project
$ git init
$ echo "# README" >> README.md
$ git add README.md
$ git commit -m "Initial commit"
```

Remember to use the SSH URL you noted in the previous section.

Connecting your local repository to a remote repository on GitHub involves adding a remote URL. This linkage allows you to push your local changes to GitHub. Establish this connection with the git remote add command, ensuring to replace [Username] and [Repository] with your GitHub username and the repository's name:

```
$ git remote add origin git@github.com:[Username]/[Repository].git
```

For cases where your repository already has a remote URL but needs an update, git remote set-url is the command of choice. This command updates your Git configuration to the new remote repository URL:

```
$ git remote set-url origin git@github.com:[Username]/[Repository].git
```

With these steps, you have successfully linked your local and remote repositories. This connection is a pivotal point in managing your project, ensuring that your local developments are mirrored on GitHub for further progress and collaboration.

As we move forward, the next step will be to push your local code to GitHub.

git push – Making your code count

Finally, it is time to push your local commits to the remote repository. This step updates the remote repository with the changes you have made locally:

```
$ git push -u origin main
```

When you use `-u` or `--set-upstream` with `git push`, you are effectively setting the upstream for the current branch in your local repository to the `main` origin.

By specifying this upstream, you simplify your future interactions with the remote repository. Once the upstream is set, you can use `git push` without additional parameters to push to the same branch on the remote repository. This means that a subsequent `git push` operation will automatically know to push your commits to the `main` origin.

Examining code on GitHub

Now, let's examine what the pushed code looks like on GitHub.

When you visit a GitHub repository, the first thing that greets you is the repository's main page. Here, you can see the most recently updated files, the README.md file (if available), and various repository details. This view provides a quick snapshot of the project's contents and purpose:

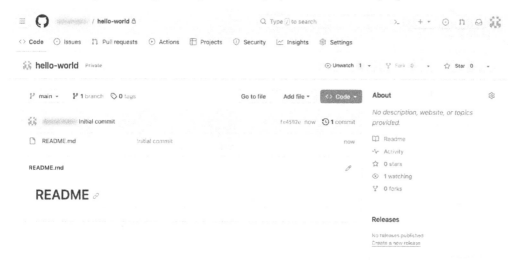

Figure 4.11 – GitHub repository page after pushing the code

Editing code on GitHub

One of the key features is the ability to interact with code directly on GitHub. You can add or edit files using the interface itself, which is particularly useful for small changes or quick fixes. Here's how to do that:

1. Click the *edit* button in the upper-right corner to enter the edit mode:

Figure 4.12 – Entering the edit mode

2. You can then edit and commit your changes. Remember that this commits directly to your code base:

Figure 4.13 – Edit page on GitHub

3. This action commits your changes directly to your remote repository. However, you also have the flexibility to select a destination and branch for your commit. While the default is typically the branch you are currently working on, you have the option to create a new branch simultaneously, which can be particularly useful when starting a new contribution. If you choose to create a new branch, you can still merge it later into the mainline:

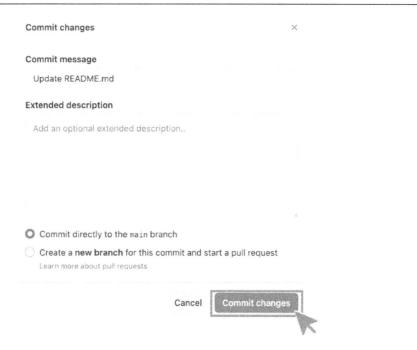

Figure 4.14 – Committing changes

4.   Now, you should see the changes reflected, as in the following screenshot:

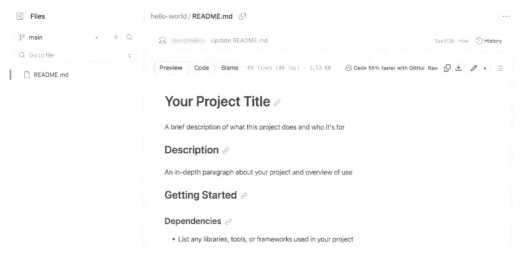

Figure 4.15 – After the commit, you will return to the code screen

Reviewing code and changes on GitHub

Now, let's look inside GitHub via the code we just updated. For a closer look at the code, GitHub provides several views in the file browser:

- **Preview** mode is the default, available for certain file types such as Markdown, and displays the file as it would appear in its formatted state:

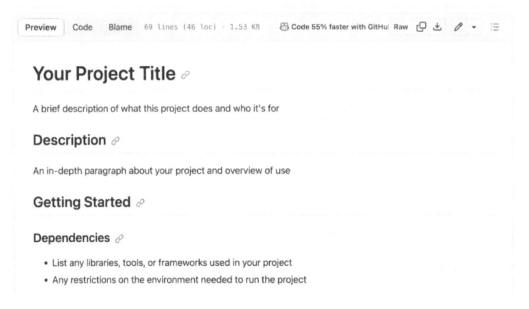

Figure 4.16 – Preview mode

- **Code** mode shows the contents of the file as it is in the latest commit, with beautiful syntax highlighting:

Figure 4.17 – Code mode

- **Blame** mode is particularly insightful, as it breaks down the file by lines, showing who last modified each line and in which commit. This is invaluable for understanding the evolution of code and tracking changes:

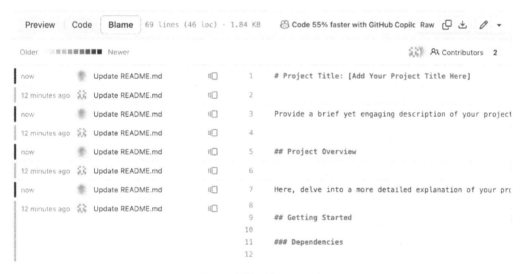

Figure 4.18 – Blame mode

This is useful when you do not want to get code locally and review it but want to take a look at the code on GitHub first. Within the GitHub repository interface, you have the ability to explore the commit history of the project. This feature allows you to delve into the specifics of each commit, examining changes made:

Figure 4.19 – Change history on GitHub

Additionally, GitHub offers the functionality to comment on these changes, enabling you to engage in discussions or provide feedback on specific alterations made in the repository:

Figure 4.20 – GitHub commit view

Managing branches on GitHub

Managing branches on GitHub is easy. Here is a brief overview of branch management on GitHub.

First, navigating between different branches in a repository is a common task. On GitHub, you can easily switch between branches using the branch drop-down menu, typically found at the top of the repository page. This feature allows you to swiftly move from one branch to another, enabling you to review different versions or stages of the project efficiently:

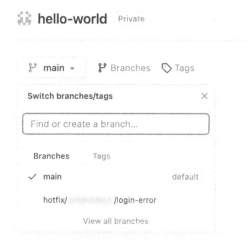

Figure 4.21 – Switching branches on GitHub

With repositories that have multiple branches, finding a specific branch can become challenging. GitHub provides a search functionality within the branch drop-down menu. This feature allows you to quickly filter and find the branch you are looking for, saving time and improving your workflow:

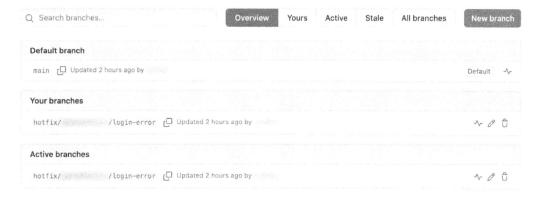

Figure 4.22 – Searching for branches on GitHub

Starting a new line of development is often done by creating a new branch. GitHub simplifies this process to create a new branch. You can name the new branch and base it on an existing one, making it straightforward to branch off for new features or experiments:

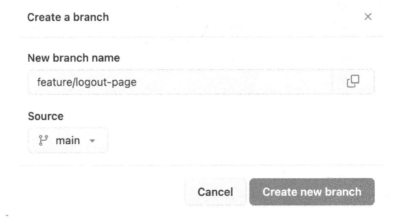

Figure 4.23 – Creating a branch on GitHub

GitHub branch management features provide a seamless and efficient way to handle multiple lines of development within a single repository. Whether you are switching to view different project states, searching for a specific branch, or creating a new branch for development, the GitHub interface makes these tasks intuitive and accessible. This streamlined approach to branch management is integral to maintaining an organized and productive development environment.

git pull – Bridging local and remote work

Now that we have seen how GitHub manages the code we push, let's get back to the command line. Get the new changes made to the local repository. We have edited README.md on GitHub, but how do we bring those changes to our local environment? The answer lies in the git pull command.

In the realm of version control with Git, staying updated with the latest changes in a remote repository is crucial for seamless collaboration and development. The git pull command is the tool designed precisely for this purpose. It serves as a bridge, bringing changes made remotely on platforms such as GitHub into your local working directory.

Using git pull is particularly important when working in a collaborative environment. Suppose your team members are committing changes to a shared repository on GitHub. In that case, regularly pulling these changes ensures that everyone's work aligns and reduces the likelihood of conflicts or inconsistencies.

To use `git pull`, navigate to your repository's directory in your command line or terminal and enter the following command:

```
$ git pull origin main
```

It is a simple yet powerful command that maintains the harmony of your collaborative efforts and keeps your local repository up to date with the latest developments.

When you execute `git pull`, what essentially happens is a two-step process. First, Git fetches the updates from the remote repository—this includes all commits and branches that have been pushed since your last update. Then, it merges these updates into your local repository. This merge is critical as it integrates remote changes with your local work, keeping your local repository in sync with its remote counterpart.

The `git pull` command might come across as straightforward at first glance, but it is actually a combination of two fundamental Git commands: `git fetch` and `git merge`. This dual nature makes `git pull` a powerful tool in the Git arsenal.

Moving on, let's delve deeper into the first component of this process: `git fetch`. This command is an essential piece of the version control puzzle, allowing you to see what others have been working on without merging those changes into your own work just yet.

git fetch – Syncing without disruption

`git fetch` plays a crucial role in how developers interact with remote repositories. At its core, `git fetch` is about safely and efficiently updating your local repository with changes from its remote counterpart.

When you run `git fetch`, Git contacts the specified remote repository and pulls down all data from it that you do not have yet. This includes new commits, branches, and tags. The beauty of `git fetch` is that it does this without making any changes to your working files. It is like taking a sneak peek at what others have been doing without actually integrating their changes into your work. This feature makes it a non-destructive operation, ensuring your current development work remains untouched.

The fetched data is stored in your local repository, but it is kept separate from your actual project files. To incorporate these fetched changes into your work, you would typically follow up with a `git merge` command, which merges the fetched branch into your current branch. Yes—`git fetch` can show its true power when used with `git merge`.

Fetch versus pull

Let's come back to `git pull` here a little bit. When you run `git pull`, it first initiates a `git fetch` operation. This part of the process reaches out to the remote repository and pulls in all new data it finds. This data includes commits, files, and references updated in the remote repository since your last fetch. It is a vital step to ensure you have all the latest information from the remote repository, but it does not automatically integrate these changes into your working files.

The second part of the `git pull` command is where `git merge` comes into play. After fetching updates, `git merge` takes these newly downloaded references and incorporates them into your local repository. This merging process is what actually updates your current working files with changes from the remote repository. It is a seamless integration of remote changes with your local work, keeping your repository in perfect sync with its remote counterpart.

Understanding the dual nature of `git pull` as a combination of fetching and merging operations reveals its true power in managing and synchronizing code changes in a collaborative environment.

Also, knowing the difference between `git fetch` and `git pull` is crucial. It allows you to more accurately control when and how changes from your remote repository are incorporated into your local work. This clear understanding is essential for smooth collaboration and adept repository management as it lets you strategically decide whether to just review changes or fully integrate them.

git clone – Bringing GitHub repos to your workspace

Speaking of cloning and downloading, these options are readily available for every repository. By going to the repository page and pressing the < > **Code** button, you will see that there are those options. Cloning creates a local copy of the repository on your machine, allowing you to work on the project offline, while downloading provides a ZIP file of the project for backup or review purposes:

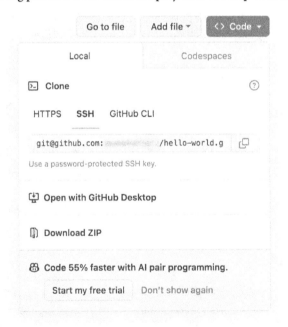

Figure 4.24 – git clone

Running the `git clone` command is a straightforward process, making it easily accessible for anyone wanting to engage with a project hosted on a platform such as GitHub. To clone a repository, all you need is the URL of the repository you want to clone:

```
$ git clone [Your SSH URL]
```

`git clone` stands out as a core command, enabling you to create a precise local copy of an existing repository. This process involves more than just duplicating current files; it replicates the repository in its entirety. This includes all file versions, the full commit history, and all branches. By using `git clone`, you bring a complete, functional version of the project onto your local machine. This not only gives you the ability to work offline but also provides a comprehensive view of the project's development history, aiding in understanding and effective contribution.

Forking – More than just copying code

In addition to `git clone`, there is another way to duplicate a repository on GitHub. This is especially useful for open source development. The concept of forking in Git, particularly on platforms such as GitHub, is a cornerstone of collaborative and open source development. Forking a repository means creating your own personal copy of someone else's project under your account:

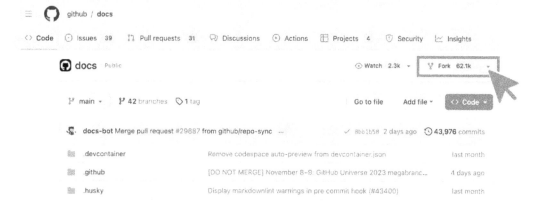

Figure 4.25 – Forking on GitHub

When you fork a repository, you create a personal copy of someone else's project within your GitHub account. While this copy starts as a mirror of the original, it operates independently, meaning you can make modifications, additions, or experiments without affecting the original project. However, it is important to understand that this independence has limits. For example, if the original repository is deleted or its visibility changes, it can affect the fork's status. Despite these dependencies, forking remains a pivotal practice in open source development, enabling developers to contribute through pull requests without needing direct write access to the source repository.

Forking is particularly significant in the open source world. It allows developers to contribute to projects by making changes in their forks and then proposing these changes to the original project through a process called a **pull request**. This is how you can contribute to a project without having direct writing access to the source repository. When you fork, a copy is made in your new environment, as shown in the following screenshot:

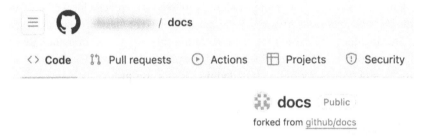

Figure 4.26 – The forked repository is managed under your environment

Forking provides a unique platform where anyone, regardless of their relationship or level of trust with the original project maintainers, can freely experiment and contribute. This approach significantly lowers barriers to entry in collaborative coding.

By forking a repository, you create an environment where you can add your ideas, enhancements, or fixes to the project without impacting the upstream repository. This is particularly empowering for new contributors who might not yet have gained the trust of the project maintainers for direct access to the main repository. It allows them to demonstrate their capabilities and contributions in a separate, personal space.

This independent yet connected nature of a fork is crucial. It enables a two-phase contribution process: first, in your own fork, where you freely experiment and make changes, and second, via a pull request, where you propose these changes to be merged into the original project. This workflow fosters a culture of open collaboration, where ideas and contributions are freely exchanged, and the best ones are seamlessly integrated into projects.

In essence, forking is more than just copying a repository; it is about participating in a larger community. Whether you are contributing to an existing project, starting a new one based on someone else's work, or just experimenting, forking is an essential aspect of working with Git and GitHub.

You have learned the basics of Git commands and how to manage Git repositories, both individually and in a collaborative remote environment. Now, you are ready to dive into GitHub Issues and pull requests, essential tools for communication in GitHub. These features, although seemingly straightforward, play a crucial role in the success of open source projects. They serve as platforms for idea generation, discussions, and reviews, fostering a culture of communal development and innovation. As we proceed, we will explore how these functionalities enhance communication and collaboration, contributing to development on GitHub.

Issues – Collaboration excellence at GitHub

GitHub Issues stands as a multifaceted tool within the GitHub ecosystem, essential for orchestrating collaborative efforts. It functions not merely as a place to report problems but as a comprehensive system for tracking various types of tasks and activities related to your projects. This includes managing bugs, proposing enhancements, and monitoring other essential tasks within your GitHub repositories.

In the DevOps environment, GitHub Issues plays a crucial role by facilitating continuous feedback and seamless collaboration. It acts as a transparent, efficient platform where developers can flag issues, team members can suggest new features, and stakeholders can engage in meaningful discussions about potential enhancements. This functionality is in perfect harmony with the core principles of DevOps, which emphasize breaking down organizational barriers, promoting open communication, and nurturing a culture of continuous improvement and adaptation.

By leveraging GitHub Issues, teams can create a shared, accessible space that fosters collaboration and ensures that everyone involved in a project is on the same page. It is not just about tracking problems; it is about building a dynamic, responsive environment where ideas can flourish and be efficiently managed.

What makes GitHub Issues unique

Let's now look at the unique role of GitHub Issues in fostering transparency and enhancing developer experience.

GitHub Issues stands as a unique tool in the landscape of software development, particularly in its approach to transparency and collaboration. This tool, integral to GitHub, has redefined how development teams, and indeed broader open source communities, communicate and collaborate on projects. The significance of GitHub Issues lies not just in its functionality as a bug-tracking or feature-request tool, but in its role in cultivating an open, transparent, and community-driven approach to software development, echoing the ethos of the open source movement.

The importance of transparency in development

Transparency in software development is about making the entire process of creating, modifying, and maintaining software visible and understandable to all stakeholders involved, from developers to end users. This transparency is crucial for several reasons:

- **Improved collaboration**: When all aspects of a project are visible, team members can collaborate more effectively. Everyone has access to the same information, leading to better decision-making and a shared understanding of goals and challenges.

- **Increased accountability**: Transparency leads to a clearer allocation of responsibilities. Team members are more accountable for their work when it is visible to others, fostering a sense of ownership and commitment.

- **Enhanced quality and innovation**: Open access to project data allows for more eyes on the project, resulting in more feedback, ideas, and critiques. This collective scrutiny not only enhances quality but also spurs innovation.

- **Trust building**: Transparency builds trust among team members and with external stakeholders, including users and customers. Trust is crucial for long-term project success and for establishing reliable, user-focused software.

GitHub Issues – A catalyst for transparent collaboration

GitHub Issues exemplifies this transparent approach. Unlike tools that allow for detailed, hierarchical permissions, GitHub Issues typically operates on a more open-access model. Every issue, its discussion thread, and the decisions made are visible to all team members, and often to the public in open source projects. This openness prevents information silos and encourages a bottom-up culture where ideas and feedback can come from any level within the organization or the community.

This approach aligns seamlessly with the ethos of open source development, which values community contribution, shared responsibility, and open dialogue. By adopting a similar model internally, companies can reap the benefits of this open source approach, breaking down organizational silos and fostering a community-like atmosphere within teams. It encourages developers to take initiative, contribute ideas, and engage in healthy, constructive debates.

Open source as a model for internal collaboration

The open source way of working, facilitated by tools such as GitHub Issues, is an excellent strategy for enhancing the developer experience. It brings the collaborative, transparent nature of open source communities into the internal workings of an organization. Developers feel more engaged and valued when they can see the impact of their work and contribute to discussions beyond their immediate tasks. This open environment nurtures a sense of community, improves morale, and can significantly boost innovation and productivity.

Moreover, the transparency and openness fostered by GitHub Issues and the open source model provide invaluable learning opportunities. Developers can learn from each other, gain insights from different perspectives, and grow by being exposed to a variety of challenges and solutions. This environment is conducive to personal and professional development, crucial for retaining talent and keeping teams motivated and productive.

GitHub Issues is a collaboration catalyst

In summary, GitHub Issues plays a pivotal role in promoting transparency and a community-driven approach to software development. Drawing inspiration from open source practices helps break down organizational barriers, fosters a collaborative and transparent work culture, and significantly enhances the developer experience. In an era where software development is increasingly about community and collaboration, GitHub Issues stands as a beacon, guiding teams toward a more open, inclusive, and effective way of working.

Let's take a look at an issue from that perspective.

Crafting an issue – Essentials for a well-structured issue

Creating your first issue on GitHub may initially seem challenging because of its simplicity, but mastering this skill is crucial for effective collaboration. A well-structured issue is key: it should be clear, concise, and actionable. The goal is to provide enough context to make your point understandable without bombarding your collaborators with excessive information. Begin by clearly identifying the issue, explaining its importance, and outlining the desired outcome.

The process begins in your GitHub repository. If you have an existing repository or have just created one, you will find the **Issues** tab in the repository menu. Here, you can initiate a new issue:

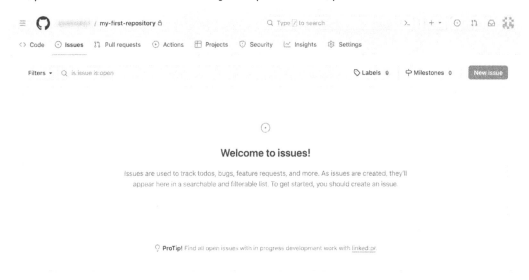

Figure 4.27 – New issue

Creating an issue is straightforward. The interface presents fields for the title and main description, along with metadata options such as assignees and labels. The focus should be on the content of the issue. GitHub supports Markdown for documentation formatting, so it is beneficial to familiarize yourself with Markdown syntax. However, remember that simplicity is key—Markdown is not as feature-rich as Microsoft Word, but it is perfect for creating clean, straightforward documentation:

Figure 4.28 – Creating an issue on GitHub

Within an issue, you can assign it to team members and also mention individuals or teams directly in the content for notifications:

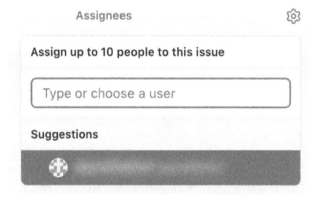

Figure 4.29 – Assigning an issue to other users

Labeling tasks (for example, as a bug, documentation, or enhancement) is also possible. While custom labels can be created, it is advisable to start with default labels and enhance them gradually. Overusing labels can lead to confusion and categorization challenges. If your team or organization has specific labeling standards, it is best to adhere to those.

The approach to using issues in GitHub is not top-down but rather encourages a community-driven, bottom-up style. Imposing strict rules from the outset can limit the freedom necessary for fostering an open, agile, and collaborative culture. Balance is crucial; as you and your team become more accustomed to GitHub workflow, you can adjust your approach accordingly:

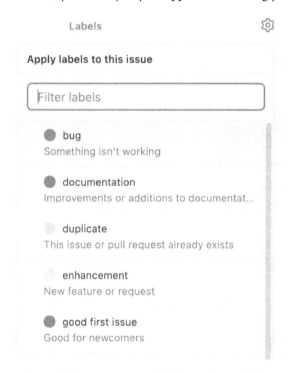

Figure 4.30 – Many types of labels can be applied

Finally, you will see the submitted issue:

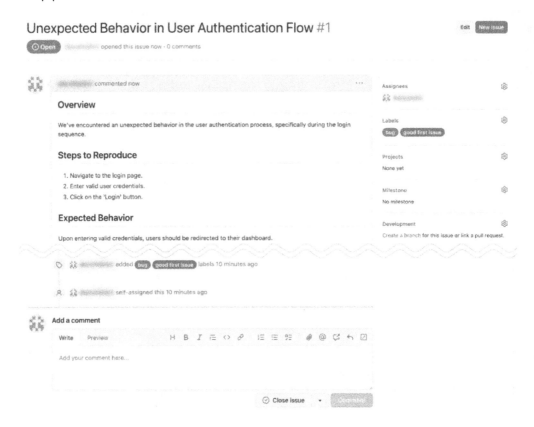

Figure 4.31 – After submission of the issue

So, as you can see, managing issues on GitHub is straightforward. The key lies in fostering collaboration and communication. In the following section, we delve into effective communication techniques and explore how to enhance collaboration within your organization using GitHub.

Effective communication

Now, there are a few things that go into making a great issue: the title, the way the description is written, and the basic way replies are made. Even if we actually try to write clearly, we tend to write messily in the midst of a busy workday. The accumulation of such contextual deficiencies can lead to miscommunication. By following some of the rules that will be covered, you will be able to communicate more wonderfully with your peers.

Writing effective titles – Key principles for clarity and impact

The title of your issue is the first thing collaborators see, making it crucial for capturing attention and conveying the issue's essence. Aim for a title that is concise yet descriptive. Avoid vague titles such as "*Problem*" or "*Feature Request*"—be specific. For instance, "*Fix Broken Link in README*" is far more informative. But why is clarity so important?

When working within an organization, you are often part of multiple repositories, each potentially containing a multitude of unresolved issues. To effectively manage and attract attention to these issues, the title plays a crucial role. It should be engaging yet accurate, clear but not exaggerated.

Here are guidelines to ensure your issue titles stand out while remaining truthful and easy to understand:

- **Concise and clear description**: Ensure your title is brief yet descriptive, using straightforward language that avoids technical jargon. This clarity helps team members quickly understand the issue.

- **Begin with a categorical keyword**: Start with a term such as "*Fix*," "*Enhance*," or "*Optimize*" to immediately convey the nature of the issue.

- **Summarize the core issue**: The title should succinctly capture the main problem or request without extraneous details.

- **Neutral and specific**: Focus on the issue, not on who reported or will resolve it. If applicable, include the specific component or feature affected for better categorization.

- **Clarity over priority**: Avoid using the title to indicate urgency or severity. Instead, employ labels or the issue's content for this purpose, ensuring the title remains unambiguous and focused.

Of course, there are exceptions, and these guidelines should be customized for each project, but effective titles on GitHub issues **speed up triage** by quickly sorting and identifying issues, **enhance discoverability** for easy issue location, and **facilitate clear communication** across the team, ensuring everyone understands the issue at a glance. This streamlined approach is key to efficient repository management.

Providing context in descriptions – Strategies for clear and concise communication

Effective issue descriptions are the cornerstone of collaborative problem-solving in DevOps. To craft a compelling and clear issue description, begin by outlining the present scenario. This sets the stage for understanding. Next, succinctly state the problem or the enhancement you are suggesting. Conclude by articulating the preferred outcome or solution. This methodical approach ensures both comprehension and a constructive dialogue direction.

Context is pivotal in issue descriptions. It gives your teammates insight into your perspective and the circumstances in which a problem arose or the necessity for a feature emerged. If possible, include steps that can reproduce the issue. This is not just about explaining a problem; it is about bringing your collaborators into your experience, enabling them to gauge the issue effectively.

You can also leverage Markdown to enhance your issue's readability and engagement. This simple markup language allows you to structure your issue with headers, organize points with bullet lists or numbered lists, and include code snippets using code blocks and syntax highlighting. These elements not only make your issue straightforward to navigate but also more appealing and easier to engage with.

Here are guidelines to ensure your issue description is clear, concise, and effectively communicates the problem or enhancement you are addressing:

- **Context and clarity**: Start with a clear background of the current situation, and define the problem or enhancement in specific terms. This sets the stage for understanding the issue.

- **Outcome and reproduction steps**: Describe the desired outcome for resolution and, if reporting a bug, provide detailed steps for reproducing it. This clarity helps others visualize the solution and understand the issue's scope.

- **Beautiful Markdown and emojis**: Employ Markdown and emojis to structure your description, making it reader-friendly with headers, lists, and code blocks.

- **Visual aids and solutions**: Include screenshots or links for additional context. Suggesting potential solutions or workarounds can also help in initiating the problem-solving process.

- **Focus and collaboration**: Keep the description focused on the issue, avoiding unrelated topics. Encourage feedback and be open to suggestions, promoting a collaborative approach to resolving the issue.

Good issue descriptions **improve understanding** by providing a clear comprehension of the issue, **facilitate efficient problem-solving** by enabling quick assessment and resolution, and **enhance collaboration** by inviting constructive feedback and joint solution-finding. This concise approach streamlines project progress and teamwork.

Issue replies for a collaborative culture

GitHub issues are more than just a tool for tracking bugs; they serve as a hub for collaboration and documentation. When you respond to an issue, you are not just addressing a specific problem or query, but you are also contributing to the project's passive documentation.

Replying to an issue is easy. Just write your reply in Markdown and reply. But even here, you need to have a philosophy:

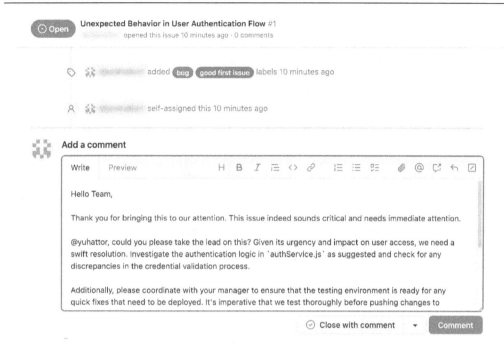

Figure 4.32 – Commenting on an issue

On GitHub, commenting on an issue is really important, not just a mail reply. Let's look at the following perspectives:

- **Passive documentation**: Passive documentation is a concept emerging from the InnerSource context, where documentation is not actively created but rather evolves naturally through interactions within the repository. In GitHub, every issue, pull request, and discussion thread becomes part of this passive documentation. This process is organic and bottom-up; as team members engage in conversations, ask for features, resolve problems, or implement solutions, their interactions get recorded. This creates a comprehensive, evolving record of decisions, discussions, and changes, contributing to a living document that captures the project's history and rationale.

- **Centralizing communication for transparency**: In a collaborative environment, communication often happens through various channels such as Slack, Teams, Jira, and GitHub. However, centralizing project-related discussions on GitHub has significant advantages. It not only creates valuable documentation but also fosters a transparent culture. All decision-making processes and collaborations are visible and accessible to all team members, fostering inclusivity and understanding. When conversations occur on other platforms such as Slack, guiding those discussions back to GitHub ensures that crucial information and decisions are documented and shared within the entire team. This approach prevents silos and ensures that everyone, regardless of when they join the project, has access to the same information.

- **Embracing positive and inclusive communication**: Effective collaboration is rooted in positive and inclusive communication. When replying to issues, it is important to acknowledge and praise good behavior, thank team members for their contributions, and maintain a respectful and supportive tone. This not only encourages a healthy team dynamic but also boosts morale and fosters a sense of belonging and appreciation. Inclusive communication means ensuring that everyone's voice is heard and valued and their contributions are recognized. This approach not only strengthens team cohesion but also drives better problem-solving and innovation.

In GitHub, replying to issues is more than just a response; it is an integral part of building passive documentation, fostering team transparency, and encouraging positive, inclusive communication. By treating issue replies as contributions to a living document, we create a rich history of the project's evolution. Centralizing communication on GitHub ensures that all team members have equal access to information, aiding in transparent decision-making. Lastly, embracing a positive communication style strengthens team bonds and ensures that everyone feels valued and heard. This holistic approach to issue replies is not only about solving problems but also about building a strong, inclusive, and transparent team culture.

Now, let's look at pull requests in the next section. This has a very similar interface to GitHub Issues, with the main difference being that it involves implementation in addition to comments.

Now, let's get down to the heart of engineering collaboration.

Pull request excellence

The GitHub pull requests feature stands as a pivotal innovation in the landscape of software development, one that can be credited with significantly shaping the **Open Source Software (OSS)** movement. Its introduction marked a transformative moment, redefining how collaboration, code integration, and **Quality Assurance (QA)** are conducted in software projects, particularly in OSS.

Pull requests in GitHub are more than just a feature; they are a foundational mechanism for collaboration in the world of software development. A pull request is essentially a request to merge a set of changes from one branch of a repository to another, typically from a feature or topic branch into the main or master branch. But the significance of pull requests goes well beyond mere code merging; they are a nexus for discussion, review, and refinement of code in a collaborative project setting.

What makes pull requests unique?

The pull request model transformed collaborative coding. It shifted the focus from individual code patches sent in isolation to a more interactive and community-driven approach. Developers could now not only submit changes but also engage in discussions about those changes directly within the GitHub platform. This fostered a culture of collaborative review and continuous feedback, essential for maintaining high code quality and aligning contributions with the project's goals. Pull requests introduced a structured, transparent method for code reviews. Code changes are now easily visible and discussable within the context of a pull request, allowing for more detailed and productive feedback. This process ensures that changes are thoroughly vetted, leading to higher code quality and more robust software projects.

Pull requests have not only revolutionized the way code is reviewed and merged but also significantly streamlined development workflows in GitHub. By integrating seamlessly with GitHub native features and a plethora of third-party tools, they support and enhance **Continuous Integration** (**CI**) and **Continuous Deployment** (**CD**) practices. This integration transforms the development process, making it more efficient, reliable, and automated.

A fascinating development in the use of pull requests is the integration of pre-release testing within the pull request thread itself. This advancement has led to a more comprehensive and cohesive approach to ensuring code quality and project management. Whenever a developer initiates a pull request, it triggers a series of automated checks and tests. These can range from code quality assessments and security vulnerability scans to performance tests. The results of these tests are then displayed directly in the pull request, providing immediate and actionable feedback.

Beyond the command line

When discussing the historical context and evolution of GitHub pull requests, it is important to note that the term *pull request* itself has roots in the `git request-pull` command in Git. This connection might lead some to view GitHub's contribution as primarily providing a user interface for an existing concept rather than inventing something entirely new. However, a deeper exploration of the history and development of pull requests reveals a more significant impact.

GitHub took a basic command-line function and transformed it into a rich, interactive, and collaborative feature within its web interface. This transformation was not just about adding a user interface layer; it was about reimagining how collaboration around code changes could be done.

Crafting a pull request

Begin by selecting or creating a repository on GitHub. For this demonstration, we will focus on the GitHub user interface rather than the command-line interface. Consider a repository with only a README.md file as a starting point. The goal is to add detailed content to this file and submit a pull request for merging:

Figure 4.33 – Repository page

The first step involves creating a branch named `adding-details-to-readme`. This branch is where you will make your edits before merging them into the main branch. While you can create and push new branches using Git commands, GitHub also offers an intuitive interface for this purpose. Use the branch drop-down button in the top-left corner to create a branch derived from the main branch:

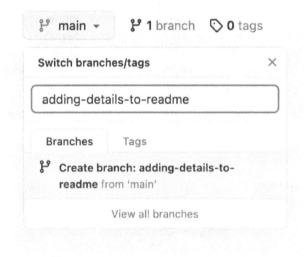

Figure 4.34 – Creating a new branch via the drop-down menu

Once a branch is created, you can make changes on any branch, not just the main or master branches:

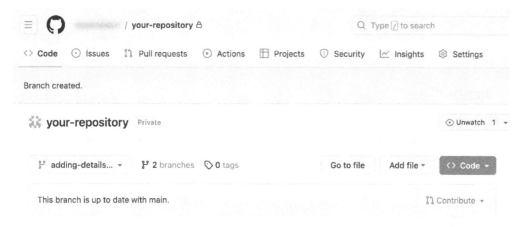

Figure 4.35 – Branch creation notification

Then, let's edit README.md. Ensure you are on the correct branch by checking the drop-down menu in the top-left corner before starting your edits. Then, use the edit button in the top-right corner to begin editing the README file:

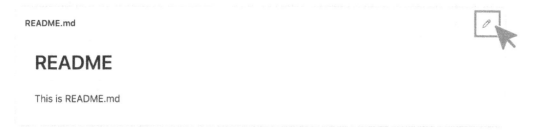

Figure 4.36 – Clicking the edit button

The README.md file is the face and gateway of your repository, welcoming team members and new contributors. Here, let your imagination run wild and craft a compelling README:

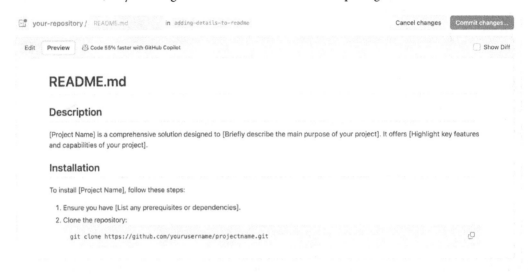

Figure 4.37 – Editing the README.md file

Well, now we are all set. Let's get your commit reflected. Since you are already in the branch for editing, you may commit your edits as they are. However, if you open the edit window and commit it while still in the main branch, you still have the option of creating a new branch. But it is safer to consciously create a branch initially and commit. On the other hand, there is a branch protection policy configuration at GitHub that prevents you from committing directly to the team's shared environment, such as main, production, and release, which will be covered in this chapter later.

The title becomes the Git commit message, so think about this carefully as you read the previous chapters and commit it:

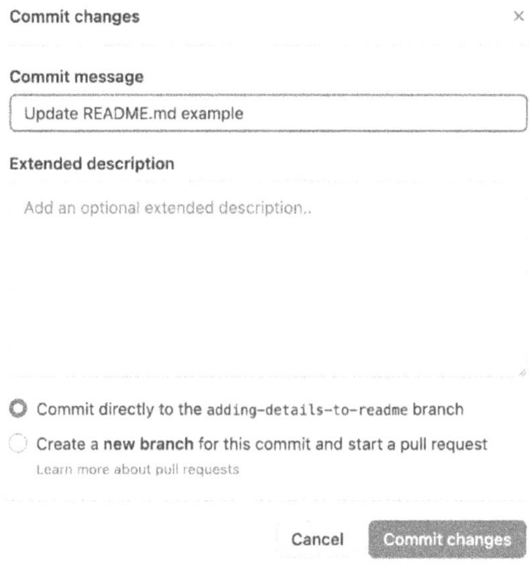

Commit changes
Commit message
Update README.md example
Extended description
Add an optional extended description..
Commit directly to the adding-details-to-readme branch
Create a new branch for this commit and start a pull request
Learn more about pull requests
Cancel
Commit changes

Figure 4.38 – Committing changes

Once your changes are committed, you will likely see an alert on the repository's home page for creating a pull request. You can also create a pull request from the **New pull request** button if an alert does not appear or you wish to select a different branch:

your-repository
Private
Unwatch 1
adding-details-to-readme had recent pushes less than a minute ago
Compare & pull request
adding-details...
2 branches
0 tags
Go to file
Add file
Code
This branch is 1 commit ahead of main.
Contribute
Update README.md example
0a2b10d now
2 commits
README.md
Update README.md example
now

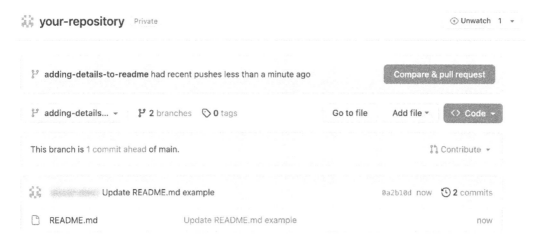

Figure 4.39 – Pull request alert

If you do not see this alert or want to select a different branch, you can start the same process by clicking the **New pull request** button under the **Pull requests** tab:

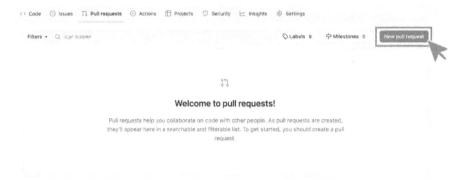

Figure 4.40 – Clicking the New pull request button

When navigating the interface, you may find yourself on the pull request page whether by following an alert or by clicking the **New pull request** button. Regardless of how you arrive, this is the place where you will check the history of your changes.

The way changes are presented in GitHub can vary. As illustrated in the screenshot, differences (or diffs) can be displayed inline, interspersed within each line of the code:

Figure 4.41 – Reviewing changes screen in the unified mode

Alternatively, GitHub offers a split view, showcasing differences side by side. This bifurcated display allows for a clearer comparison between the original and modified code:

Figure 4.42 – Reviewing changes screen in the split mode

When satisfied, let's write your pull request. A good pull request includes a clear title, a detailed description, and designated reviewers. As for reviewers, you can specify individuals or teams. The content here is somewhat like what you would write in an issue:

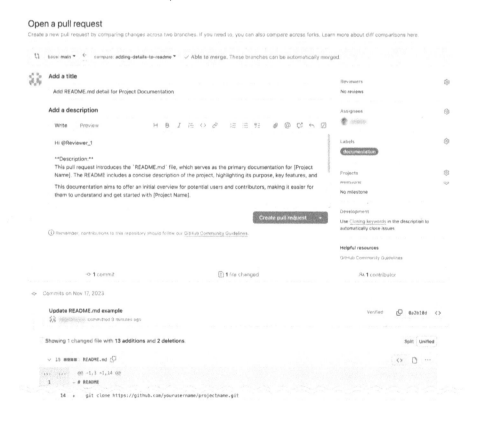

Figure 4.43 – You can check the differences between the commits

Now, your writing skills are put to the test once again. The content to be concerned with when writing here is the same as what we were concerned with regarding issues in the previous section. Write in an easy-to-read, Markdown format. However, in this context, understanding the distinct objectives of these tools is crucial. The primary aim of a pull request is to be merged, typically addressed to specific individuals authorized to approve it. In contrast, an issue can be directed toward a wider and undefined audience. Therefore, when writing a description for this pull request, it is crucial to consider who will be reviewing it and how to write it.

If the review is to be conducted by a specific person, there might be some shared understanding or context, which could reduce the need for extensive comments in the review. The basic technique is the same as for an issue, but it is important to tailor your approach to your target audience.

You might notice that there are two options available when creating a pull request, which can be accessed via the drop-down button on the right. You can either create a standard pull request or opt for a draft pull request. Draft pull requests may not be applicable to private repositories depending on your plan, but anyone can try it for public repositories. I encourage you to check it:

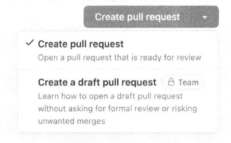

Figure 4.44 – There is another option: Create a draft pull request

Both draft and regular pull requests do not differ much in terms of the user interface. However, a draft pull request is used to indicate that the pull request is not yet finalized or that the overall work is still in progress, incomplete, or in a specific stage of development.

It allows for intermediate reviews, signifying that it is not intended for formal review yet. Reviewers usually appreciate receiving interim results or reports. Early reviews can provide valuable insights and share progress with the team, which is beneficial.

In the case of a draft pull request, the merge cannot be done immediately by mistake, as follows:

Figure 4.45 – Draft pull request explicitly indicates it is not ready for review

In an extreme scenario, you can create a pull request even without writing a single line of code with the `git empty commit` command. This can be incredibly useful from the early stages of development, allowing team members or a pair-programming partner to review the code, helping to identify mistakes early. Therefore, it is highly recommended to make use of draft pull requests as well.

An empty commit in Git is a commit that does not contain any changes; it is like sending a message without altering any files. This can be particularly useful for initiating discussions in the early stages of development without the need for actual code changes. To create an empty commit, you can use the `git commit --allow-empty -m "Your message"` command, which enables you to make a commit with a message but no content changes. This feature is handy for creating pull requests that serve as placeholders for future code reviews or to mark specific milestones in the development process. It is recommended to keep this empty commit in mind along with the draft pull request.

Now, once you have conducted appropriate communication and completed the review, it is time to merge. The great thing about GitHub here is not the command interface, but the ability to perform merges on the user interface. You can go ahead and merge as it is, but let's look at the options before doing so:

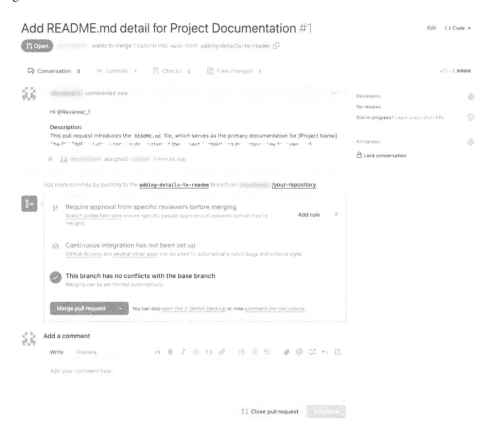

Figure 4.46 – Merge can be done with the web user interface

Upon inspecting the **Merge** dropdown, you will find three options. These are creating a merge commit, then squashing to combine commits into one and merge, and finally, performing a rebase merge. While these merging techniques were covered in a previous chapter and will not be elaborated on here, the beauty of GitHub lies in the flexibility it offers to choose each of these options for managing your Git history. If you want to preserve the history of contributions, you will first incorporate the commits, ensuring as much of the change history remains as possible. On the other hand, if you prefer a cleaner history, options such as **Squash and merge** and **Rebase and merge** are also available to consider.

It is important to note, however, that GitHub's **Rebase and merge** option is not identical to the traditional `git rebase` command. **Rebase and merge** on GitHub effectively reapplies each commit from the feature branch onto the base branch individually, without creating a merge commit. This allows for a linear history while preserving the chronological order of commits. Whether you aim to maintain a detailed record of contributions or prefer a streamlined history, GitHub provides the tools to accommodate your project's needs:

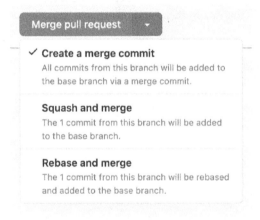

Figure 4.47 – Merge options

This time, we chose to create a merge commit. Creating a merge commit is easy; simply write a title and a description. Then, click on the **Confirm merge** button to merge:

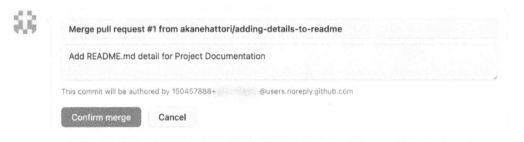

Figure 4.48 – Creating a merge commit

Then, you will confirm that the merge was successfully done on the GitHub platform:

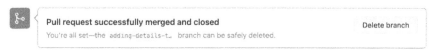

Figure 4.49 – Checking if the merge was successful

You have observed the simplicity of managing pull requests on GitHub. This platform demonstrates how intricate actions and reviews, traditionally executed via the command line, can be efficiently conducted within a unified platform enhanced by a streamlined user interface.

Moving forward, we will delve deeper into the nuances of proficient pull request management. Our focus will be on how you can adeptly leverage these features within a DevOps-centric communication framework to drive the success of your projects or products. Additionally, we will discuss key aspects that call for your attention and consideration.

Pull request review 101

First and foremost, it is essential to grasp how to conduct reviews on GitHub and then explore best practices that merit attention. When you begin learning GitHub, you might not immediately engage in full-fledged code reviews. However, understanding how reviews should be conducted can influence your expectations and the content you include when writing a pull request.

Remember—these are practices that can be gradually improved and, ultimately, should be optimized for your team.

Review basics

Accessing the review interface on GitHub is straightforward. From the pull request page, open the **Files changed** tab to see how many files have been modified:

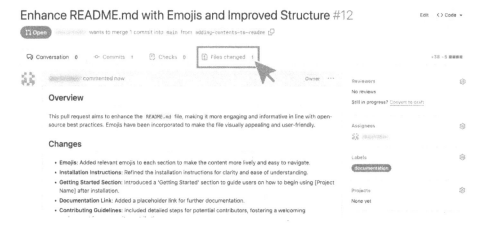

Figure 4.50 – Tab for reviewing pull requests

Once you have opened the **Files changed** tab, examine the contents. In addition to the line-by-line difference screenshot shown next, there is a view option that arranges changes side by side, which is highly recommended. Lines prefixed with − indicate deletions, while those with + are additions:

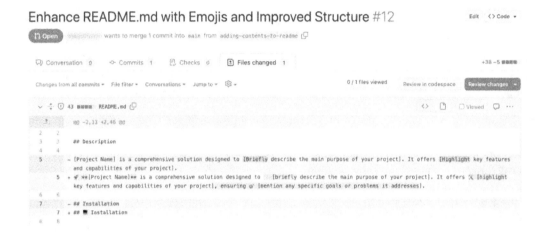

Figure 4.51 – Viewing line-by-line differences on GitHub

To comment on specific line changes, use the + button on the left. This also allows for selecting multiple lines, facilitating efficient discussion initiation:

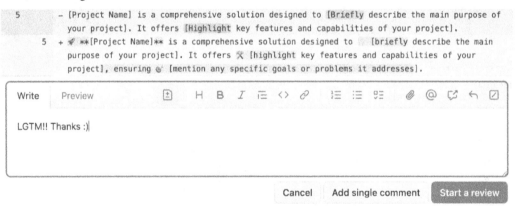

Figure 4.52 – Reviewing changes

When reviewing, you may want to propose specific changes. This can be done by pressing the **Suggestion** button on the screen, which copies the content of the relevant line. Edit this content in your comment, but be aware that while comments can be added to deleted lines, suggestions cannot:

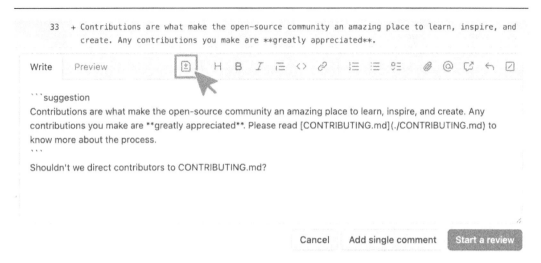

```
 33   + Contributions are what make the open-source community an amazing place to learn, inspire, and
         create. Any contributions you make are **greatly appreciated**.
```

Write   Preview

```
```suggestion
Contributions are what make the open-source community an amazing place to learn, inspire, and create. Any
contributions you make are **greatly appreciated**. Please read [CONTRIBUTING.md](./CONTRIBUTING.md) to
know more about the process.
```
```

Shouldn't we direct contributors to CONTRIBUTING.md?

Cancel   Add single comment   Start a review

Figure 4.53 – Proposing changes using the Suggestion button

If you find a suggestion to be good, press the **Add single comment** button to comment. For multiple review comments, use the **Start a review** button, which is handy when there are many edits. Review comments, including suggestions, appear both in the pull request thread and interspersed between code differences, making code reviews more straightforward:

```
 33   + Contributions are what make the open-source community an amazing place to learn, inspire, and
         create. Any contributions you make are **greatly appreciated**.
```

now   Collaborator ...

Suggested change

```
 33   - Contributions are what make the open-source community an amazing place to learn,
         inspire, and create. Any contributions you make are **greatly appreciated**.

 33   + Contributions are what make the open-source community an amazing place to learn,
         inspire, and create. Any contributions you make are **greatly appreciated**. Please
         read [CONTRIBUTING.md](./CONTRIBUTING.md) to know more about the process.
```

Commit suggestion ▾   Add suggestion to batch

Shouldn't we direct contributors to CONTRIBUTING.md?

☺

Reply...

Resolve conversation

Figure 4.54 – Suggestion appears as a comment

After completing the review, you will see **Commit suggestion** and **Add suggestion to batch** buttons. GitHub's brilliance lies in allowing these changes to be committed directly through the user interface, rather than needing to do so via the command-line interface or an editor. **Commit suggestion** commits an individual change, while **Add suggestion to batch** enables recording multiple changes as a single commit. This prevents unnecessary commits when your pull requests receive many changes. Pressing the **Commit suggestion** button brings up a screen for entering a commit message and description, after which the change is committed to the pull request branch:

Figure 4.55 – Committing changes

Once the review is complete, it is time for you to conduct a review. Note that approving a review does not automatically merge the pull request, but it does mark it as approved by you. Here, you can choose between **Commit**, **Approve**, and **Request changes**. The **Comment** option is for just only making a comment, **Approve** indicates approval, and **Request changes** is used to suggest necessary amendments:

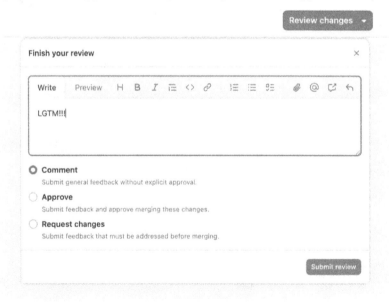

Figure 4.56 – Three options for the review

If you approve, your comment and approval status are posted in the thread like this:

Figure 4.57 – Post-review status

Thus, GitHub simplifies the review process and enables many functionalities through its GUI. The blend of code changes and related comments enriches the context, allowing reviewers, reviewees, and current or future team members seeking historical context to understand and interact with the information effectively.

Mastering this feature can lead to highly transparent communication within your team.

Let's look at what to consider when reviewing or being reviewed

Review best practices

In the dynamic landscape of software development, GitHub reviews stand as a pivotal component in bridging individual effort and collective excellence. These reviews extend beyond mere code examination to fostering a collaborative and learning-rich environment. Mastering GitHub reviews is crucial for teams aiming for high-quality development processes. Here are some guidelines on how to achieve that:

- **Cultivating the reviewer's mindset**: The effectiveness of GitHub reviews starts with the reviewer's mindset. Emphasizing prompt feedback is key, as it maintains the momentum of development. However, speed should be balanced with thoroughness, recognizing that the code is a collective asset of the team. This mindset fosters a constructive and ego-free approach to reviews, seeing them not just as a task but as an opportunity for meaningful dialogue and documentation for current and future team members.

- **Enhancing communication in reviews**: Effective communication is central to GitHub reviews. Utilizing Markdown for clarity and structured feedback ensures that reviews are accessible and understandable. Being specific and concise in comments avoids confusion and expedites the review process. Positive reinforcement and constructive feedback, often supplemented with emojis, create a welcoming and psychologically safe review environment, encouraging prompt and enthusiastic adoption of changes.

- **Promoting diversity and authorship in reviews**: Diversity in the review process introduces varied perspectives, enriching the review and safeguarding against blind spots. Encouraging developers to revise their code based on feedback fosters empowerment and skill development. Additionally, preserving authorship, even in practices such as squash merging, is crucial for maintaining individual motivation and accountability.

- **Maintaining standards in urgent scenarios**: Even in urgent scenarios, such as hotfixes, the quality and thoroughness of reviews should not be compromised. Upholding standards under pressure is essential, as each review contributes to the team's overall work ethic and code quality.

- **Integrating automation for efficiency**: Incorporating automation into the review process, through automated tests, syntax checks, and linter rules, streamlines the review process. This allows human reviewers to focus on more complex aspects of the code. Employing templates for reviews also ensures consistency and thoroughness, maintaining a high quality of review across the board.

In conclusion, reviews on GitHub are more than just a mechanism for code QA; they are a vital part of fostering team growth, learning, and collaboration. By adopting these best practices, teams elevate not just their code but also their working environment, promoting mutual respect, continuous improvement, and a collaborative spirit. A well-executed review is indeed a step toward a more cohesive, efficient, and resilient development process.

We have now gone through an overview of pull requests, basic usage, and best practices. So far, it seems like you have a pretty good grasp of how to collaborate on GitHub. From here, we will look at other features of GitHub to help you collaborate better.

Getting the best out of GitHub

Exploring additional features in GitHub can greatly enhance your repository management experience. While a detailed exploration of each feature would be extensive, a brief introduction to each can highlight their significance.

GitHub Projects – Managing your issues and pull requests in one place

GitHub Projects is a tool that allows you to manage issues, issue drafts, and pull requests in one place.

GitHub Projects will allow for more flexible management than just GitHub issues and pull requests. It represents a significant evolution in how development teams can organize, track, and manage their work on GitHub. Unlike the linear and somewhat limited scope of issues and pull requests, GitHub Projects offers a multifaceted approach to project management, aligning seamlessly with the collaborative and iterative nature of modern software development:

Figure 4.58 – GitHub Projects table view

At the heart of GitHub Projects lies the Kanban board, a highly visual tool that enhances workflow visualization. This board allows teams to create custom columns that mirror their workflow stages—from **To Do** to **In Progress** and **Done**. The simplicity of dragging and dropping issues and pull requests across these columns significantly improves workflow transparency and helps in tracking the progress of tasks more intuitively:

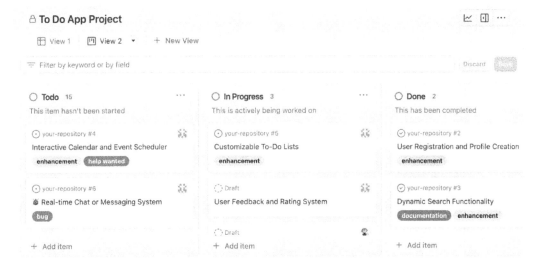

Figure 4.59 – GitHub Projects Kanban board view

Collaboration is further enhanced through tools such as assignees and milestones. Assignees ensure that responsibilities are clearly defined, while milestones help in tracking progress toward key objectives or deadlines. This structured approach to collaboration ensures that every team member is aligned with the project goals and understands their role in achieving them.

Integrated project reporting is another facet that sets GitHub Projects apart. It provides a comprehensive overview of the project's progress. DevOps metrics are invaluable for assessing team performance and identifying areas for improvement. This data-driven approach to project management enables teams to make informed decisions and optimize their workflows:

Figure 4.60 – GitHub Projects status chart

GitHub Projects also offers a range of project templates—from predefined ones for common project types such as bug tracker or Kanban to the ability to create custom templates tailored to specific team workflows. These templates save time and provide a consistent structure that teams can rely on.

Moreover, the inclusion of issue and pull request filters within the project board enhances the ability to manage tasks efficiently. Teams can filter by labels, assignees, milestones, and more, allowing them to quickly find and focus on tasks that matter most.

One of the most significant advantages of GitHub Projects is its ability to manage issues and pull requests from multiple repositories in a single project. This feature is particularly beneficial for larger projects that span multiple repositories, providing a holistic view and cohesive management experience.

GitHub Projects goes beyond the traditional confines of issue tracking and pull request management, offering a comprehensive, flexible, and highly collaborative platform for project management. By using its features, development teams can enhance their productivity, improve collaboration, and drive their projects toward successful outcomes, all within the familiar ecosystem of GitHub. This alignment with the principles of DevOps culture—prioritizing collaboration, efficiency, and transparency—makes GitHub Projects a great tool in the modern software development landscape.

GitHub Codespaces – Transforming development workflows with cloud-based environments

GitHub Codespaces revolutionizes the way developers work by offering fully configurable, cloud-based development environments directly within GitHub. It marks a significant step in the evolution of development workflows, making it easier for teams to collaborate and streamline their DevOps practices.

GitHub Codespaces streamlines development with critical features:

- **Quick Start and Uniform Workspaces**: Enables instant setup of cloud-based environments, aligning team efforts and reducing setup complexity

- **Collaboration and Pull Request Integration**: Facilitates easier code reviews and discussions within the Codespaces environment, enhancing teamwork across locations

- **Secure and Isolated Environments**: Offers secure, containerized workspaces for each user, protecting project integrity and data security

As an implementation of Visual Studio Code available in the browser, GitHub Codespaces offers the features and extensions available in VS Code. Although there are limitations to the extensions available in the Codespaces version, this familiarity is a tremendous advantage. It allows developers to leverage a powerful and popular development tool with the added benefits of cloud accessibility and integration:

Figure 4.61 – GitHub Codespaces

Starting a new codespace is straightforward. With just a few clicks, developers can spin up a development environment that is automatically configured with the settings and tools specified in the repository's `.devcontainer` configuration. This ensures consistency across development environments, a fundamental aspect of DevOps practices that emphasizes reproducibility and reduces *"works on my machine"* issues.

One of the most significant benefits of GitHub Codespaces is the elimination of the need to clone heavy files and set up complex development environments locally. This not only saves significant new engineers' onboarding time but also simplifies the process of switching between different projects, each with its unique environment requirements. By hosting the development environment in the cloud, Codespaces significantly reduces the overhead of managing local development setups.

Performance and customization are key aspects of GitHub Codespaces. Developers can choose hardware specifications for their codespaces, ensuring they have the necessary resources for their tasks. Customization extends to the development environment itself, with support for Visual Studio Code extensions and personalized editor settings, reinforcing the DevOps focus on developer experience. From an administrative perspective, GitHub Codespaces allows organization leaders to set specific policies regarding the development environment, including constraints on the types of machines users can select for their codespaces. This capability ensures that development environments align with organizational standards and resource management strategies, offering a balanced approach to cost and performance within the company's guidelines:

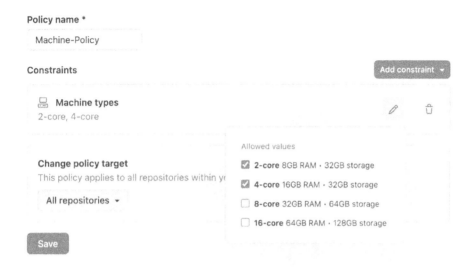

Figure 4.62 – Restricting access to machine types

Also, it offers a remarkable blend of collaboration and security, striking a perfect balance for modern development teams. Integrating pull requests directly into the Codespaces environment significantly enhances the collaborative process, making it easier for teams to propose, discuss, and merge changes efficiently, regardless of their physical locations. This streamlined workflow for code reviews and collaboration is coupled with a powerful security advantage. Codespaces reduce the risks associated with employees downloading whole source code data locally, addressing common security concerns that arise from local file storage and management. Each user's workspace is securely isolated, further mitigating potential security issues tied to local development practices. This thoughtful integration of collaboration and security within Codespaces not only boosts productivity but also strengthens the safeguarding of project data, offering a secure, collaborative development solution.

GitHub Codespaces is more than just a development environment; it is a catalyst for enhancing DevOps practices. By offering a flexible, collaborative, and integrated platform, it empowers teams to innovate faster, collaborate more effectively, and deliver higher-quality software, all within the GitHub ecosystem. This makes GitHub Codespaces an indispensable tool in the modern software development and DevOps landscape.

GitHub Discussions – Fostering community and collaboration

GitHub Discussions serves as a vital platform for building and nurturing community within GitHub repositories. It represents a significant advancement in how developers, contributors, and users interact and collaborate. This feature extends beyond the traditional issue and pull request communication, offering a dedicated space for questions, ideas, and discussions. GitHub Discussions creates an environment where the broader community—including those who may not be directly involved in code contributions—can engage, share insights, and provide feedback:

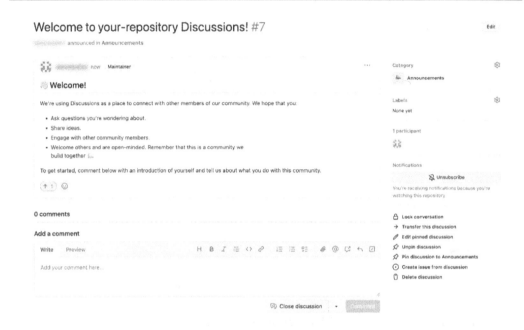

Figure 4.63 – GitHub Discussions thread

A key aspect of GitHub Discussions is its ability to organize communication effectively. Discussions can be categorized into different types, such as Q&As, announcements, or general discussions. This categorization helps to maintain clarity and focus, making it easier for users to find relevant conversations and contribute meaningfully:

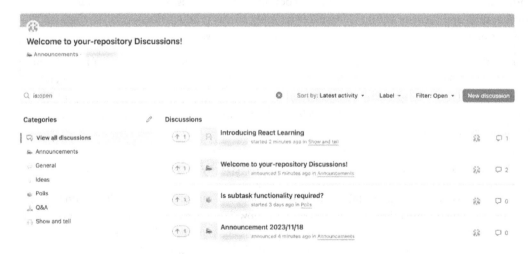

Figure 4.64 – GitHub Discussions categories

GitHub Discussions also plays a crucial role in knowledge sharing and preservation. Unlike transient communication channels such as chat rooms, discussions are persistent and searchable, making them a valuable resource for current and future community members. This archival quality ensures that knowledge shared in discussions continues to benefit the community long after conversations have taken place.

In summary, GitHub Discussions is not only a powerful tool for fostering community engagement and collaboration but also plays a crucial role in maintaining the organization and clarity of GitHub issues. As projects grow and evolve, the volume and diversity of issues can become overwhelming, leading to clutter and confusion. GitHub Discussions acts as a catalyst for communication, enabling teams to channel various topics and conversations into a more structured and appropriate space.

This capability of GitHub Discussions to segregate broad, general discussions from more specific, technical conversations typically housed in GitHub Issues is invaluable. It helps in keeping the **Issues** section focused and manageable, reducing noise and making it easier for teams to track and address specific code-related tasks.

Moreover, by providing a dedicated platform for wide-ranging discussions, GitHub Discussions smooths the path for collaboration in numerous ways. It not only ensures that valuable insights and ideas are shared and preserved but also prevents the dilution of technical discussions in the **Issues** section. This distinction between general discussions and specific issues is essential for maintaining an efficient workflow and aligning with DevOps practices, which emphasize streamlined processes and clear communication.

Therefore, GitHub Discussions is more than a mere addition to the GitHub ecosystem; it is an integral component that enhances the overall functionality and effectiveness of project management on the platform. It aids in keeping GitHub issues clean and focused while offering a robust environment for broader, community-driven conversations, thereby smoothing collaboration and driving projects toward success.

GitHub repository excellence

There are many configurations in GitHub repositories that can promote collaboration. These settings can reduce the need to fear failure and make the review process more standardized. We will not cover all of them here, but some of the major ones are particularly important.

Repository rules – Streamlining workflow and ensuring code quality

Branch rules are important for managing a repository in a way that strikes a balance between security and collaboration. While GitHub allows setting permissions for the repository or specific functions, it does not offer code-based permissions. Relying solely on write permissions can restrict participation and hinder open communication. Branch rules allow repository administrators to enforce specific policies on branches, particularly critical ones such as the main or master branches. These policies include requirements for pull request reviews, status checks, and restrictions on who can push to the branch. By setting up these rules, teams can ensure that the code merged into important branches meets predetermined quality standards and that the process aligns with the team's workflow.

The ruleset allows for a variety of settings. They can be applied only to specific branches, or administrators can be authorized to bypass them:

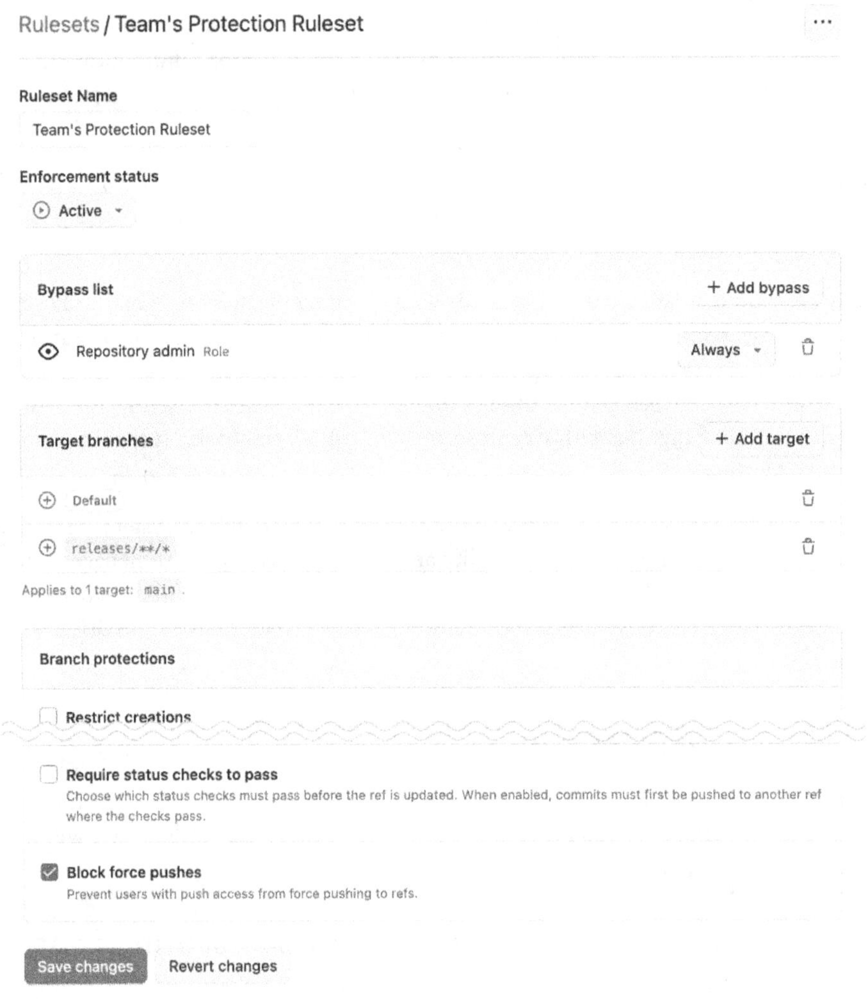

Figure 4.65 – Setting up branch rules in GitHub

One of the primary benefits of branch rules is the enforcement of code review. By requiring that pull requests receive a certain number of approvals before merging, teams can ensure that every change is scrutinized and validated. This peer review process not only improves code quality but also fosters knowledge sharing and collaboration among team members:

✅ **Require a pull request before merging**
Require all commits be made to a non-target branch and submitted via a pull request before they can be merged.

Additional settings   ∧

Required approvals

2 ▾

The number of approving reviews that are required before a pull request can be merged.

☐ **Dismiss stale pull request approvals when new commits are pushed**
New, reviewable commits pushed will dismiss previous pull request review approvals.

☐ **Require review from Code Owners**
Require an approving review in pull requests that modify files that have a designated code owner.

☐ **Require approval of the most recent reviewable push**
Whether the most recent reviewable push must be approved by someone other than the person who pushed it.

☐ **Require conversation resolution before merging**
All conversations on code must be resolved before a pull request can be merged.

Figure 4.66 – Code review requirements in branch rules

Status checks are another critical part of branch rules. These checks can include automated tests, code linter results, or any other type of automated process that verifies the quality and functionality of the code. By requiring these checks to pass before merging, teams can prevent bugs and issues from making their way into the main code base, thus maintaining high standards of code quality:

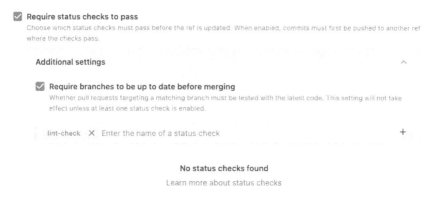

✅ **Require status checks to pass**
Choose which status checks must pass before the ref is updated. When enabled, commits must first be pushed to another ref where the checks pass.

Additional settings   ∧

✅ **Require branches to be up to date before merging**
Whether pull requests targeting a matching branch must be tested with the latest code. This setting will not take effect unless at least one status check is enabled.

| lint-check ✕ Enter the name of a status check   +

No status checks found
Learn more about status checks

Figure 4.67 – Status checks in branch rules

Branch rules are a fundamental configuration in GitHub for safeguarding code quality and enforcing workflow discipline. They enable teams to automate and enforce critical aspects of their development process, aligning with the principles of DevOps. By utilizing branch rules, teams can ensure that their code base remains stable, secure, and consistent, thereby supporting the delivery of high-quality software in a collaborative environment. This makes branch rules an essential element in modern software development and an invaluable asset in the DevOps toolkit.

CODEOWNERS – Streamlined review and ownership

The CODEOWNERS file in GitHub is a simple yet powerful tool for automatically assigning reviewers to pull requests and clarifying ownership of specific code areas. This file, placed in the root, docs/, or .github/ directory of the repository, lists individuals or teams alongside file patterns. When changes are made to files matching these patterns, the specified code owners are requested for review:

Figure 4.68 – Example of a CODEOWNERS file

The benefits of using a CODEOWNERS file include the following:

- **Automated reviewer assignment**: Streamlines the pull request process by automatically assigning the right reviewers, ensuring that changes are checked by the appropriate experts

- **Clear ownership**: Clarifies who is responsible for specific parts of the code base, aiding in quicker decision-making and more efficient maintenance

This aspect of CODEOWNERS is particularly important as it directly relates to deployment safety. In environments where CI/CD is the norm, ensuring that only well-reviewed and approved code is deployed is critical. This adds a layer of security and efficiency to the deployment process, embodying the preventive and proactive principles central to effective DevOps practices.

Issue and pull request templates

Templates in GitHub enhance collaboration and maintain consistency across various aspects of project management:

Figure 4.69 – Issue template menu

Issue templates guide contributors in creating detailed and structured issue reports. By providing specific templates for different types of issues (bug reports, feature requests, and so on), you ensure that all necessary information is included, facilitating easier understanding and quicker resolution:

Issue: Bug report

Create a report to help us improve. If this doesn't look right, choose a different type.

Add a title

    Title

Add a description

| Write   Preview | | H B *I* ≔ <> *ℰ*   ≔ ≔ ≝   @ @ ㇏ ↩ ☑ |

Describe the bug
A clear and concise description of what the bug is.

To Reproduce
Steps to reproduce the behavior:
1. Go to '...'
2. Click on '....'
3. Scroll down to '....'
4. See error

Expected behavior

Figure 4.70 – Example of an issue template

Pull request templates ensure that every pull request adheres to the project's standards and requirements. These templates typically include checklists, sections for describing changes, referencing relevant issues, and any additional notes. This standardization simplifies the review process and enhances the quality of contributions.

Each of these components plays a vital role in shaping a well-organized, accessible, and contributor-friendly GitHub repository. By implementing these standard base documentations and templates, you lay down a strong foundation for collaboration and project management, resonating with the best practices in DevOps and open source culture.

Summary

In this chapter, you have gained valuable insights into fundamental aspects of collaborating on GitHub, setting a strong foundation for DevOps practices. While we have explored various topics around Git, GitHub, and DevOps, this chapter has specifically focused on how to effectively use GitHub for collaboration, a crucial skill in the world of DevOps.

This knowledge is not just theoretical but highly practical, setting the stage for the next phase of our journey—applying these Git techniques and GitHub skills in the actual DevOps release process. As we transition to the next chapter, we will build upon this foundation, diving deeper into how these skills and practices are directly applied and leveraged in DevOps workflows, ultimately enhancing the efficiency and effectiveness of the software development and deployment process.

Ready to embark on this next phase? Let's move forward to the next chapter, where we will see these principles in action, witnessing the transformative impact of Git and GitHub in the realm of DevOps.

Driving CI/CD with GitHub

This chapter is designed to unravel the layers of GitHub Actions, from its core concepts to advanced deployment strategies. You will encounter a detailed exploration of GitHub Actions' capabilities, structure, and best practices. We delve into the essence of workflows, jobs, steps, and actions, each dissected to reveal their importance in automation. Practical insights on reducing redundancy, managing secrets and variables, and the art of debugging will enhance your workflows' efficiency and security. Permissions and approval processes are also covered, ensuring that you wield control over your **Continuous Integration/Continuous Delivery (CI/CD)** pipeline with precision.

Deployment strategies unfold with clarity, presenting blue-green, rolling, and canary deployments, each with their steps, real-world applications, and switchover methods. The world of feature release strategies is also demystified, providing you with a detailed explanation of feature flags and release trains.

We will cover the following main topics in this chapter:

- GitHub Actions – Mastering workflow automation
- Deployment strategies
- Feature release strategies

GitHub Actions – Mastering workflow automation

GitHub Actions represents a transformative shift in how software development and deployment processes are automated. As a native feature of GitHub, this world-class CI/CD platform facilitates the creation, management, and execution of workflows directly within your GitHub repository. GitHub Actions provides a simple and clear workflow, as the following screenshot shows:

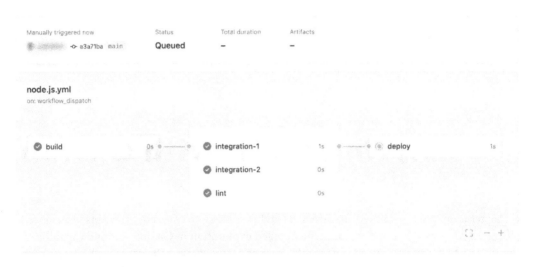

Figure 5.1 – GitHub Actions built-in visualization

This chapter delves into the intricacies of GitHub Actions, providing a detailed understanding of its capabilities, implementation, and best practices.

Comprehensive overview of GitHub Actions

GitHub Actions offers a wide range of benefits to enhance your software development workflow. Here is a closer look at what it brings to the table:

- **Automation**: GitHub Actions automates repetitive tasks such as code building, testing, and deployment. It responds to events such as code pushes and issue creation, reducing the need for manual intervention.

- **Versatility**: It can be used for various purposes, including building containerized applications, deploying web services, managing dependencies, and more. This flexibility makes it adaptable to different development needs.

- **CI/CD automation**: GitHub Actions streamlines the CI and CD processes. It automatically builds and tests code changes, ensuring code quality, and simplifies the deployment pipeline, leading to faster and more reliable releases.

- **Improved collaboration**: It automates code review processes, performs automated testing, and sends notifications based on workflow results. This fosters better collaboration among team members, as they can focus on addressing critical issues and improvements.

- **Customization**: GitHub Actions allows for workflow customization through YAML configuration. Developers can tailor workflows to suit their specific requirements and seamlessly integrate with third-party tools and services for extended functionality.

Creating workflows is as simple as placing a YAML file in the `.github/workflows` directory of your repository, as shown in the following screenshot. This setup enables CI tasks, feedback integration into pull requests, and defining conditions for pull request merging:

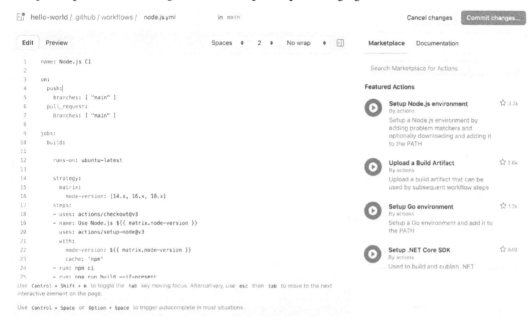

Figure 5.2 – Easy development experience with YAML

To illustrate the power and versatility of GitHub workflows, let's consider a typical CI workflow for a Node.js application. Triggered by every push to the `main` branch and pull requests, this workflow may include jobs such as **build**, **test**, and **deploy**. Each job serves a specific purpose – building the project, running tests, and deploying the application, respectively. Within these jobs, steps, and actions are carefully orchestrated to ensure that each phase of the CI process is executed flawlessly. From checking out the code and setting up the Node.js environment to running tests and deploying the application, each step and action plays a critical role. We will now delve into the detailed structure.

The following is a typical example of a GitHub Actions workflow. The workflow is written in YAML, which may seem difficult. But if you look at each line one by one, it is simple and very easy. Note that this example is for building a Node.js application and will not work if you just paste this file. If you want to try it, try copying the entire project from the Packt repository (`https://github.com/PacktPublishing/DevOps-Unleashed-with-Git-and-GitHub/tree/main/chapter5`):

```
name: Node.js CI
on:
  push:
```

```
    branches: [ "main" ]
jobs:
  build:
    runs-on: ubuntu-latest
    strategy:
      matrix:
        node-version: [16.x, 18.x]
    steps:
    - uses: actions/checkout@v3
    - name: Use Node.js ${{ matrix.node-version }}
      uses: actions/setup-node@v3
      with:
        node-version: ${{ matrix.node-version }}
        cache: 'npm'
    - run: npm ci
    - run: tsc
    - run: node dist/test
```

Deep diving into GitHub workflow structure

The GitHub workflow stands as the epitome of modern automation in software development, a feature that fundamentally transforms the landscape of how developers approach CI/CD processes. This exploration delves into the intricacies of GitHub workflows, breaking down their structure and functionality to understand how they revolutionize software development practices.

When you see a YAML file, you may think that it is difficult to understand. Yes, it might be more intuitive if you could tweak it in the GUI. But the GitHub Actions workflow is really simple.

The workflow can be broken down into the following elements:

- **Workflow**: The backbone of automation, defining the entire process
- **Job**: A group of steps executed in the same environment
- **Steps**: The smallest unit of a workflow, each representing an individual task
- **Actions**: Reusable unit, combined into steps, to perform specific tasks

It would be easier to understand if we think of each of these as the following blocks:

```
on: push

jobs:

  deploy:
    runs-on: ubuntu-latest

  steps:

    - uses: actions/checkout@v3
```

Figure 5.3 – GitHub Actions workflow structure

We will cover these elements in detail in the following subsections.

Workflow – The automation framework

At the heart of GitHub Actions lies the concept of the **workflow**. It is more than just a sequence of tasks; it is an automated, structured, and highly customizable set of procedures, all defined within a YAML file. This file, living in the `.github/workflows` directory of a GitHub repository, is the blueprint of your automation strategy. It is here where the magic begins—with each GitHub event, such as a push or a pull request, these workflows spring into action, setting the cogs of automation in motion.

A GitHub Actions workflow can engage with a variety of event types, each triggering different automated sequences that are defined in the YAML file. The following subsections cover detailed explanations of the event types that can be used to trigger workflows.

Webhook events trigger

A variety of triggers are possible, but we will mention a few typical ones here:

- **Pull request operations**: Workflows can be configured to trigger on pull request events, such as when pull requests are opened, updated, merged, or closed. This enables automated testing, code reviews, and merge conflict checks, ensuring that changes are validated before integration into the `main` branch.

- **Issue operations**: Similar to pull requests, workflows can react to issue activities such as creation, assignment, labeling, and closing. This is ideal for automatic issue response templates, prioritization, and triaging.

- **Push events and others**: Perhaps the most common trigger, a push event, occurs when commits are pushed to the repository. Workflows initiated by push events can handle a multitude of tasks, including code scans, building, testing, and deploying applications.

The following example triggers an event when pushed to `main`:

```
on:
  push:
    branches: [ "main" ]
```

Scheduled events trigger

Workflows can be scheduled to run at specific times using the Cron syntax. This feature is akin to an alarm clock that activates your workflows at predetermined intervals, useful for nightly builds, regular cleanups, or periodic syncing tasks. In this example, the workflow is triggered daily at 5:30 and 17:30 UTC:

```
on:
  schedule:
    - cron: '30 5,17 * * *'
```

Manual events trigger

`workflow_dispatch` allows workflows to be manually triggered from the GitHub UI or API. This offers the flexibility to run workflows on demand, which is particularly useful for ad hoc tasks such as manual deployments, data imports, or any operation where manual oversight is necessary before execution.

The following is an example of a setup for manual operation:

```
on: workflow_dispatch
```

Job – The execution unit

Within each workflow, we encounter **jobs**. Think of a job as a coherent group of steps that execute collectively on the same runner. A runner in GitHub Actions is a server that has the GitHub Actions runner application installed. It is essentially where your jobs are executed. Each runner can be thought of as a clean, isolated **Virtual Machine** (**VM**) that is provisioned for each job or workflow run. The beauty of jobs in a GitHub workflow is their ability to run concurrently across different runners unless they are explicitly defined to be dependent on one another. Each job can operate on a variety of GitHub-hosted VMs, each catering to different operating systems, or even on self-hosted machines, offering an unprecedented level of flexibility.

In the following example, the `build` job is a fundamental component of the workflow process, generally responsible for compiling code or generating build artifacts. The name `build` can be replaced with any job name you like. In your setup, the `runs-on` key specifies the execution environment for the following example job, which is the `ubuntu-latest` runner. This choice instructs GitHub Actions to execute the `build` job on the most recent version of Ubuntu Linux available on the platform. Apart from this, you can choose macOS and Windows. Also, your local machines or on-premises machines can be registered as self-hosted runners, giving you the flexibility to use them in a variety of environments, including those with strict network requirements or larger workloads:

```
jobs:
  build:
    runs-on: ubuntu-latest
```

The `strategy` feature in GitHub Actions simplifies testing across multiple environments using the `matrix` option. This option allows you to define a combination of different configurations (such as operating systems, programming language versions, or dependencies) that you want your workflow to run on. Instead of setting up multiple jobs manually for each configuration, the matrix option dynamically generates a job for each combination you specify. This approach avoids the redundancy of manual setup and ensures your code works on various versions of dependencies, such as Node. js. It is a proactive way to catch compatibility issues early, affirming your application's stability across different environments. This is optional, but good to keep in mind:

```
jobs:
  build:
    strategy:
      matrix:
        node-version: [16.x, 18.x]
```

In addition, container settings can be made as follows. If you want a specific container environment, you can use this to implement CI/CD in a flexible environment:

```
jobs:
  your-container-job:
    container:
      image: node:18
```

You can also specify the conditions under which jobs will run as follows:

```
jobs:
  production-deploy:
    if: github.repository == 'georgehattori/hello-world'
```

Steps – The building blocks

Diving deeper, each job comprises **steps**, fundamental tasks, or operations. Each step in a job is executed sequentially, ensuring a controlled progression of tasks. These steps can be as simple as a script or command execution or as complex as running a series of actions. Steps are the building blocks of a workflow, piecing together the larger picture of automation:

```
steps:
- uses: actions/checkout@v3
- uses: actions/setup-node@v3
```

Actions – Customized task executors

The most granular elements within these steps are **actions**. Actions are the workhorses of GitHub workflows, encapsulating specific functionalities in reusable units. From custom actions tailor-made for specific tasks to a plethora of ready-to-use actions available in GitHub Marketplace, the possibilities are endless. Actions come in various forms, including JavaScript actions for direct execution on the runner, Docker container actions for containerized operations, and composite run steps actions, which combine multiple run commands. This versatility allows for a high degree of customization, enabling developers to craft workflows that align perfectly with their development needs.

The following snippet from a GitHub Actions workflow is tailored for Node.js projects, utilizing a series of commands and actions to prepare the runtime environment and build the application:

```
- uses: actions/checkout@v3
- name: Use Node.js 14
  uses: actions/setup-node@v3
  with:
    node-version: '14'
    cache: 'npm'
- run: npm ci
- run: npm run build --if-present
- run: npm test
```

Let's take a closer look at the GitHub Actions specifics:

- name: This is essentially a label for readability within the workflow file. It helps you and anyone else reading the workflow understand what the step is intended to do. Here, it specifies that the step will set up Node.js version 14.

- uses: This key specifies an action to be used. Actions are reusable pieces of code that can perform complex tasks. actions/setup-node@v3 refers to the third major version of the setup-node action, which is designed to configure a Node.js environment. When you specify an action with uses, GitHub Actions will fetch that piece of code and execute it as part of the step.

- with: This part of the step feeds input parameters to the action specified in uses. It customizes the behavior of the action. For setup-node, you are providing two pieces of information: the Node.js version (node-version: '14') and the package manager cache settings (cache: 'npm'). The cache option tells the action to cache the dependencies, which can speed up future job runs. This is a predefined parameter in the action that is available in the marketplace or is open source. You can create your own and distribute it to the world, or create it for internal use and have your internal users use it.

- `run`: This is a directive for running command-line scripts, and it is where you can execute shell commands. In this case, `npm ci` is a command that installs all dependencies for your project as specified in your `package-lock.json` file. And after that, it builds and tests the project.

GitHub Actions may seem complicated at first, but once you get the hang of it, it is easy. It is essentially a mechanism to control the flow of scripts.

Furthermore, GitHub workflows are not just about the tasks they perform; they are about streamlining and simplifying the development process. The ability to reuse parts of workflows, such as setup and test steps, in different contexts, such as pull request validation, exemplifies the platform's emphasis on efficiency and reusability. This aspect is crucial in an era where Agile development and rapid iteration are the norms.

Now, let's embark on the journey of utilizing GitHub Actions. With a vast array of templates readily available, the best way to start is by diving right in and trying them out. These templates cater to a wide range of automation needs, from streamlining repetitive tasks and automating code testing and building in CI to facilitating code deployment across various environments and implementing crucial security checks and measures. The large selection of GitHub Actions templates is easily accessible at GitHub, as shown in the following screenshot:

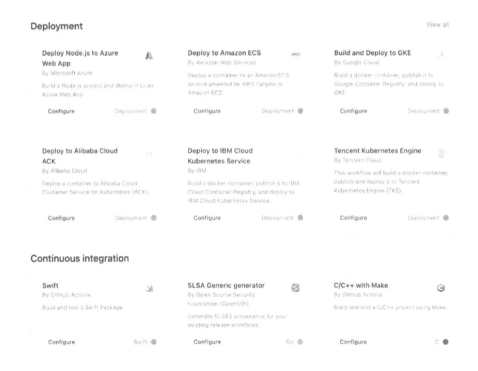

Figure 5.4 – Extensive templates for GitHub Actions

By leveraging these templates, you will be able to harness the full potential of GitHub Actions efficiently and effectively. Embrace this powerful tool and watch as it transforms your development workflow, making it more streamlined, secure, and robust.

GitHub Actions best practices

There are several best practices for GitHub Actions that are worth discussing. These include reducing redundancy, which helps streamline your workflows by eliminating unnecessary repetition. Secrets and variable management are crucial for maintaining security and efficiency in your actions. Debugging GitHub Actions workflows is an essential skill, allowing you to identify and fix issues quickly. Managing permissions effectively ensures that the right levels of access are maintained, while the implementation of approval processes with environments helps in controlling the deployment flow and maintaining the integrity of different deployment stages. Learning and applying these best practices can significantly enhance your proficiency with GitHub Actions.

Now, let's look at them one by one.

Reducing redundancy

Harnessing the power of GitHub Actions efficiently demands a focus on reducing redundancy, a crucial best practice in workflow automation. This involves three key options:

- **Utilizing GitHub Marketplace**: Here, you can tap into a vast array of existing actions created by the community, suitable for a wide range of common automation tasks. This approach saves time and leverages the collective expertise of other developers.

- **Creating custom actions**: For unique requirements not covered by Marketplace actions, custom actions offer a tailored solution. They allow you to address the specific needs of your project with precision.

- **Implementing reusable workflows**: Develop workflows that can be applied across multiple projects. This not only streamlines the workflow setup process but also ensures consistency and easier maintenance.

By integrating these, you can optimize your use of GitHub Actions, leading to more efficient, consistent, and maintainable automation processes in your **Software Development Life Cycle (SDLC)**. Various actions are available as open source projects, as follows:

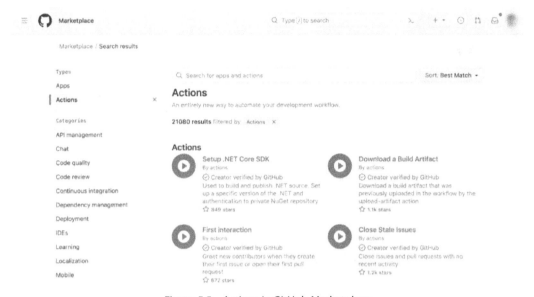

Figure 5.5 – Actions in GitHub Marketplace

Custom actions and reusable workflows are the next areas of learning for the reader. We will not go into depth here, but for extended use of GitHub Actions, there are links to detailed resources in the *Further reading* section at the end of the chapter.

Secrets and variable management

In GitHub Actions, managing secrets and variables is essential for both security and workflow customization:

- **Secrets**: Secrets are used to store sensitive information such as API keys, passwords, and tokens. They are encrypted and secure. In your workflow files, you reference secrets using ${{ secrets.NAME }}, ensuring they are not exposed in logs or to unauthorized users. Once a secret is registered, it cannot be retrieved, and the registered value will not appear in the console output of GitHub Actions.

- **Environment variables**: Environment variables hold non-sensitive configuration data, such as file paths or configuration settings. Environment variables can also be retrieved as ${{ env. My_Variable }}. You set environment variables directly in your workflow files, and they can be different for each job or step.

The following is an example of using a registered secret in GitHub Actions, allowing you to inject values from outside the workflow in a flexible manner:

```
steps:
  - shell: bash
    env:
      MY_SECRET: ${{ secrets.MySecret }}
    run: |
      sample-command "$MY_SECRET"
```

Proper management of secrets and variables is key to maintaining the security and efficiency of your GitHub Actions workflows. Secrets and variables can be set from the GitHub configuration page as follows:

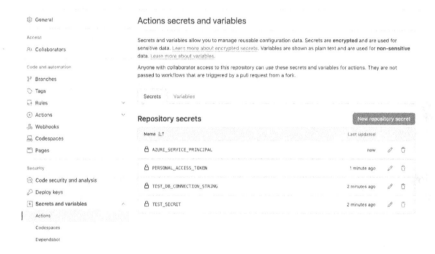

Figure 5.6 – Secrets and variables configuration for GitHub Actions

Debugging GitHub Actions workflows

Debugging in GitHub Actions is an essential practice to ensure your workflows run as expected and to identify and resolve any issues that arise. Here are some key points to help you effectively debug your GitHub Actions workflows:

- **Step debug logging**: For more detailed logs, you can enable step debug logging in your GitHub Actions workflows. To do this, create a repository secret named ACTIONS_STEP_DEBUG with the value true. This will provide you with more detailed information during the execution of your actions, making it easier to pinpoint where and why a problem is occurring.

- **Run logs access**: GitHub Actions automatically generates logs for each run. These logs can be accessed in the **Actions** tab of your GitHub repository. They provide a detailed record of what happened during each step of your workflow.

- **Local testing with act**: Tools such as act (https://github.com/nektos/act) allow you to run your workflows locally on your machine. This can be particularly helpful for testing complex workflows without having to push changes to your repository. It enables a faster iteration cycle in fixing and optimizing your actions.

- **Manual workflows**: Utilizing the workflow_dispatch event trigger in your workflow file allows you to manually trigger workflows. This can be useful for testing changes without the need to trigger workflows on push or pull request events.

Other things to keep in mind when creating GitHub Actions workflows include the following:

- **Simplifying workflows**: Break down complex workflows into smaller, more manageable parts to isolate and identify issues.

- **Utilizing action outputs**: Use outputs from actions for diagnostic purposes. These can give insights into the behavior of different steps.

- **Iterative approach**: When making changes to a workflow, do it incrementally. Test each change thoroughly before implementing the next. This approach helps isolate the impact of each change, making debugging easier.

Debugging GitHub Actions workflows effectively requires a combination of utilizing detailed logs, testing workflows locally, simplifying complex setups, and manually triggering workflows. These practices help to quickly identify and resolve issues, ensuring your CI/CD processes are robust and reliable.

Permissions

Managing permissions in GitHub Actions is critical for maintaining the security and integrity of your workflow processes. This section focuses on setting and managing the appropriate permissions for actions within your GitHub workflows:

- **Automatic token scoping**: GitHub Actions automatically restricts permissions granted to GITHUB_TOKEN, a special GitHub-generated token used by workflows. By default, this token is scoped to the repository containing your workflow, ensuring actions cannot inadvertently affect other repositories or sensitive data.

- **Granular control**: You can customize the permissions of GITHUB_TOKEN within your workflow file for specific jobs or the entire workflow. This allows you to restrict or extend the token's capabilities based on the needs of individual jobs, enhancing security and minimizing risk. Permissions are set in the workflow file using the permissions key. You can specify permissions for various GitHub API scopes, such as contents, issues, deployments, and more. The following is an example of such a setup:

```
# Sets permissions of the GITHUB_TOKEN
permissions:
  contents: read
```

```
        pages: write
        id-token: write
```

- **Minimal access**: Apply the **Principle of Least Privilege (PoLP)** by granting permissions that are only just sufficient for a particular action or job to function. Avoid giving broad or admin-level permissions unless absolutely necessary.

By meticulously managing permissions in GitHub Actions, you can safeguard your workflows against unauthorized access, mistakes, and potential security vulnerabilities. This involves setting precise token permissions, securely managing secrets, and regularly auditing access levels to align with PoLP. Implementing these practices will significantly strengthen the security posture of your CI/CD pipeline.

Approval processes with environments

In the dynamic world of software deployment and CI, GitHub Actions brings a crucial element of control and oversight through its **Environments** feature. This innovative functionality significantly elevates the way teams handle their deployment workflows, particularly in terms of approval processes and adherence to specific operational conditions.

Environments in GitHub Actions serve as dedicated spaces within the workflow, each tailored to specific stages such as testing, staging, or production. What sets these environments apart is their capacity to be customized with unique rules and access controls. They become not just segments of the workflow but controlled realms, each with its distinct set of permissions and secrets. This ensures that sensitive information and actions are confined to where they are most relevant, bolstering the security of the entire process.

Central to the value of environments is their role in facilitating approval workflows. Imagine a scenario where any deployment to production requires a careful review. Environments make this possible by integrating a manual approval process. When a deployment reaches the production stage, it triggers a pause in the workflow, awaiting the green light from authorized personnel. This pause is not just a halt in operations; it is a gatekeeper ensuring that every change undergoes scrutiny before it affects the live environment. The approval flow with **Environments** is seamlessly integrated into the GitHub Actions experience, as shown in the following screenshot:

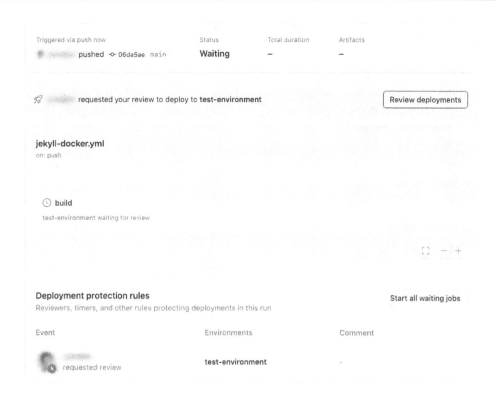

Figure 5.7 – Approval on Environments

Beyond mere approval, environments in GitHub Actions allow for sophisticated condition settings. Jobs within an environment can be configured to run only in specific circumstances, such as on certain branches or in response to particular events. This level of detail in control ensures that the workflow adheres to the precise operational standards of a project, avoiding any unintended deployments or actions.

The introduction of protection rules within these environments further fortifies the workflow. By setting requirements such as mandatory reviewers for changes, organizations can enforce compliance and maintain high-security standards. This is not just about keeping the workflow secure; it is about aligning it with organizational protocols and best practices.

An environment, therefore, is not just an addition to GitHub Actions; it is a paradigm shift in how deployment workflows are managed. It introduces a layer of security, control, and compliance that is indispensable in modern software development. Environments ensure that every step in the CI/CD pipeline, especially those involving sensitive stages such as production, is executed under stringent scrutiny and within the bounds of defined operational guidelines. This is GitHub Actions not just facilitating automation, but doing so with a keen eye on safety, reliability, and organizational integrity. From the **Environments** configuration, you can add protection rule settings such as adding an approver:

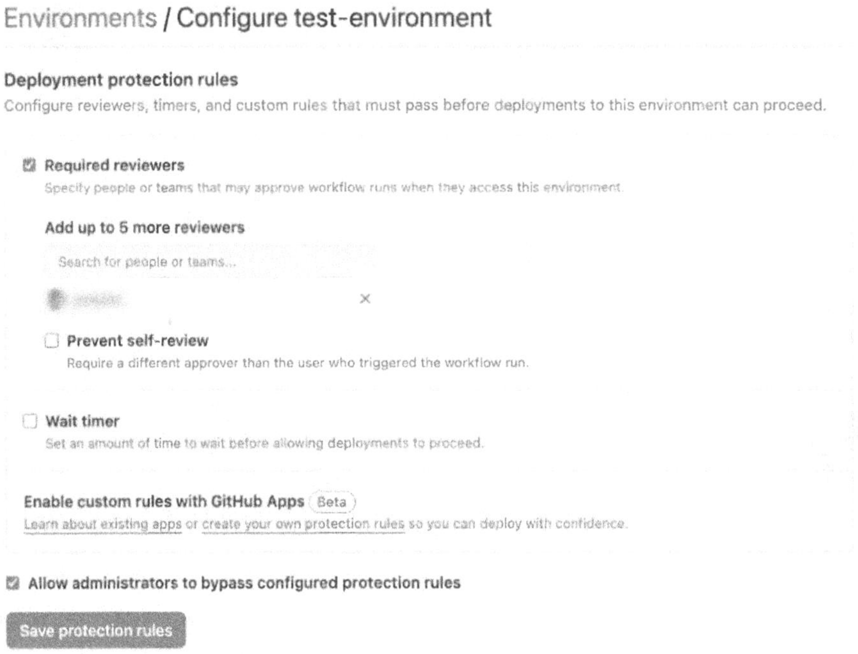

Environments / **Configure test-environment**

Deployment protection rules
Configure reviewers, timers, and custom rules that must pass before deployments to this environment can proceed.

☑ **Required reviewers**
Specify people or teams that may approve workflow runs when they access this environment.

Add up to 5 more reviewers

Search for people or teams...

☐ **Prevent self-review**
Require a different approver than the user who triggered the workflow run.

☐ **Wait timer**
Set an amount of time to wait before allowing deployments to proceed.

Enable custom rules with GitHub Apps (Beta)
Learn about existing apps or create your own protection rules so you can deploy with confidence.

☑ **Allow administrators to bypass configured protection rules**

Save protection rules

Figure 5.8 – Environments configuration

GitHub Actions stands out as a versatile tool, adaptable to a wide range of development scenarios, making it an indispensable asset for modern software development teams. Whether it is automating routine tasks, ensuring code quality, or deploying applications, GitHub Actions provides the tools and flexibility required for high-quality software delivery.

Now, let's look at some applied practices for deploying with GitHub Actions.

Deployment strategies

It is important to embrace *failure* as a system in DevOps. In the dynamic world of DevOps, embracing failure is not just recommended; it is essential. Contrary to traditional perspectives where failure is often seen as a setback, in DevOps, failure assumes a transformative role. It is not merely an incident or an unexpected result; it is an integral part of DevOps.

In conventional deployment methodologies, extensive checks and balances are the norm, aimed at minimizing the occurrence of failure. However, the fast-paced nature of modern development such as Agile alters this approach significantly. In modern development, the landscape is ever-evolving, and services undergo constant changes. If these changes are not made swiftly and effectively, it could lead to service degradation or failure. Therefore, it becomes crucial to build a system that is resilient and can adapt to these rapid changes.

In this context, the goal is not to prevent failure outright, but to create an environment where failures are manageable and their impacts are minimized. This involves adopting strategies that anticipate failures and implement mechanisms to quickly recover or roll back changes when necessary. It is about building robustness and resilience into the system, ensuring that it can withstand and recover from failures, rather than simply aiming for a failure-free operation. This section delves into how to accept failure as a systemic necessity in DevOps.

Traditionally, the realms of infrastructure and application deployment have existed as separate domains. However, the advent of DevOps has ushered in an era where these boundaries blur into a unified landscape. Nowadays, infrastructure configuration is also defined by **Infrastructure as Code (IaC)**. This means that infrastructure and apps can be released at the same time. You need to deploy both infrastructure and apps stably in both aspects in the context of DevOps.

Let's look at some practices that are particularly common when deploying services.

Blue-green deployment

Blue-green deployment is a strategy in software deployment that minimizes downtime and risk by maintaining two identical production environments. This method allows for safe and seamless transitions between software versions. As shown in the following diagram, the load balancer or **Platform as a Service (PaaS)** services' capabilities switch traffic:

Figure 5.9 – Blue-green deployment

In this strategy, the blue environment hosts the current live version, while the green environment is used for the new version. Once the new version in the green environment is fully tested and ready, traffic is switched over from blue to green.

Key benefits of this approach include the following:

- **Easy rollback**: If issues are discovered in the green environment after going live, traffic can be quickly redirected back to the stable blue environment.

- **Minimal downtime**: Blue-green deployment allows you to release new versions of your software without any downtime for end users. The new version is deployed alongside the old one, and the switch is made instantly.

- **Easy testing**: Developers and **Quality Assurance** (**QA**) teams can thoroughly test the new version in a production-like environment without affecting end users.

The terminology of blue-green is often perceived as a synonym for environments such as staging, QA, and production, but it is not exact. Unlike a traditional staging-to-production promotion, both the blue and green environments in this method are production-grade.

Despite its advantages, there are notable challenges:

- **Requirement of two production environments**: This can be resource-intensive and costly. Maintaining two full-scale production environments can be expensive, even in a cloud computing context.

- **Challenges with irreversible changes**: If changes such as database schema updates are not backward compatible, rollback can be complicated.

- **Stateful application considerations**: Synchronizing stateful data between environments can be complex.

Typical steps

A practical example of blue-green deployment for a web application, where the current live version is 1.3 in the blue environment and the goal is to deploy version 1.4, can be outlined as follows:

1. **Deployment**: Initiate by deploying the new version, 1.4, to the green environment. This environment is a replica of the existing blue environment but hosts the new version.

2. **Validation**: Conduct comprehensive testing in the green environment. This step is critical to ensure that the new version operates correctly and meets all necessary requirements.

3. **Traffic switch**: Once validation is successful, the next step is to switch user traffic. This is done by updating the load balancer settings to redirect traffic from the blue environment (version 1.3) to the green environment (version 1.4).

4. **Monitoring**: After the traffic switch, closely monitor the green environment for any operational issues or unexpected behavior. This monitoring phase is crucial to quickly identify and address any problems that may arise post-deployment.

5. **Finalization**: If the green environment with version 1.4 runs smoothly and no significant issues are detected, the deployment is deemed successful, and the green environment becomes the new production environment. However, if there are critical problems, you have the option to promptly revert traffic to the stable blue environment (version 1.3), minimizing disruption and risk.

This methodical approach ensures a smooth transition between application versions, maintaining system stability and availability throughout the deployment process.

Real-world scenario

Achieving a successful blue-green deployment strategy requires a comprehensive understanding of your infrastructure and the tools available within your platform. The implementation approach can differ significantly based on whether you are using **Infrastructure as a Service (IaaS)** with VMs or PaaS with load balancers.

Here is a closer look at the different methods:

- **DNS load balancers**: In this approach, the changeover between blue and green environments is managed through DNS rewriting. This method is often used when the environments are hosted on different servers or clusters.

- **Layer 4 network load balancers**: These perform the switchover by **Network Address Translation (NAT)** translation. It is a suitable option for switching between environments hosted within the same network infrastructure.

- **Layer 7 application load balancers**: Here, the routing to different application versions is managed at the application layer. This method provides more granular control over traffic distribution and is often used in complex deployments.

Many PaaS solutions come with built-in load-balancing capabilities, simplifying the blue-green deployment process. In these setups, the load balancer can be easily configured to switch traffic between the blue and green environments. In such cases, users can set up switching simply by configuration without being aware of the presence of a load balancer.

In more advanced environments, such as **Kubernetes (k8s)**, network resources are managed as IaC, providing the capability for dynamic allocation. This enables the implementation of blue-green deployments through modifications to IaC configuration, typically achieved by editing YAML files. While numerous PaaS offerings abstract away network configuration complexities from users, certain platforms, such as Kubernetes, maintain network configurations internally within a single cluster, thereby enabling the same blue-green deployment approach to be applied seamlessly within the cluster.

Switching methods

Now, how do we switch environments? There are several possible ways, so let's take a look:

- **Separate script or graphical UI (GUI) for load balancer configuration**: Some teams prefer to handle the switchover separately from the main deployment script. This can be done using a dedicated script or through a GUI, providing more control and oversight during the switch.

- **Load balancing configuration in deployment script**: This method involves scripting the load balancer setting changes directly in the deployment script. It is a streamlined approach that can automate the switchover process as part of the deployment pipeline.

- **Automation**: Automation encompasses the automated testing of the new version, ensuring that the switch only occurs when the new version performs successfully. This involves setting specific conditions for the release to proceed, often relying on components such as **End-To-End (E2E)** tests and monitoring for errors in the new environment.

It is important to note that the timing of the switchover and the handling of existing connections can vary based on the system and service used. Each method has its nuances and requires careful planning to ensure a smooth transition with minimal disruption to the users.

Rolling deployment

A rolling deployment is a deployment strategy used in distributed systems whereby updates are applied incrementally across the nodes of a cluster. This method reduces downtime and ensures **High Availability (HA)** while updating applications or systems.

It is used in clusters such as Kubernetes for stable releases with no downtime. A rolling deployment involves gradual releases, as shown in the following diagram:

Figure 5.10 – Rolling deployment

This way, we can safely update each release one by one.

Typical steps

The process of a cluster rolling deployment generally involves the following steps:

1. **Preparation**: Before starting the update, ensure the system is ready for the upgrade. This includes taking backups of critical data and preparing the new version of the software or configuration to be deployed.

2. **Update the first node**: Begin the rolling update by selecting a single node. Instead of taking this node out of service before applying the update, the update is applied while the node is still in service. A new instance with the updated configuration or software is started alongside the existing ones.

3. **Health check**: Once the new instance is up and running, perform a thorough health check. This step is crucial to ensure that the new instance is correctly configured and capable of handling the intended workload without issues.

4. **Traffic shift**: After confirming that the new instance is healthy, gradually redirect traffic from the old instance to the new instance. This may involve adjusting load balancer settings or service discovery configurations to point to the new instance.

5. **Remove old instance**: Once the new instance is successfully handling traffic, the old instance can be safely removed from service. This ensures there is no downtime, as the service continues uninterrupted during the update.

6. **Gradual rollout**: Continue with the rolling update by repeating the process for each node in the cluster. Update nodes one by one, ensuring each new instance is healthy and capable of handling traffic before decommissioning the old ones.

7. **Monitoring**: Throughout the update process, continuously monitor the system for any issues. Pay close attention to performance metrics and error logs to quickly identify and address any problems.

8. **Finalization**: After all nodes have been updated and old instances removed, the rolling update is complete. Conduct a final review to ensure the entire system is stable, performing as expected, and that all instances are running the new version.

Real-world scenario

In real-world scenarios, a cluster rolling deployment is particularly vital in environments where continuous availability is crucial. This approach is commonly used in cloud computing services, data centers, and large-scale web applications. For example, updating a Kubernetes cluster or a database cluster often employs this strategy to avoid downtime and service disruptions. Also, be aware that rolling upgrades include both the application context and the infrastructure context. In the case of Kubernetes, in addition to cluster-side upgrades, there is also such a procedure for application upgrades.

This may be done through in-place upgrades while the service is running, but in mission-critical services, such as financial services, it may be applied in conjunction with other release strategies. This is like a blue-green deployment with a cloud load balancer in front of the cluster itself and distributed.

While it is true that some of these have a discourse of losing the benefits of rolling upgrades in some cases, it means that the configurations that open source projects and service vendors generally consider best practices do not necessarily match configurations that can realistically be taken.

Switchover methods

The method of a rolling deployment varies in difficulty depending on whether the system supports it as a feature. In a cluster orchestrator such as Kubernetes, updates can be rolled out using automated orchestrators, which manage the process of updating nodes and conducting health checks, while there are cases where a rolling deployment is still a reality, traditionally done by hand.

For example, if a single-tenant service is hosted in an isolated environment for an individual company and each environment requires updates, then deploying customers in several tiers is categorized and updates are done gradually. While this is also a type of rolling deployment, explicitly referring to DevOps practices will often refer to automated practices.

A cluster rolling deployment is essential for maintaining the reliability and stability of distributed systems during upgrades or maintenance. By updating nodes sequentially, this strategy minimizes the risk of system-wide failures and ensures that services remain available to users throughout the process.

Canary deployment

A canary deployment is a technique whereby new versions of the software are rolled out gradually to a small subset of users before being deployed to the entire user base. This approach allows developers to test the new version in a real-world environment with minimal risk.

In a canary deployment, instead of releasing a new version to all users at once, the update is first introduced to a small group of users – the **canaries**. This group acts as an early indicator for any potential issues, hence the name *canary*, akin to the canaries used in coal mines to detect harmful gases. By monitoring the behavior and performance of the software with these initial users, developers can identify and address any issues before a full rollout. As shown in the following diagram, the switching is implemented gradually, and once stability is confirmed, the range is expanded:

Figure 5.11 – Canary deployment

This is essentially the same as a rolling deployment but differs in duration and the activities and objectives associated with it. Rolling deployments are intended to replace older versions of applications sequentially with newer versions by completely replacing the infrastructure on which the application is running, and health checks are performed and completely replaced within a short period of time. In most cases, this is done in a few minutes to a few hours. For large systems, it might take several days.

Canary releases, on the other hand, take a relatively long period of time to observe how the system behaves in response to user behavior and to use that feedback for a stable release.

Although canary releases are sometimes confused with beta releases targeted at a subset of users, it should be noted that canary releases are clearly a practice with release stability as a major objective. The methodology for targeted beta releases is covered in the *Feature flag* section.

Key benefits of a canary deployment include the following:

- **Risk mitigation**: By limiting the exposure of the new version, any negative impact is contained and affects only a small portion of the user base

- **Real-world testing**: Provides an opportunity to observe how the new version performs under real-world conditions

- **User observation**: Early observation from a subset of users can be invaluable for making adjustments before the wider release

- **Gradual rollout**: Offers a controlled way to manage the release process, reducing the likelihood of widespread issues

However, it also has its challenges:

- **Segmentation**: Deciding which users should be part of the canary group can be challenging.

- **Monitoring complexity**: Requires robust monitoring tools to effectively track the performance of the new version.

- **Consistent user experience**: Ensuring a consistent experience for all users, regardless of the version they are using, can be difficult. For example, when a new backend service is developed, it must be released with the assurance that the current service will continue to work properly.

Typical steps

Let's take a look at each of these steps:

1. **Deployment**: Initially, deploy the new version to a small percentage of your infrastructure, which will serve a fraction of your user base.

2. **Monitoring and analysis**: Observe the behavior of the application closely. Use metrics, logs, and user feedback to evaluate performance and identify any issues.

3. **Expansion**: If the initial deployment is successful, gradually increase the percentage of users accessing the new version. Continue monitoring and analyzing user feedback and system performance.

4. **Full rollout**: Once confident that the new version is stable and well received, proceed with the full rollout to all users.

5. **Roll back if necessary**: If significant issues are identified during the canary phase, roll back the changes quickly to minimize impact.

Real-world scenario

Canary releases will be applied differently depending on the number of users and services to be deployed.

For example, when Microsoft applies canary releases to deploy Azure features, the canaries can be selected from a particular data center or a particular cluster of data centers. This is because it clearly narrows down the affected users and minimizes the impact. Another advantage of this clear user focus is that the situation can be observed on an ongoing basis. When stability is confirmed by deploying to a particular cluster or data center, the next step is to expand the deployment to a wider target.

In the absence of the ability to target specific data centers or clusters, canary releases are frequently executed in a more randomized manner, leveraging the capabilities of cloud platforms. For instance, consider the approach of directing a random subset of users, say 5%, to a newly configured environment. This method employs a weight-based distribution strategy, where initially a small percentage such as 5% is chosen, subsequently increasing to 10%, 25%, and eventually 100% as confidence in the new environment grows. During this process, the load balancer is configured to allocate the defined percentage of user requests to the staging or new environment. Many cloud load balancers use this weight-based method.

To enhance user experience consistency, some services use cookies to ensure subsequent requests from the same client are directed to the same instance. However, the primary method of traffic allocation under this model is largely random. For instance, in the scenario where 5% of users are routed to a new environment and an error exists in the new version, there is a proportional 5% likelihood of users encountering the error, but all the users have that possibility.

Alternatively, a more deterministic method involves the use of header-based routing. This technique involves inserting specific information into the request header, which is then utilized to direct traffic. This approach reduces randomness by enabling targeted trials for specific users or user groups. The feasibility of implementing this method depends on the capabilities of the cloud service being used.

Both methods provide mechanisms for the gradual exposure of new updates or features, but each with its own level of control. For example, DNS load balancers do not read header information, so they basically only distribute weights, but they may be able to distribute by country. Layer 7 application load balancers, on the other hand, can read header information and other information.

Canary selection methods

In canary deployments, managing how users are exposed to the new version is crucial. Various methods can be employed to control this exposure:

- **Weight-based approach**: This method involves allocating a certain percentage of traffic to the new version. For example, initially, 5% of users may be directed to the new environment, gradually increasing to 25%, 50%, and ultimately 100% as confidence in the new version grows. Load balancers are often configured to handle this distribution of traffic based on predefined weights.

- **Header-based routing**: This technique utilizes specific information added to the request headers to direct traffic to the appropriate version. This method is less random than weight-based routing and allows for more targeted testing, such as exposing the new version to certain user groups or individuals based on header criteria.

- **Cookie-based routing**: Some services use cookies to ensure that subsequent requests from the same client are consistently directed to the same version (either new or old). This approach helps maintain a consistent user experience and is particularly useful for session persistence.

- **Geography-based distribution**: In some cases, traffic can be distributed based on the geographical location of the users. Some DNS load balancers, for example, can route traffic differently based on the country or region, which can be useful for global services looking to roll out updates in specific areas first.

Choosing the right switchover method is a critical decision in canary deployments, as it directly impacts the ability to effectively test the new version and respond to any issues that may arise during the initial rollout phase.

A canary deployment is a strategic approach to software releases, offering a balanced mix of risk mitigation and real-world testing. By gradually introducing changes, it allows for a more measured and informed approach to software deployment.

We have seen how to deploy applications and how to release them seamlessly and securely. Now that we have looked at strategies for how to deploy, we will next look at how to release at a more functional level.

Feature release strategies

So far, we have focused on releasing the infrastructure and the service as a whole, but now, we will focus on releasing the features within the service. For feature releases, we introduce a release style called the feature flag and release train.

Feature flag

Feature flag deployment is a technique used in software development and delivery that involves toggling on or off certain features of an application without deploying new code. This method allows for more granular control over feature release, testing, and rollback, enabling a more dynamic and flexible approach to software management.

The main drawback of using feature flags for anything is that feature flags can easily become a technical liability. Unused feature flags can clutter up the code base. Feature flags enable features for specific users or groups, as shown in the following diagram:

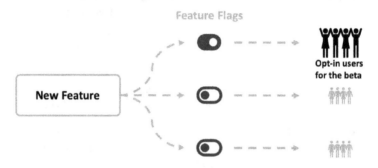

Figure 5.12 – Feature flag

Dark launches are typically released to user groups that do not know they are being tested and have not been told about the new feature at all. The advantage of this, on the other hand, is that it can be applied to any user group that wishes to do so, and not just to certain categories of users.

Typical steps

The implementation of feature flags typically involves the following steps:

1. **Implementation of feature flags in code**: Developers write conditional code for new features, controlled by feature flags. These flags can be toggled on or off, determining whether the feature is active.

2. **Integration with feature management system**: The feature flags are then integrated with a feature management system, which allows for controlling and changing the flags without needing to modify the code base.

3. **Testing**: Before enabling the feature for all users, it is often tested with a limited audience, similar to a canary release. This testing can be targeted based on user segments, geography, or other criteria.

4. **Gradual rollout**: After initial testing, the feature can be gradually rolled out to more users, allowing for careful monitoring of its impact and performance.

5. **Monitoring and feedback**: Continuous monitoring is essential to quickly identify any issues. Feedback from users during the rollout phase is also valuable for further refinement.

6. **Full rollout or rollback**: Depending on the feedback and performance, the feature can be fully rolled out to all users or rolled back by simply toggling the feature flag off.

Real-world scenario

Feature flags are an integral tool for modern software teams, enabling them to deliver features more efficiently and with greater control. This approach reduces risks associated with deploying new features and allows for more Agile product development and iteration. Their application extends across various aspects of software development, including A/B testing and dark launches.

The following subsections are real-world examples illustrating these applications.

A/B testing

Let's say a software team at an e-commerce company might use feature flags to test two different checkout page designs. They would create two variants: Design A (the current design) and Design B (the new design). By employing feature flags, they can expose Design B to a small, randomized group of users while the rest continue to see Design A. The team then monitors **Key Performance Indicators (KPIs)** such as conversion rates, **Average Order Value (AOV)**, and user feedback. This data helps them understand which design performs better in terms of user engagement and sales conversion. Based on the results, they can decide to either roll out Design B to all users, iterate on it, or revert to Design A, all with minimal disruption to the overall user experience.

Dark launch

A social media platform might use dark launches to test a new feature, such as an enhanced image recognition algorithm. They release the feature *in the dark*, meaning it is live but not visible to users. The platform then collects data on how the new algorithm performs in terms of accuracy and speed compared to the old one, without users being aware of the change.

This approach allows the platform to gather real-world data on the feature's performance and iron out any issues before making it visible to users. If the new algorithm does not perform as expected, they can refine or roll it back without impacting the user experience.

Feature flag deployment empowers teams to test and release features with higher confidence and control. By decoupling deployment from release, it allows for more flexibility, quicker iteration, and reduced risk in software development processes.

Release train

A release train is a concept in software development that emphasizes regular, scheduled deliveries of new features, enhancements, and fixes. It aligns multiple teams and processes to ensure a coordinated and predictable release cycle, significantly improving the efficiency and reliability of software deployments. As shown in the following diagram, the release train only releases those that meet the deadline:

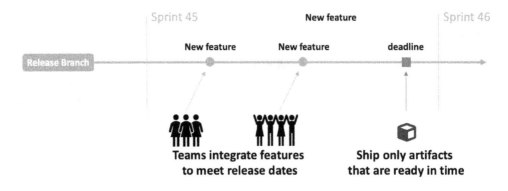

Figure 5.13 – Release train

Typical steps

The release train approach typically involves the following steps:

1. **Planning and coordination**: Establish a release schedule that all teams adhere to. This schedule includes fixed intervals (for example, bi-weekly, monthly) at which new features and updates are released.

2. **Development and testing**: Teams work on their respective features and fixes within the defined timeline. CI and **Continuous Testing (CT)** are employed to ensure code quality and compatibility.

3. **Integration and staging**: All features, enhancements, and fixes are integrated into a staging environment. This stage is crucial for identifying any integration issues and ensuring that all components work together seamlessly.

4. **Release review**: Conduct a review meeting with all stakeholders to ensure that the release is ready to be deployed. This meeting assesses the quality, functionality, and potential impact of the release.

5. **Deployment**: Once approved, the release is deployed to production according to the schedule. The deployment process is typically automated to reduce human error and increase efficiency.

6. **Monitoring and feedback**: After the release, continuous monitoring is essential to quickly identify and address any post-deployment issues. Feedback from users and stakeholders is collected for future improvements.

Real-world scenario

In a large software organization, the release train approach can significantly streamline the deployment process. For instance, a company developing a suite of business applications might have multiple teams working on different modules such as finance, HR, and operations. By adopting the release train model, the organization ensures that updates across all modules are released in a coordinated manner. Every month, new features and updates from each team are integrated, tested, and then deployed simultaneously. This synchronization avoids complexities and conflicts that can arise when different teams deploy updates independently.

Moreover, this approach provides customers with a predictable update schedule, enabling them to plan for the adoption of new features and updates. It also allows for more efficient allocation of resources within the organization, as teams can plan their workloads in accordance with the release schedule.

In essence, the release train model fosters a disciplined, predictable, and efficient release process, benefiting both the development teams and the end users.

Summary

This chapter has equipped you with the knowledge and skills to transform your development workflow into a model of automation excellence. The journey through the pages of this chapter has taken you from the foundational elements of GitHub Actions to strategic deployment and release techniques that stand at the forefront of modern software practices. To go further from here, you need to deepen such things as testing and concurrency. These things are not only connected to how the pipeline is put together but also to the philosophy of testing and integration. I hope you will continue to learn more.

By embracing the practices and strategies outlined herein, you are now poised to craft workflows that are not only efficient and robust but also secure and compliant with the highest standards. Let this chapter be a constant companion as you continue to innovate and excel in the evolving landscape of software development. In the upcoming chapter, we will delve into the critical areas of DevOps metrics, DevSecOps, and scaling collaboration, exploring how these concepts play a pivotal role in enhancing the efficiency and security of software development and deployment processes.

Further reading

- *About custom actions*: https://docs.github.com/en/actions/creating-actions/about-custom-actions
- *Reusing workflows*: https://docs.github.com/en/actions/using-workflows/reusing-workflows

Part 3:
Beyond DevOps

This part provides a detailed examination of DevOps, emphasizing the role of metrics, the incorporation of DevSecOps practices, and strategies for scaling collaboration in organizations. It then shifts focus to the integration of AI in software development, exploring tools such as GitHub Copilot and best practices for coding with AI assistance, including prompt crafting and AI-friendly programming principles. Finally, it reflects on the transformative impact of technologies such as Git, GitHub, DevOps, and AI in software development, contemplating the future influence of AI on software engineering practices.

This part has the following chapters:

- *Chapter 6, Enriching DevOps Implementation*
- *Chapter 7, Accelerate Productivity with AI*
- *Chapter 8, Reflection and Conclusion*

6

Enriching DevOps Implementation

In this chapter, we take a holistic approach to DevOps, examining the critical role of metrics in enhancing development processes, the integration of security practices through DevSecOps, and strategies for scaling collaboration effectively within organizations. We will delve into how metrics, enabled by tools such as GitHub, drive visibility and performance, explore methods to seamlessly embed security into the development lifecycle, and discuss fostering a collaborative, trust-based culture, emphasizing InnerSource principles to effectively scale DevOps practices. This comprehensive overview aims to provide a nuanced understanding of the multifaceted nature of modern DevOps.

We will cover the following main headings in this chapter:

- Leveraging metrics in DevOps
- DevSecOps – Security as a continuous matter
- Scaling the collaboration

Leveraging metrics in DevOps

What does it mean to measure metrics in DevOps? Measuring metrics in DevOps is about quantifying various aspects of the software development and delivery process to improve efficiency, quality, and collaboration. Metrics provide a data-driven approach to assess performance, identify bottlenecks, and inform decision-making. They are critical for continuous improvement, enabling teams to track progress against objectives and align efforts with organizational goals.

In DevOps, metrics can be categorized into different types. Performance metrics, such as deployment frequency and change lead time, measure the efficiency of the deployment pipeline. Quality metrics, such as defect rates and mean time to recovery, assess the stability and reliability of the software. Process metrics look at the efficiency of development processes, and people metrics focus on team performance and satisfaction.

Tools and automation are essential for effectively measuring these metrics. **Continuous Integration/Continuous Deployment (CI/CD)** tools such as **GitHub Actions**, issue tracking systems, and application performance monitoring tools are commonly used to collect and analyze data. We will now cover some well-known metrics measurements and ideas.

Four keys – DORA metrics

The **DevOps Research and Assessment (DORA)** metrics, introduced in the influential book *Accelerate* by Nicole Forsgren, Jez Humble, and Gene Kim, have become a key framework in software development. These metrics, often referred to as the **four keys**, go beyond being mere indicators; they offer a comprehensive approach to assessing and improving DevOps practices.

The following list helps with understanding DORA metrics:

- **Deployment frequency**: This measures how often you successfully release to production. Aim for regular, smaller deployments. This approach reduces risks and encourages a culture of continuous feedback and improvement.

- **Lead Time for changes**: This tracks the time from code commit to production deployment. Shortening this time by streamlining development and QA processes can boost your team's efficiency and ability to adapt to market changes.

- **Change failure rate**: This metric assesses the percentage of deployments that fail in production. Improving testing, quality assurance, and monitoring can lower these failures, enhancing the quality of your releases.

- **Mean Time To Recovery (MTTR)**: This measures the average time to recover from a failure in production. Developing robust incident response strategies and investing in automation can help reduce this time, ensuring greater system reliability.

There are the following reasons why so many teams love and use these metrics:

- **Objective insights**: DORA metrics provide clear, quantifiable insights into your team's performance, supporting data-driven decisions

- **A path to improvement**: Identifying strengths and weaknesses through these metrics helps target areas for improvement in your DevOps practices

- **Industry benchmarking**: These metrics allow you to compare your practices with industry standards, aiming to reach and maintain best practices

However, as with any metric, these indicators are a means to measure, not a goal in themselves. Let us note the following:

- **Context matters**: Always interpret these metrics within your organization's unique context and goals

- **Beyond the numbers**: Remember to balance these quantitative measures with qualitative aspects such as team morale and customer satisfaction

- **Stay adaptable**: As your organization and the industry evolve, so should your approach to these metrics

Teams are often classified into four performance levels—elite, high, medium, and low—based on these metrics. The ultimate goal is to reach **elite** status, which signifies a high-performing, agile, and efficient DevOps environment.

The DORA metrics offer a valuable lens through which to view and enhance your DevOps practices. Thoughtfully applying these metrics can lead to a more efficient, quality-driven, and effective software development process, positioning your organization to excel in the ever-changing landscape of technology.

SPACE framework

While DORA metrics focus on the specific operational aspects of DevOps, the SPACE framework, introduced by Dr. Nicole Forsgren and her colleagues, complements this by broadening the perspective to encompass **Developer Experience (DevEx)**. This dual approach allows organizations to balance technical excellence with a deep consideration of the human factors that drive successful software development.

Developed by Dr. Nicole Forsgren, along with her collaborators, the SPACE framework provides a multi-dimensional view of software development, considering aspects beyond the traditional scope of DevOps. **SPACE**, an acronym for **satisfaction and well-being, performance, activity, communication and collaboration, and efficiency and flow**, offers a holistic strategy to improve both the technical and human sides of development teams.

Here are the elements of the SPACE Framework:

- **Satisfaction and well-being**: Prioritizing the mental and emotional health of developers, recognizing that their satisfaction and well-being directly impact productivity, innovation, and effectiveness.

- **Performance**: Reframing traditional performance metrics to include not just speed and output but also quality and the overall impact on project and organizational goals.

- **Activity**: Focusing on optimizing the daily workflows and tasks of developers to align with both the project's objectives and individual career aspirations.

- **Communication and collaboration**: Encouraging open communication and effective collaboration is crucial for breaking down silos and fostering cohesive progress in development projects.

- **Efficiency and flow**: This involves aiming for a state of flow in work processes where developers can work seamlessly, leading to improved creativity and high-quality output.

The SPACE framework adds a vital dimension to DevOps strategies by emphasizing that technical efficiency and success cannot be fully realized without considering the well-being and satisfaction of the team. This holistic view is key to setting leading organizations apart, as it acknowledges the importance of a positive developer experience for sustainable growth and innovation.

Here are the benefits of integrating the SPACE framework in DevOps:

- **Comprehensive development strategy**: By including human-centric aspects, the SPACE framework ensures a more balanced and thorough approach to software development.

- **Enhanced team dynamics**: Focusing on satisfaction, communication, and collaboration leads to a more motivated, cohesive, and effective team.

- **Benchmarking across multiple dimensions**: SPACE allows organizations to benchmark not only their technical performance but also their cultural and human-centric practices against industry standards.

Integrating the SPACE framework with DORA metrics provides a more complete picture of an organization's DevOps practices. It ensures that while operational efficiency and technical benchmarks are met, the human aspects that are pivotal to the success and satisfaction of the development team are also given due attention. This dual approach paves the way for a more successful, well-rounded, and sustainable DevOps strategy.

Metrics at GitHub

In the multifaceted domain of DevOps, there exists a wide spectrum of metrics, each offering different approaches and insights. This document hones in on the collaborative dimensions of Git and GitHub, emphasizing metrics that are key to understanding and enhancing teamwork within these platforms. Grasping the nuances of these specific metrics and how they function is essential for effectively utilizing Git and GitHub in a DevOps setting, ensuring a more cohesive and productive collaboration.

GitHub Insights

GitHub offers an array of features that provide deep insights into various aspects of software development, aiding teams in enhancing their development. It tracks changes over time in various areas such as contributions, code frequency, and repository health. Each of these features plays a crucial role in understanding project dynamics, team collaboration, and community engagement.

GitHub metrics can track how healthy collaboration is between repositories, their contributors, and teams. In addition, it also provides a bird's eye view of library dependencies with regard to security.

The following is a brief overview of the GitHub Insights features:

- **Pulse**: **Pulse** is a feature that gives a quick overview of the activity in a repository over a specific period. It helps teams track the progress of their project, showing what has been completed and what is still pending, including merged pull requests, proposed changes and opened or closed issues. **Pulse** is instrumental in giving a snapshot view of the project's health and momentum:

Figure 6.1 – Pulse in GitHub Insights

- **Contributors**: The **Contributors** section offers insights into who is contributing to a project and how. It tracks individual contributions, such as commits, pull requests, and issues created. This feature is crucial for recognizing the efforts of team members and understanding the distribution of work within the team:

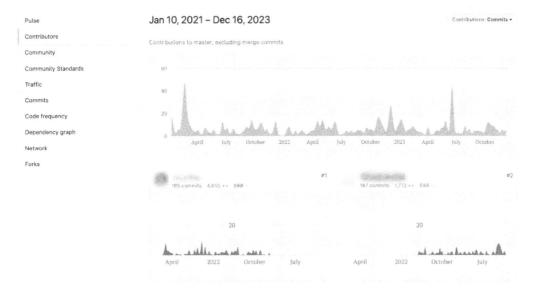

Figure 6.2 – Contributors in GitHub Insights

- **Community**: This section assesses the health of a project's community by tracking aspects such as user engagement and contributor activity. It encourages open source best practices, helping to ensure that the project is welcoming and inclusive, which is essential for fostering a vibrant and sustainable community:

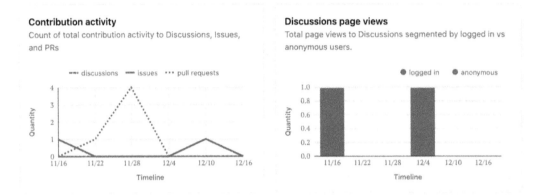

Figure 6.3 – Community in GitHub Insights

- **Community Standards**: This section provides a checklist to help maintain a healthy and welcoming environment for contributors. This includes a code of conduct, contributing guidelines, issue and pull request templates, and more. Adhering to these standard documentations is to build a respectful and collaborative community:

Figure 6.4 – Community standards in GitHub Insights

- **Traffic**: Traffic analytics provide data on how many people are viewing and interacting with a repository. It includes information on clones, views, visitors, and referring sites. Understanding traffic helps gauge the popularity and reach of a project, informing strategies for future growth and engagement:

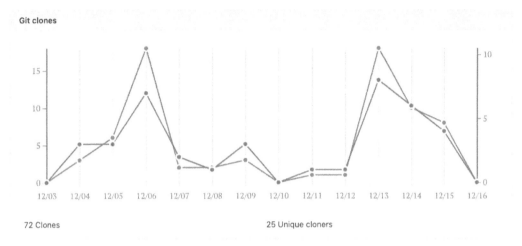

Figure 6.5 – Traffic in GitHub Insights

- **Commits**: The **Commits** feature gives a detailed history of changes made to the project. It allows teams to track progress, review changes, and understand the evolution of the codebase over time. This feature is essential for maintaining a comprehensive and traceable record of the development process:

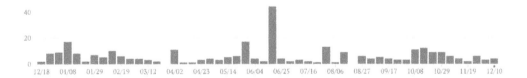

Figure 6.6 – Commits in GitHub Insights

- **Code frequency**: This graphs the volume of additions and deletions to the codebase over time. This visual representation helps teams understand coding patterns and periods of high activity:

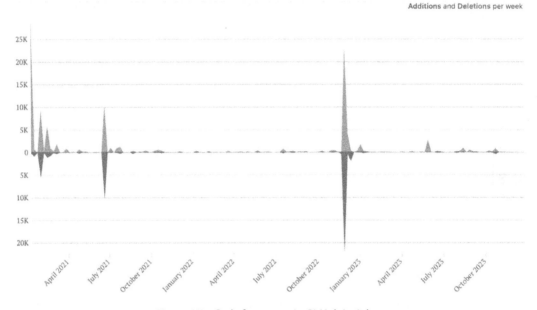

Figure 6.7 – Code frequency in GitHub Insights

- **Dependency graph**: The **Dependencies** tab shows the repository's dependencies and the projects that depend on it. This is crucial for managing third-party libraries, understanding potential security vulnerabilities, and ensuring the integrity and reliability of the code:

Figure 6.8 – Dependency graph in GitHub Insights

- **Network**: The **Network** feature visualizes the repository's fork network, showing the branches and forks from the original repository. This can reveal how changes are being merged back into the main project and how the community is contributing and branching off:

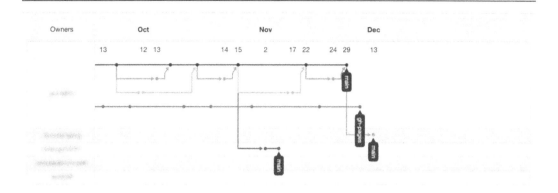

Figure 6.9 – Network in GitHub Insights

- **Forks**: The **Forks** feature indicates how many times the repository has been forked by other users. This metric is a strong indicator of a project's impact and reach within the GitHub community. It can signal active engagement and potential areas for collaboration:

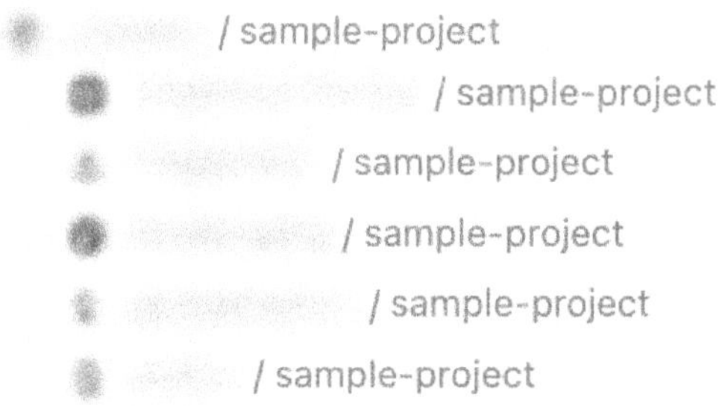

/ sample-project

/ sample-project

/ sample-project

/ sample-project

/ sample-project

/ sample-project

Figure 6.10 – Forks in GitHub Insights

By utilizing these features, teams and project maintainers can gain a comprehensive understanding of their project's performance, community engagement, and collaborative dynamics. These insights are invaluable for making informed decisions, fostering community growth, and driving continuous improvement in the development team.

These configurations prove particularly effective for community-based development initiatives such as open source, as well as for InnerSource efforts that integrate aspects such as community-based culture within a corporate setting. Visualizing contributions offers a practical way to grasp an overview of who is contributing and how. The balance of documentation on GitHub holds significant importance for fostering team collaboration, highlighting the critical role of managing both excess and deficiency. However, it is important to note that these insights may not universally apply to all projects.

Depending on the needs, integrating methodologies, such as the four keys or employing the SPACE framework in combination, can offer tailored approaches to enhance project outcomes.

Issue metrics

Measuring issue metrics is a crucial aspect of maintaining a healthy and efficient software development environment. These metrics provide invaluable insights into how quickly and effectively a team addresses issues, which is a key component of the overall DevEx. By tracking metrics such as the number of open issues, the time taken to close an issue, and the backlog of issues, teams can gauge their responsiveness and problem-solving abilities. This, in turn, directly impacts the team's productivity, satisfaction, and the quality of the software they produce.

The GitHub Action `issue-metrics`, available at `github/issue-metrics` (https://github.com/github/issue-metrics), serves as a powerful example of how teams can automate and simplify the process of tracking issue-related metrics.

The following GitHub Action measures several key metrics by searching for issues, pull requests, and discussions in a repository:

Metric	Average	Median	90th percentile
Time to first response	0:38:20	0:38:20	0:38:20
Time to close	None	None	None

Metric	Count
Number of items that remain open	6
Number of items closed	3
Total number of items created	9

Title	URL	Author	Time to first response	Time to close
Proposed Change: Adding examples	https://github.com/PacktPublishing/DevOps-Unleashed-with-Git-and-GitHub/issues/42	foo_bar	0:38:14	None
Monthly Metrics: Contributors 2023-11-01..2023-11-31	https://github.com/PacktPublishing/DevOps-Unleashed-with-Git-and-GitHub/issues/41	github-actions[bot]	None	None

Figure 6.11 – issue-metrics works with GitHub Actions

It generates a comprehensive report in the form of a GitHub issue, offering a clear and organized view of the data. The items to be analyzed can be filtered using a search query, making the tool adaptable to various needs and contexts.

Here are the available metrics:

- **Time to first response**: Measures the duration from the creation of an issue to the initial comment or review, giving insights into the team's initial engagement with new issues.

- **Time to close**: Tracks the period from the creation of an issue to its closure, indicating the overall speed of issue resolution.

- **Time to answer (discussions)**: Specifically for discussions, this metric measures the time from creation to an answer, reflecting the team's engagement in discussions.

- **Time in label**: Monitors the duration from when a label is applied to an issue or pull request to when it is removed. This requires the `LABELS_TO_MEASURE` environment variable to be set.

Leveraging a tool such as `issue-metrics` can significantly enhance a team's ability to monitor and improve their issue-handling processes. This not only boosts the efficiency of the development cycle but also plays a vital role in maintaining a positive developer experience and a healthy team dynamic. There is a lot of data that can be taken from GitHub. Let's find out what works for your team.

Pull request metrics

Pull request metrics are crucial in understanding the dynamics of code reviews and the team's capacity to adapt to and integrate new changes. Metrics such as the time taken to merge a pull request and the ratio of opened-to-closed pull requests provide valuable insights into the efficiency of the code review process, the team's responsiveness, and their collaborative effectiveness. These metrics are particularly useful in identifying bottlenecks and fostering improvements in collaboration and code quality. Since the closure of an issue often coincides with the closure of a pull request, you should be sure to measure not only the issue but also the pull request when you measure it. You can also use the `issue-metrics` GitHub Action to measure pull requests.

In the context of InnerSource, which, as mentioned in *Chapter 4*, refers to the adoption of open source practices within an organization, these metrics take on additional significance. InnerSource metrics focus on aspects such as cross-team collaboration, the reuse of code across projects, and the contribution rates from different teams. In GitHub organizations, the concept of **teams** allows for defining groups of members belonging to specific functional or organizational areas. By analyzing pull requests, organizations can measure the extent of collaboration that occurs outside these defined teams. This is particularly valuable for gauging the effectiveness of InnerSource initiatives, as it reflects cross-team interaction and distributed contribution models.

Quantifying the number of collaborations that transcend team boundaries is a crucial metric for organizations promoting InnerSource and distributed contribution models. It highlights how open collaboration practices are being embraced across different segments of the organization and can pinpoint areas where more effort is needed to break down silos.

In conclusion, leveraging metrics in DevOps is about more than just tracking numbers. It is about using data to drive better software delivery practices, enhance team collaboration, and continuously improve the overall health of development processes. By carefully selecting and analyzing these metrics, organizations can create a more efficient, responsive, and collaborative development environment.

DevSecOps – Security as a continuous matter

In the traditional approach to software development, security was often relegated as a final step, typically handled by a dedicated security department or outsourced to external vendors. This method, while standard, led to security considerations being somewhat isolated from the core development process. Security assessments were conducted at specific checkpoints, often resulting in the identification of vulnerabilities late in the development cycle when they were more challenging and costly to address.

However, the landscape of software development and security has undergone a significant transformation. In today's fast-paced, continuously evolving digital environment, treating security as an afterthought is no longer viable. Security concerns need to be interwoven throughout the development process, not tacked on at the end. This shift in perspective and practice gave rise to the concept of DevSecOps.

DevSecOps represents a fundamental change both culturally and technically in how security is perceived and implemented in software development. It is a methodology that integrates security practices within the DevOps process, making security a continuous concern rather than a discrete or final phase. In DevSecOps, security is not solely the responsibility of a separate team but is a shared responsibility, deeply embedded within the DNA of the project lifecycle from its inception.

Security shift-left

The concept of **shift-left** predates DevSecOps but has been significantly embraced and refined within the DevSecOps framework. Traditionally, security was often a separate concern, managed by specialized teams, and typically addressed late in the development cycle. However, in the DevSecOps era, this paradigm has shifted significantly. Security is no longer a distinct responsibility of a dedicated security department but has become a shared and integral part of the development team's workflow.

This integration of security early in the development cycle is not just a procedural change; it is a fundamental redefinition of how security is handled. The proactive stance of shift-left is essential in today's fast-paced development environments because it enables teams to detect and address security issues much earlier. This approach is typically more cost-effective and less complex than trying to rectify security issues post-deployment. This proactive strategy is pivotal for several reasons:

- **Early detection of vulnerabilities**: Integrating security practices from the beginning enables teams to identify and mitigate potential vulnerabilities early. This not only reduces the risk of security breaches but also lessens the complexity involved in fixing issues later in the development cycle.

- **Cost-effective security management**: Addressing security issues in the later stages of development or after deployment can be significantly more expensive. Early integration helps minimize these costs by preventing the escalation of security flaws into more serious problems.

- **Cultural shift in development practices**: Shift-left advocates for a culture change where security is the collective responsibility of the entire development team, not just a concern for security specialists. This fosters a more holistic view of security in the development process.

DevSecOps plays a crucial role in operationalizing the shift-left approach. It involves integrating security tools and practices into the CI/CD pipeline, ensuring that security checks and balances are an integral part of the development workflow. This includes automated security testing, regular code reviews for security vulnerabilities, and ongoing monitoring of the software in production.

Security features in GitHub

As for GitHub security capabilities, several features stand out for their effectiveness in enhancing the safety and integrity of software development. These include **Dependabot**, **code scanning**, **secret scanning** (including push protection), and **dependency review**. Each of these functionalities plays a critical role in fortifying the security posture of projects managed on GitHub.

Notably, while code scanning, secret scanning (with push protection), and dependency review are part of the **GitHub Advanced Security** suite, at the time of writing, they are available for free for public repositories. This accessibility underscores GitHub's commitment to providing robust security tools to a wide range of developers and organizations. By leveraging these tools, teams can significantly enhance their security practices, ensuring that vulnerabilities are identified and addressed promptly.

Let's take a look at the major security features of each.

Dependabot – Streamlining dependency management and security

In today's fast-paced software development ecosystem, where open source software is extensively utilized, ensuring that dependencies are up-to-date and secure has become increasingly challenging. Manually tracking each dependency for updates or vulnerabilities is no longer feasible, given the sheer volume and frequency of updates in the open source world. This is where Dependabot, integrated into GitHub, becomes indispensable. Dependabot, a feature integrated into GitHub, plays a vital role in automating this aspect of software maintenance, ensuring that projects remain secure and up-to-date with minimal manual intervention. It automates the monitoring and updating of dependencies, a task crucial for maintaining the security and integrity of applications, thereby addressing a key need in modern software development where rapid and continuous deployment is the norm.

Here's how Dependabot enhances the development workflow to keep dependencies updated:

- **Automatic scanning for vulnerabilities**: Dependabot continuously monitors the dependencies in your codebase, checking for any known vulnerabilities. This includes not just the direct dependencies of your project but also the transitive dependencies (the dependencies of your dependencies).

- **Automated pull requests for updates**: When an outdated or vulnerable dependency is detected, Dependabot does not just stop at notifying you. It goes a step further by automatically creating pull requests to update the dependency to a newer, more secure version.

- **Customizable configuration**: Developers have control over how Dependabot operates within their projects. You can configure settings such as the frequency of checks, which dependencies to include or exclude, and how to handle versioning updates.

Configuring Dependabot for optimal performance

Dependabot is a critical tool for keeping your project dependencies secure and up-to-date. To maximize its effectiveness, it is important to understand and configure its various settings:

- **Dependabot alerts**: Set up alerts to be notified about vulnerabilities in your dependencies. You can manually generate Dependabot pull requests to address these vulnerabilities. Configuring alert notifications ensures you are promptly informed about potential security issues.

- **Dependabot rules**: This feature allows you to manage how alerts are handled. You can review and adjust these settings to ensure Dependabot responds to security issues in a way that aligns with your project's needs.

- **Dependabot security updates**: Enabling this option lets Dependabot automatically attempt to create pull requests for every open alert with an available patch. For more granular control, you can disable this and specify your preferences using Dependabot rules.

- **Grouped security updates (Beta)**: This setting groups all updates that resolve a Dependabot alert into a single pull request per package manager and directory. It is useful for managing multiple updates efficiently.

- **Dependabot version updates**: Dependabot can also be configured to automatically open pull requests to keep your dependencies up-to-date with their latest versions. This is managed through the `dependabot.yml` file, where you can specify parameters such as frequency, directories to check, and package tools to use.

Here is Dependabot's configuration menu. You can enable or disable each of the settings:

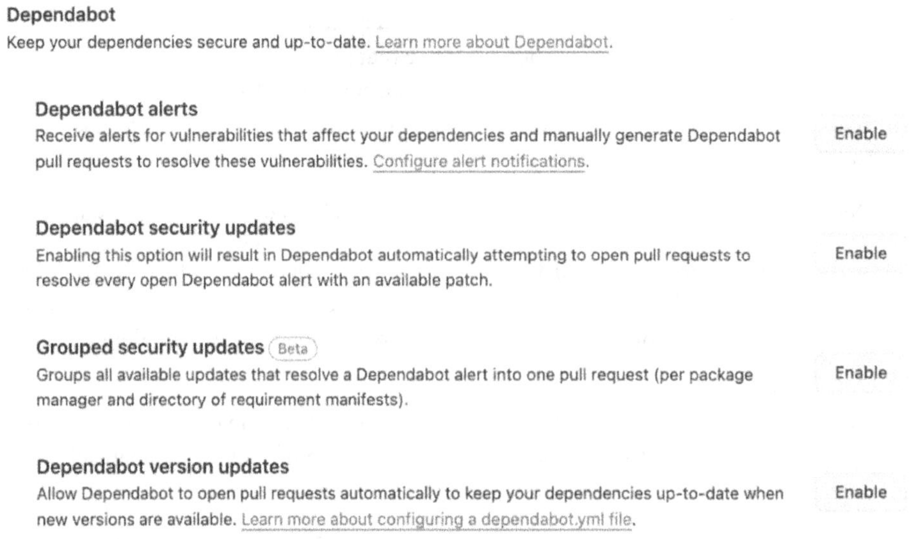

Dependabot
Keep your dependencies secure and up-to-date. Learn more about Dependabot.

Dependabot alerts
Receive alerts for vulnerabilities that affect your dependencies and manually generate Dependabot   Enable
pull requests to resolve these vulnerabilities. Configure alert notifications.

Dependabot security updates
Enabling this option will result in Dependabot automatically attempting to open pull requests to   Enable
resolve every open Dependabot alert with an available patch.

Grouped security updates (Beta)
Groups all available updates that resolve a Dependabot alert into one pull request (per package   Enable
manager and directory of requirement manifests).

Dependabot version updates
Allow Dependabot to open pull requests automatically to keep your dependencies up-to-date when   Enable
new versions are available. Learn more about configuring a dependabot.yml file.

Figure 6.11 – Dependabot configuration

Properly configuring Dependabot not only helps to maintain the security of your project but also ensures that your dependency management process is smooth and aligned with your project's workflow.

Best practices for optimal adoption

In the context of automated dependency management, Dependabot's role extends beyond merely updating packages. For its full potential to be realized, there are crucial complementary practices and configurations that teams need to adopt:

- **Integration with test automation**: The automatic updating of packages by Dependabot necessitates a robust suite of automated tests. This is essential because each dependency update, while potentially fixing vulnerabilities, also carries the risk of introducing new issues or incompatibilities. A comprehensive set of automated tests ensures that any changes introduced by dependency updates do not break existing functionality. Therefore, high test coverage is not just beneficial but a fundamental requirement for leveraging Dependabot effectively.

- **Efficient notification management**: Another important aspect is the efficient configuration of Dependabot notifications. Without proper management, Dependabot can generate an overwhelming number of alerts, leading to notification fatigue among team members. This scenario often results in important updates being overlooked or ignored, undermining the tool's effectiveness; to avoid this, it is crucial to set up suitable notification configurations that strike a balance between staying informed and avoiding excessive alerts.

- **Fostering a responsive culture**: Finally, it is vital to cultivate a culture where Dependabot alerts are given prompt attention. Ignoring alerts can lead to accumulating vulnerabilities, rendering the automated updates ineffective. Teams should prioritize addressing Dependabot pull requests promptly or set configurations that align with their capacity to handle updates. This might involve scheduling updates at a manageable frequency or categorizing the severity of updates to prioritize them effectively.

In summary, while Dependabot significantly streamlines dependency management, its effectiveness hinges on supporting practices such as high test coverage, efficient notification management, and a proactive response culture. These elements work together to ensure that automated dependency updates enhance, rather than disrupt, the software development process.

Code scanning – Implementing and leveraging automated security analysis

Incorporating code scanning into your software development process is a proactive step towards enhancing the security and quality of your codebase. GitHub provides an effective and user-friendly way to implement this through its code scanning features. This process involves the automated analysis of your code for potential vulnerabilities and coding errors, and it plays a crucial role in the early detection and resolution of security issues.

Getting started with code scanning

Enabling code scanning is very simple. The first step is to enable code scanning in your GitHub repository settings. This setting is found under the **Security** tab in the repository settings:

Figure 6.12 – Code scanning configuration

Code scanning can be performed using GitHub Actions or by integrating third-party tools. GitHub Actions offer a seamless way to automate code scanning within the GitHub environment. For specific needs or preferences, third-party tools can also be integrated into your workflow.

By clicking **Explore workflows**, You will get to the marketplace page and can look for GitHub Actions:

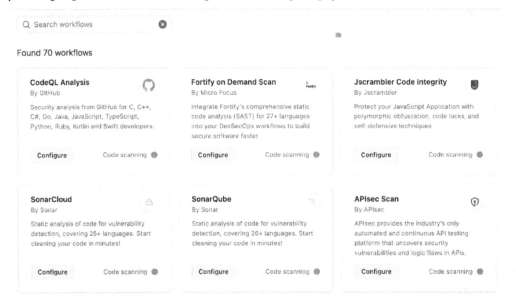

Figure 6.13 – Explore workflows

For the default configuration, click **Set up** in the code scanning configuration menu, *Figure 6.12*, and then **Default** will bring up the basic setup screen. You can configure the language settings and enable CodeQL (at the time of writing, JavaScript, TypeScript, and Python are supported):

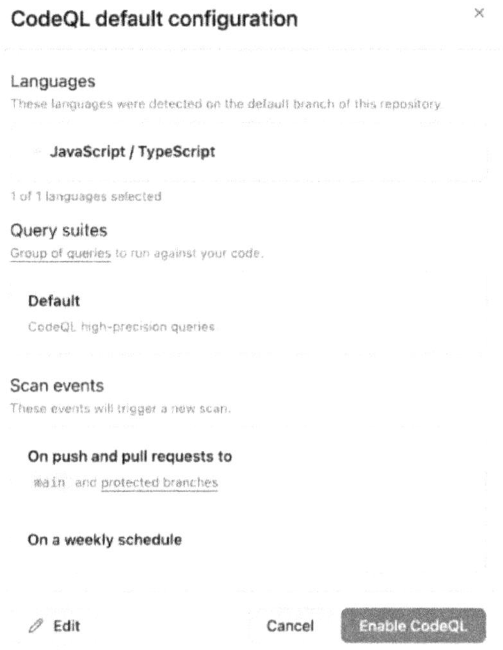

CodeQL default configuration   ×

Languages
These languages were detected on the default branch of this repository.

JavaScript / TypeScript

1 of 1 languages selected

Query suites
Group of queries to run against your code.

Default
CodeQL high-precision queries

Scan events
These events will trigger a new scan.

On push and pull requests to
main and protected branches

On a weekly schedule

  🖉 Edit   Cancel   Enable CodeQL

Figure 6.14 – CodeQL default configuration

Once set up, an initial analysis is performed. You can see the progress of the execution of the CodeQL analysis as follows:

Figure 6.15 – CodeQL Setup

This will run as GitHub Actions, but there will be no YAML file under the `.github/workflows/` directory, and the backend will handle and apply the settings:

Figure 6.16 – CodeQL Setup completion

If the scan result has no security issue, the code scanning shows that it is healthy on the page under the **Security** tab:

Figure 6.17 – When all tools are working as expected

If any vulnerabilities are found, code scanning will let you know the details:

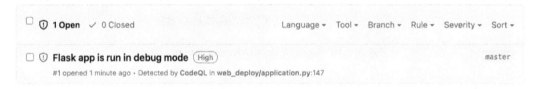

Figure 6.18 – Security vulnerability notification

You can create an issue directly from the scan result page. To dismiss a code scanning result in GitHub, first select the alert you wish to address. Then, choose the appropriate dismissal reason: select **False positive** if the alert is invalid, **Used in tests** if the alert pertains to code not used in production, or **Won't fix** if the alert is irrelevant to your project. This process helps to refine the focus of code scanning to relevant and actionable security alerts.

Figure 6.19 – Security alert contents

If you want to make these settings more detailed, you can choose **Advanced** instead of **Default** on the configuration page and use YAML to make your own settings. If the language requires a build to be analyzed, an **Advanced** setup will be required regardless of what level of detail the user would like to set code scanning at. You will see the same interface or setup regularly in GitHub Actions, where you can configure triggers and other settings as you would for typical GitHub Actions and also have the flexibility to handle more complex workflows:

Figure 6.20 – CodeQL Advanced configuration

Benefits of code scanning

Starting with code scanning in GitHub involves enabling the feature in your repository and configuring the necessary tools, either through GitHub Actions or third-party integrations. The benefits of implementing code scanning are substantial, ranging from the early detection of vulnerabilities to seamless integration with the development process, ultimately leading to a more secure and robust codebase.

Here are the benefits of code scanning:

- **Scanning for vulnerabilities and errors**: The primary function of code scanning is to systematically analyze the codebase for known vulnerabilities and coding errors. This includes scanning for issues such as SQL injection, **Cross-Site Scripting** (**XSS**), and other common security vulnerabilities.

- **CodeQL for semantic analysis**: An integral part of GitHub's code scanning feature is CodeQL, a powerful tool for semantic code analysis. CodeQL interprets the code as a database, enabling more complex and thorough queries to identify vulnerabilities that simpler scanning methods might miss.

- **Integration with GitHub workflow**: The integration of code scanning tools within the GitHub workflow ensures that security checks are a seamless part of the development process without causing significant disruption or delay.

Secret scanning and push protection

In today's cloud-centric software development landscape, the importance of securing sensitive information such as API keys, tokens, or credentials cannot be overstated. GitHub recognizes this imperative with its secret scanning and push protection features, which are crucial for bolstering the security of your repositories.

The practice of hardcoding secrets in code is a risky endeavor. As developers increasingly utilize cloud environments, the chances of inadvertently including crucial secrets in repository code are higher. Despite being vigilant, there are instances where sensitive information can mistakenly be uploaded to a repository. In the world of Git, where the core function is to maintain code history and not alter it, removing secrets once they are committed can be challenging and sometimes nearly impossible. The impact of such exposure is significant, as it can lead to security breaches and compromise of sensitive data.

This is where the need for preventive measures such as **Secret scanning** and **Push protection** becomes evident:

Secret scanning
Receive alerts on GitHub for detected secrets, keys, or other tokens.   Disable
GitHub will always send alerts to partners for detected secrets in public repositories. Learn more about partner patterns.

Push protection
Block commits that contain supported secrets.   Disable

Figure 6.21 – Secret scanning configuration

Secret scanning – Proactive detection of exposed secrets

Secret scanning is a feature that actively scans your repositories to identify exposed secrets. This functionality is easily activated through your repository settings. Once enabled, it continuously monitors your codebase and, upon detecting exposed secrets, alerts you promptly. This immediate notification system allows developers and repository administrators to take swift action to secure their repositories and the associated services, thereby preventing potential security breaches.

Push protection – Preventing accidental exposure

Complementing secret scanning is the push protection feature. This feature adds a crucial layer of precaution to your repository's security measures. When activated in your repository settings, this feature operates during push operations. It does not perform a blanket check of all code but scrutinizes the changes being pushed for the presence of potential secrets or sensitive data. If such risks are detected, the push is blocked, thereby preventing the accidental introduction of vulnerabilities into your repository.

Together, secret scanning and push protection form a comprehensive defense mechanism for your repositories. Secret scanning vigilantly identifies and alerts exposed secrets, while push protection acts as a safeguard, preventing the unintentional inclusion of sensitive information in your codebase. These features are indispensable for maintaining the integrity and security of your software projects, ensuring that your code remains secure from inadvertent vulnerabilities.

Dependency review – Ensuring secure and informed dependency management

Dependency review is designed to detect security risks in code dependencies, as defined in the manifest files. It supports various programming languages, with JavaScript's `package.json` and Python's `requirements.txt` being notable examples.

This becomes particularly crucial during the pull request process. When changes are made to manifest files, dependency review automatically checks if these changes introduce any security risks. If any risks are detected, the CI job associated with dependency review will fail, signaling potential security concerns. This integration into the pull request workflow allows for an automated and proactive approach to ensuring that any updates or additions to dependencies do not compromise the project's security.

Dependency analysis during pull requests

Seeing the dependency review is straightforward; you can utilize it in diff mode within a pull request to visually verify differences by using the rich diff setting on the edited package manifest file:

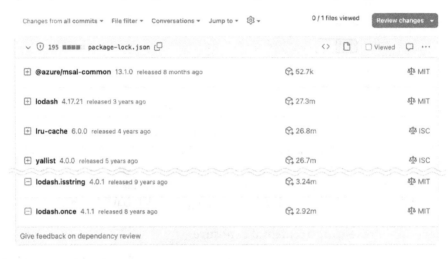

Figure 6.22 – Dependency review in the rich diff mode

Additionally, dependency review is seamlessly integrated into the pull request process on GitHub. You can use `actions/dependency-review-action` (`https://github.com/actions/dependency-review-action`) for this integration:

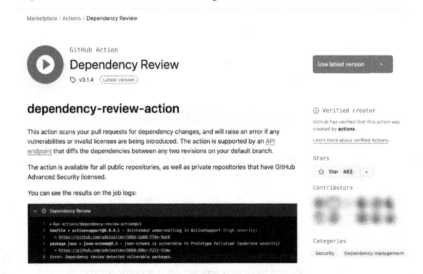

Figure 6.23 – Dependency review with GitHub Actions

This integration allows teams to do the following:

- **Review dependency changes**: When a pull request involves adding or updating dependencies, dependency review provides a clear and detailed view of these changes. This includes information about the new or updated packages, their versions, and the impact of these changes on the project.

- **Analyze security implications**: One of the tool's key strengths is its ability to analyze how changes in dependencies could affect the project's security. It flags potential vulnerabilities introduced by new or updated dependencies, enabling teams to assess and address security risks proactively.

- **Make informed decisions**: By providing comprehensive insights into dependency changes and their implications, dependency review empowers teams to make informed decisions. Teams can evaluate the necessity, benefits, and potential risks of incorporating new or updated dependencies into their projects.

The integration of dependency review into the pull request process serves as a proactive measure to ensure that all dependency changes are scrutinized for security implications before they are merged into the codebase. This proactive approach is crucial for maintaining the security integrity of applications, especially in an environment where dependencies can often be a source of vulnerabilities.

Scaling the collaboration

As organizations evolve, the imperative to expand DevOps beyond its traditional scope becomes increasingly apparent. This section addresses the critical concept of scaling collaboration, an element pivotal for transcending standard DevOps practices and embracing a more inclusive organizational approach.

Our journey so far has taken us through the realms of Git, GitHub, GitHub Actions, and the DevSecOps worldview, focusing on their individual and collective metrics. The next progressive step is to scale these collaborative frameworks. Scaling collaboration entails not just enhancing communication within the Dev and Ops teams but also broadening your collaborative impact to being organization-wide. It is about nurturing a mindset dedicated to positive contributions across all organizational levels. It would be great if we could collaborate with different teams, not just Dev and Ops.

Why scaling collaboration is imperative

In the context of DevEx, the need for scaled collaboration becomes even more pronounced with the increasing adoption of microservices in cloud architecture, which inherently intertwines with DevOps. When various people have dependencies on each other, their own work may be potentially stopped by the development of others. We have arrived in a world where we need to redefine how we should collaborate well with people who have different development styles and priorities and how we should relate to the rest of the people on our team. The demand for advanced collaborative strategies is at its peak. Additionally, the emergence of platform engineering highlights the growing complexity within technology infrastructure management, further amplifying the cognitive load on teams. This environment of managing sprawling repositories and engaging in continuous collaboration necessitates a shift towards viewing code management as a shared organizational resource and collaborating well.

In the absence of sustainable codebase management, organizations face several challenges:

- **Increased code burden**: Concentrating code maintenance responsibilities on a few individuals can lead to burnout and create critical bottlenecks. Code maintenance is sometimes neglected. It is often the case that after code is shipped, human resources are reduced, and the burden of maintenance becomes more and more dependent on a small number of individuals.

- **Code duplication**: A lack of continuous code management often results in missing out on leveraging past work, leading to the repetitive and unnecessary reinvention of solutions.

- **Code as a liability**: Neglected code management can transform code into a burdensome liability, characterized by difficulties in upkeep and an increase in unmaintained code and noise.

Adopting a **distributed contribution model** is essential in such scenarios. This model broadens the scope of collaboration and amplifies its impact across the organization.

Now, you need to cultivate a collaborative organizational culture. Expanding collaboration is synonymous with fostering a healthier organizational culture. When team members across the board leverage platforms such as GitHub for open, transparent collaboration, it naturally cultivates a highly collaborative atmosphere. Such a cultural transformation is instrumental in rendering the organization more agile, innovative, and effective.

In conclusion, scaling collaboration in the realm of DevOps is about more than enhancing communication; it is about embracing distributed contribution models and nurturing a culture of open collaboration. This approach is key to dismantling silos, spurring innovation, and ensuring a responsive and efficient development environment, paving the way for a more unified and productive organizational fabric.

InnerSource – Distributed collaboration model

InnerSource, a term coined by Tim O'Reilly in 2000, represents a significant shift in how companies approach software development. It is about leveraging open source development methodologies within the confines of an organization, culturally transforming to a shared economy model similar to open source. This approach is a journey towards breaking down organizational silos while respecting the unique culture and internal limitations of the enterprise. InnerSource aims to loosen up siloed organizations and enable collaboration with a high degree of transparency. It allows engineers within the organization to work more comfortably and happily, and enabling lateral collaboration can create synergy between organizations. Such synergy will ultimately lead to innovation and organizational strength. What we can achieve with InnerSource is not only about breaking down the silos of the development team but also about going beyond that.

As discussed in *Chapter 1*, InnerSource hinges on several key principles:

- Openness
- Transparency
- Prioritized mentorship
- Voluntary code contribution

These principles may sometimes be overlooked in the DevOps context, yet they are inherently woven into many existing practices. For example, **Extreme Programming** (**XP**) involves the concept of **collective code ownership** (also known as **team code ownership** and **shared code**). Platform engineering, another critical area, assumes the avoidance of reinventing the wheel. Importantly, diving into platform engineering often necessitates InnerSource-style collaboration, as it is about distributed contribution rather than a single team bearing all responsibilities.

But what exactly constitutes InnerSource? A common misconception is that merely using GitHub equates to practicing InnerSource. Well, GitHub is for teams to share code, and using the issue and pull request features makes it operate like open source-style development. However, as Silona Bonewald, a founding member of InnerSource Commons, points out, the challenge is not just about using GitHub to increase transparency in code. The real task is to find and nurture the source of open source within the company, developing it as a community-centric endeavor.

Here is a quote from a well-known book on InnerSource. This quote represents the essence of InnerSource.

> *The idea that GitHub is all that's needed to be InnerSource is a concept we fight against daily. Most people do not realize that it takes much more than GitHub to find, create, and grow open source communities. The communities create the software, not the other way around, but more often than not, large companies lack a sense of holistic community.*
>
> *– Understanding the InnerSource Checklist, Siona Bonewald.*

Using GitHub does not automatically lead to a distributed collaboration model. In the first place, the concept of InnerSource predates GitHub, emerging at a time when such platforms were not yet the norm. InnerSource is fundamentally about culture; it is a way of thinking and collaborating that goes beyond tools and platforms.

Crucial repository capabilities for effective InnerSource

These are the necessary repository functions to enable InnerSource collaboration and foster a co-operative environment:

- **Discoverability**: This involves making codebases, documentation, and related materials easily findable and navigable. First of all, this implies the ability to search and, moreover, to discover value. No matter how great a library is, it is meaningless if searchers do not know how to use it.

- **Composability**: This involves allowing quick and easy use of source code in various contexts. It needs to be versatile enough to be incorporated into many different things. Simple, function-specific repositories are preferred over monolithic repositories. Of course, if many people are going to use it, it can be large, and I am not claiming that a monolithic repository cannot adopt InnerSource. However, it would be even better if each component were loosely designed, easy to use, and easy to manage.

- **Contributability**: This involves facilitating simple ways for contributors to report issues, suggest new features, and make upstream commits. This begins with writing the CONTRIBUTING. md file. It is good to have a low hurdle to contact the owner or maintainer of a given repository. Creating a welcoming atmosphere is important.

- **Maintainability**: This involves ensuring that code can be continuously maintained and is essential. Just as many people are reluctant to use an open source repository that stopped being updated several years ago, the same is true of InnerSource. People will not use a repository that is no longer maintained. In other words, InnerSource is not suited to project types, i.e., projects that have a deadline and a cutover and that have clearly stated when they will stop updating. Repositories need to be maintained on a continuous basis. If you find a useful InnerSource seed in such a project, find a way to continue to maintain it organizationally rather than stopping development. These are considered essential for success. This is also closely tied to the culture of the team. I encourage you to think about what would be a good fit for your team.

Code ownership

In InnerSource, the source code is viewed as belonging to the organization. The code is for everyone. However, this does not necessarily mean giving up all ownership.

There is a concept of **weak code ownership**. In this ownership style, the code is assigned to owners, but developers can change the code owned by others. If someone wants to make a change to someone else's code, they should have a conversation with the code owner first.

Apart from that, there is also the concept of **collective code ownership**, which is the idea of completely abandoning ownership of the code, but the meaning of "*everyone owns the code*" means that, at the same time, "*nobody owns the code.*" This can lead to problems of accountability and maintenance continuity. In many cases, InnerSource organizations adopt weak code ownership and promote collaboration between the host team and guest team.

An asynchronous way of working

Enabling asynchronous collaboration will be necessary to promote the adoption of InnerSource in the organization. This derives from contexts such as open source development, where teams are distributed around the world and people in different time zones collaborate, but there are many other positive aspects as well.

There are many reasons why silos can be created within an organization, the most prominent of which is probably due to internal politics and other attempts to hide information.

The adoption of InnerSource brings transparency to the organization, but complete transparency is brought about by asynchronous ways of working. In fact, it is difficult to ensure transparency in a synchronous process. How can those who could not attend the meeting see the content of the meeting and participate in the decision-making process? How can they later learn the background of the decisions that were made without being recorded?

In open source, most conversations can be found in GitHub issues and pull requests, and these discussions can be traced back to the past. This reduces the barrier to participation for those who wish to get involved, thanks to a culture of documentation. The accumulated conversations serve as a form of documentation, often referred to as passive documentation. Such conversation histories are valuable because they represent an accumulation of trust. Users and contributors to the InnerSource repository have different needs, priorities, and ways of engaging with it. As these individuals collaborate, embracing asynchronous collaboration becomes important to ensure everyone's participation.

InnerSource program office

Implementing InnerSource at an organizational level often requires an **InnerSource Program Office (ISPO)**, which might evolve from traditional OSPO roles or be part of development technology teams. Their role is to seamlessly integrate the distributed contribution model throughout the organization.

The ISPO ensures the following:

- Sharing of InnerSource policies
- Conducting mentoring and training
- Advisory on InnerSource strategies
- Developing incentive models
- Organizing support activities
- Ensuring proper tooling

Key metrics for evaluating InnerSource include the number of repositories with multiple contributors from different teams, the presence of CONTRIBUTING.md and README.md files, and the number of forks and cross-team pull requests.

InnerSource patterns

InnerSource patterns (https://patterns.innersourcecommons.org/) are essentially codified best practices in InnerSource, structured in a specific format for ease of understanding, evaluation, and application in diverse contexts. These patterns, which are detailed in this book, represent the most mature and effective practices identified and collected by the InnerSource Commons

Community. They serve as a valuable guide for implementing InnerSource methodologies, providing practical and proven solutions to common challenges faced in collaborative software development.

Figure 6.24 – InnerSource patterns

Adopting InnerSource patterns can significantly increase the adoption and effectiveness of InnerSource within an organization. To effectively use these patterns, do the following:

1. **Identify relevant patterns**: Assess the challenges your organization faces with InnerSource and identify patterns that address these specific issues

2. **Adapt to your context**: Customize the pattern to fit the unique circumstances and culture of your organization

3. **Implement and evaluate**: Apply the solution proposed in the pattern and continually assess its effectiveness, making adjustments as needed

Key InnerSource patterns for effective collaboration

As of January 2024, 24 mature patterns are covered, with more being added as they develop. InnerSource patterns provide structured approaches to common challenges in collaborative development. I will not list them all here, but I will introduce five typical patterns that have proven effective in many different organizations and contexts.

These are my favorites and would be a good entry point for you to see what the patterns are all about:

- **Trusted Committers**: This pattern is useful for projects receiving consistent external feedback and contributions. It involves recognizing and rewarding the contributions of external collaborators, beyond individual contributions, by designating them as "Trusted Committers." This role involves responsibilities such as mentoring and quality control, further integrating contributors into the project.

- **InnerSource license**: When different legal entities within the same organization want to share source code, legal and accounting concerns may arise. An InnerSource license provides a legal framework for such sharing, clarifying rights and obligations and facilitating new forms of collaboration within the organization.

- **InnerSource portal**: To facilitate discovery of InnerSource projects, an InnerSource Portal can be established. This intranet site lists all available InnerSource projects, making it easier for potential contributors to find projects of interest and for project owners to attract external participation.

- **Standard base documentation**: For new contributors, understanding project maintenance, available tasks, and contribution processes can be challenging. Providing standardized documentation in files such as `README.md`, `CONTRIBUTING.md`, and `COMMUNICATION.md` enable self-service for new contributors, allowing them to find answers to common questions independently.

- **30-day warranty**: This pattern addresses the hesitation teams might have in accepting outside contributions. By offering a 30-day warranty, the contributing team commits to fixing any bugs in their code post-integration. This increases trust and makes the acceptance of external contributions more likely.

These InnerSource patterns offer practical solutions to foster collaboration, streamline contribution processes, and build trust in InnerSource initiatives. By implementing these patterns, organizations can create a more open, efficient, and co-operative development environment.

In conclusion, InnerSource is not just a methodology but a cultural paradigm that emphasizes open, transparent, and community-centric software development within an organization. Its successful implementation hinges not just on tools such as GitHub but on the broader cultural embrace of open source principles and practices.

Setting up GitHub for scalable collaboration

Creating an environment that supports a distributed contribution model is crucial. This is true for both DevOps and InnerSource approaches. However, configuring GitHub optimally is essential to enable this model of collaboration. A non-optimal setup can severely restrict development efforts, especially in enterprises where there's often a tendency to overemphasize security, leading to overly stringent configurations that hinder collaboration. The key challenge lies in finding the right balance between security and collaboration. Projects should be structured to maximize participation, necessitating the thoughtful management of visibility and access. This means implementing a GitHub configuration that provides controlled visibility, protecting sensitive code while still promoting knowledge sharing and collaboration.

Organizations need to walk the fine line between a security-first perspective and a collaboration-first perspective. This involves managing the risk associated with sensitive code while also encouraging internal code sharing to boost productivity and innovation. The visibility needs can vary across different InnerSource projects, and understanding these nuances is critical to effective collaboration.

Choosing the right configuration

When configuring GitHub, GitHub provides three layers of configuration. Each of these levels is **enterprise**, **organization**, and **repository**. It is vital to understand how these levels interact:

- **Enterprise level:** Exercise caution with restrictive settings at this level. Overly restrictive configurations can create friction for developers, leading to shadow IT practices. Default nudges can be more effective than complete restrictions.

- **Organization level:** Empowering repository owners to manage visibility and permissions is often more effective than imposing broad policies from the top. This approach avoids the pitfalls of overly narrow policies and adapts to evolving organizational needs.

- **Repository level:** For sensitive repositories, consider implementing stricter controls within certain organizations instead of applying blanket constraints across all enterprise code.

Selecting the appropriate base repository permissions is crucial. Options such as **Read** allow every enterprise member to view every repository, which may be suitable in some contexts. However, **No Policy** or **No Permissions** offers more flexibility, allowing different organizations within the enterprise to choose their own base permissions.

Forking vs. branching for internal collaboration

In the distributed collaboration model, both forking and branching are valuable methods for code development, with each offering distinct benefits. Forking enables quick, one-off contributions without needing permission from repository owners, making it ideal for minor changes or spontaneous contributions. This method is particularly beneficial for InnerSource as it offers a lower-friction way to make small contributions compared to branch-based development.

The choice between forking and branching often depends on the project's nature and the GitHub instance's configuration—internal or public-facing. In internal instances, forking is less risky, but in public-facing instances with compliance and regulatory concerns, forking might need to be limited. It is important to combine configuration with architecture to enable forking as an option without increasing the risk of accidental disclosure.

Base permissions in GitHub

Base permissions in GitHub are crucial as they define the collaboration environment within an organization and can be set at various levels.

- **Enterprise level**: At the enterprise level, base permissions apply to all repositories and define default access for all enterprise members. **Read** permissions grant every member read access to every repository, which is suitable in certain environments. However, **No Policy** often provides more flexibility for each organization, allowing each organization within the enterprise to tailor repository permissions to their needs. It is crucial to carefully select these settings to avoid overly restrictive policies that can hinder collaboration and innovation. **No Policy** or **Read** are common choices, enabling different organizations to set varying base permissions, ranging from wide to narrow internal sharing.

- **Organization level**: At the organization level, there is no **No Policy** option, and the choices range from **Read** to **No Permission**. Selecting **Read** allows wide sharing within the organization, while **No Permission** offers more controlled access, accommodating a range of sharing levels within the organization. The goal for base permissions is to enable low-friction repository creation and read access at scale while allowing repository owners to make informed choices on sharing their repositories. They should have the flexibility to choose the sharing level appropriate for the type of code in their repository without being forced into wide or narrow sharing based on the GitHub organization's typical usage.

The ultimate goal in setting base permissions is to create an environment that supports both easy repository creation and access and gives repository owners the autonomy to decide on sharing levels. This approach ensures that repositories are shared in a way that suits their specific needs and type of code rather than being limited by overarching organizational policies.

Summary

This chapter begins with an exploration of DevOps metrics and also mentions DevSecOps. Concepts such as InnerSource, known for their strong compatibility with DevOps and their ability to enhance collaboration beyond a single team to the entire organization's excellence, are introduced.

DevOps is fundamentally a culture that can be refined by adopting individual practices, re-evaluating tool usage, and properly setting up metrics. This refining process is ongoing. There are a variety of books available, so we encourage you to learn more and find the best form of DevOps for your team.

Further reading

- *Accelerate: The Science of Lean Software and DevOps: Building and Scaling High Performing Technology Organizations* by Nicole Forsgren, Jez Humble, and Gene Kim (`https://en.wikipedia.org/wiki/Accelerate_(book)`)

- The SPACE of Developer Productivity by Nicole Forsgren, Margaret-Anne Storey, Thomas Zimmermann, Brian Houck, and Jenna Butler (`https://queue.acm.org/detail.cfm?id=3454124`)

- *Getting Started with InnerSource* by Andy Oram (`https://www.oreilly.com/radar/getting-started-with-innersource/`)

- *Understanding the InnerSource Checklist* by Silona Bonewald (`https://innersourcecommons.org/learn/books/understanding-the-innersource-checklist/`)

- *InnerSource Patterns* by the InnerSource Commons Community (`https://patterns.innersourcecommons.org/`)

7

Accelerate Productivity with AI

In this chapter, we embark on a journey to explore the exciting realm of AI-powered software development. In reality, although the application of large language models in coding is gradually becoming more apparent, it remains largely in the research and development phase. While we have focused on practical content so far, this chapter shifts our attention to the theories that facilitate a wonderful collaboration with AI. We aim to provide insights that will help you understand the context of AI in development correctly and master its use. With this foundation, let's explore the world of AI-powered coding together.

The essence of AI's role in coding fundamentally boils down to the age-old notion of *how to write good code*, which, in turn, relies on knowledge, skills, and experience. If you are looking for a universal magical technique to make AI write remarkable code, you might find that, in reality, such a thing probably does not exist. Furthermore, even when mentioning specific product features, it is important to recognize that the rapid pace of evolution in this field may quickly render newly acquired skills obsolete.

This book has consistently focused on the theme of collaboration. In this context, we maintain that focus, aiming to understand how to collaborate effectively with AI. The gateway to all communication starts with understanding your counterpart. By gaining a correct understanding of AI, setting appropriate expectations, and focusing on extracting the right information from AI, you will be able to refine your interactions with AI tools, regardless of how these tools evolve. As the author, it is my belief that we should aim to fundamentally understand AI rather than focusing solely on individual tips and tricks.

We will explore best practices for engaging with AI tools, with an emphasis on the subtleties of coding with AI assistance. AI-powered coding represents an exciting frontier with many uncharted territories. We encourage you to grasp the fundamentals and embark on coding alongside AI.

We will cover the following main headings in this chapter:

- AI innovation in coding
- Exploring the capabilities and interaction with AI in coding
- Strategies for maximizing AI efficiency

AI innovation in coding

The introduction of LLMs by OpenAI has marked a pivotal moment in the evolution of software development. We delve into the aftermath of this groundbreaking innovation, exploring how it has reshaped the coding landscape.

The impact of LLMs on coding

We can say the advent of LLMs has fundamentally changed how programming is approached and executed. With the capacity to understand and generate human-like text, these models have opened up new avenues in coding, making it more efficient and accessible. LLMs have significantly sped up the process of writing code. Developers can now leverage AI to quickly generate code snippets, reducing the time spent on routine or repetitive coding tasks. The introduction of LLMs has enabled developers to tackle coding challenges more creatively. By providing suggestions and alternative solutions, these models have become valuable tools in the problem-solving arsenal of programmers.

LLMs have introduced a new realm of AI-powered development, where developers collaborate with AI tools to enhance their coding workflow. This collaboration ranges from generating code snippets to offering insights into complex coding problems. For novice developers, AI serves as an educational tool, helping them learn coding patterns and best practices. This reduces the entry barriers to programming, making it more approachable for beginners. Additionally, for experienced developers, this AI integration is a powerful catalyst, enabling them to achieve more by augmenting their skills with advanced code suggestions, automating routine tasks, and providing deeper insights into code optimization and problem-solving. The combination of seasoned developer expertise and AI efficiency creates a synergy that pushes the boundaries of what can be accomplished in software development.

The introduction of modern LLMs has revolutionized coding, transforming it from a purely manual endeavor to a more collaborative, efficient, and innovative process. This change has not only accelerated development but has also opened up new possibilities for creativity and problem-solving in the realm of software engineering. Additionally, this area is being extended right now to a variety of tasks, not only coding but also review and documentation.

Understanding LLMs – A basic introduction

In the context of AI-powered programming, LLMs have emerged as a pivotal innovation, reshaping our approach to software development. But what are LLMs? Let's get to know this first.

LLMs are advanced AI models designed to understand, interpret, and generate human-like text. These models are large not only in their size (often comprising billions of parameters) but also in their scope of training data and capabilities.

LLMs such as **Generative Pre-trained Transformer (GPT)** are trained on vast datasets comprising a wide range of internet text. This training enables them to predict and generate text based on the input they receive, making them highly versatile in language understanding and generation. The core technology behind LLMs involves neural network architectures, specifically transformer models, which have revolutionized **Natural Language Processing (NLP)**. These networks are adept at handling sequential data, making them ideal for language tasks.

To fully harness their potential, it is essential to understand what LLMs are fundamentally designed to do and what they are not. While AI may seem like magic, it is more akin to a mirror reflecting your own input; it is not a panacea that solves everything. You must approach it with the right expectations, guide it properly, and cleverly extract value. Now it is time to take a look at the essential characteristics of LLMs:

- **Word prediction engines**: At their core, LLMs are sophisticated engines designed to predict the next word in a sequence. This prediction capability is based on the extensive training they receive from vast datasets, enabling them to generate contextually relevant and coherent text.

- **Probabilistic, not deterministic**: Unlike deterministic models that always produce the same output for a given input, LLMs are probabilistic models. This means that they predict what comes next based on the probability of various possible continuations, leading to potential variations in output for the same input. This aspect underscores the inherently stochastic nature of LLMs, highlighting that the same "*context*" or input can lead to different outcomes, depending on the probabilistic determination of what comes next.

- **Not a Google search alternative**: It is crucial to note that LLMs are not replacements for search engines such as Google. They do not learn in the traditional sense or retain information for future output. Each response generated by a typical LLM is based on the input provided at that moment, without any memory of past interactions.

- **Generation, not retrieval**: LLMs operate by generating responses each time rather than retrieving stored information. This means that their outputs are created anew based on the patterns they have learned during training.

LLMs have a critical role in the context of coding, primarily due to their ability to predict the next sequence of characters or words. These models are not just versatile in handling natural languages, such as English, but extend their capabilities to a wide array of programming languages. In fact, the application of LLMs to programming languages is where their effectiveness is most recognized and highly anticipated.

LLMs' adaptability to different programming languages stems from their training on diverse datasets, which include not only natural language texts but also vast repositories of code. This enables them to understand the syntax and semantics of various programming languages, making them incredibly useful for tasks such as code completion, bug fixing, and even generating entire blocks of functional code.

Moreover, LLMs can assist developers in translating requirements into code, providing suggestions based on best practices, and even offering creative solutions to complex programming challenges. Their predictive ability ensures that they can recommend the most relevant code snippets, streamline the coding process, and significantly enhance coding efficiency and accuracy.

In addition to the key capability, understanding the limitations and handling misconceptions is also important:

- **Not infallible**: The accuracy of LLMs is not absolute. While they can produce remarkably relevant and sophisticated outputs, there are instances where their predictions can be off the mark. They can sometimes create outputs that seem plausible but are actually inaccurate or nonsensical; a phenomenon sometimes referred to as **hallucination**.

- **Need for human oversight**: This potential for error underscores the importance of human oversight. Users of LLMs should be vigilant and discerning, capable of identifying and correcting instances where the model's output may be misleading or incorrect.

- **Appropriate use and expectation setting**: Understanding these limitations is key to setting realistic expectations and finding the most effective use cases for LLMs. They should be viewed as tools that augment and assist in tasks such as coding or text generation rather than as standalone solutions that operate with complete autonomy and accuracy.

In essence, LLM is a powerful innovation, offering significant capabilities in text generation and language understanding. However, their effective use requires an awareness of their limitations and the critical role of human oversight in guiding their output.

Application of LLMs in coding

The integration of LLMs in the world of coding has seen one of its most significant applications in the form of AI-powered coding tools such as GitHub Copilot. This section explores how AI is redefining the coding experience.

AI-powered tools designed to assist developers in writing code leverage the power of LLMs to provide real-time code suggestions, automating some aspects of coding and enhancing overall productivity. These tools, trained on a vast array of code repositories, interpret the context from the current coding environment and offer suggestions for the next lines of code, function implementations, or even entire classes and modules.

The fundamental capability of these AI tools is that they work as plugins to editors such as Visual Studio Code, providing AI assistance as you code within the editor. The vision behind these tools includes integrating AI into all phases of the software development cycle, with a significant focus on their integration into the editor as a major feature. This approach represents a broader effort to harness AI for enhancing software development processes, aiming to make coding more efficient and accessible to developers at all skill levels.

Transforming the coding process

AI-powered tools assist in enhancing the development process by streamlining a variety of coding tasks. Traditionally, coding involves research, reading documentation, and ensuring the correctness of the code. These tools help optimize these activities in several key areas:

- **Increasing speed and efficiency**: Developers can speed up the coding process with these tools. They help reduce the time spent on repetitive code patterns and offer quick solutions and suggestions, freeing up developers to tackle more complex and innovative work.

- **Facilitating learning and exploration**: For newcomers or those delving into new programming languages or frameworks, these AI tools serve as educational aids. They provide syntactically accurate code snippets and show best practices in action.

- **Reducing cognitive load**: AI-powered tools tackle the more routine aspects of coding, alleviating the mental burden developers face. This reduction in cognitive load enables developers to concentrate their mental energy on tackling more intricate and challenging problems.

- **Expanding possibilities**: Through their suggestions, these tools not only assist with code completion but also stimulate creative thinking. They introduce developers to alternative problem-solving approaches and expose them to new coding patterns and practices they might not have previously encountered or considered. This expansion of possibilities can lead to more innovative solutions and a broadening of the developer's skill set.

By minimizing the need for frequent diversions to look up information and by offering pertinent code suggestions, these AI-powered tools support a more focused and efficient workflow. This not only leads to better code quality but also enhances developer productivity, establishing these tools as essential components in contemporary software development.

Collaborative code creation

When comparing code completion tools to chat-based tools, it is clear that each provides a unique set of offerings to developers. Here are the major differences:

- **Code completion experience**: Tools equipped with code completion capabilities can predict the next words or code blocks directly within the editor. They offer incremental suggestions that users can quickly accept or reject, streamlining the coding process. This is somewhat similar to mob programming alongside an experienced engineer or engaging in pair programming with real-time screen sharing, which promotes an interactive and dynamic coding environment:

```
Cᵉ ItemManager.cs U  ●

Cᵉ ItemManager.cs

23    private void Awake()
24    {
25       Instance = this;
26       waitingItemSOList = new List<ItemSO>();
27    }
28
29    private void Update() {
30       spawnItemTimer -= Time.deltaTime;
         if (spawnItemTimer < 0f) {
            spawnItemTimer += spawnItemTimerMax;
            if (waitingItemSOList.Count < waitingItemsMax) {
               SpawnItem();
            }
         }
      }
31

⌥ main*  ↻   ⚠ 0   Git Graph        ⊕   Ln 30, Col 5   Tab Size: 2   UTF-8   LF   C#
```

Figure 7.1 – Code completion experience in GitHub Copilot

- **Chat experience**: In contrast, the chat experience resembles consulting with a senior engineer via platforms such as Slack or Teams or even delegating implementation tasks. Some tools also feature a chat interface, enabling developers to tap into both direct code assistance and conversational guidance:

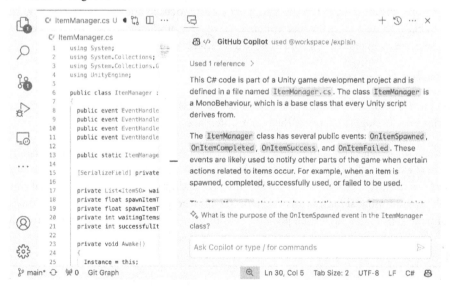

Figure 7.2 – Chat experience in GitHub Copilot

GitHub Copilot, the developer-centric designed tool, supports both chat and code completion experiences. ChatGPT, known for its versatility beyond coding, requires users to carefully craft prompts to guide their responses. In contrast, AI-powered developer tools stand out for enhancing the developer experience within the editor, focusing on how engineers can seamlessly integrate their current work context with AI assistance.

They are engineered to support developers by intuitively understanding the context of their work and making it easier to communicate this context to the AI with fewer prompts. The more code developers write, the more these tools can tailor their assistance to align with the developers' objectives and the specifics of their work context.

Prompt and context

The concept of **prompts** has gained widespread attention with the advent of generative AI technologies. Among the various terms you might have encountered, "Prompt Engineering" stands out as a particularly common reference. However, what is prompt engineering really? Prompt engineering is the art of designing inputs or prompts for AI models to generate desired outputs. It is about crafting questions or statements in a way that guides the AI to understand and respond in a specific manner. This is crucial because the quality and relevance of AI outputs are highly dependent on how the prompts are structured. At the same time, however, it is also true that there are excessive expectations for this, and it was treated like a buzzword in the early days.

The term prompt engineering seems to me to be a mixture of diverse things. I will explain them here.

Two types of prompt engineering

In the evolution of AI and machine learning, prompt engineering has emerged as an important discipline that shapes how we interact with and extract value from AI models. There are two types of prompt engineering. Although not an academic classification, I will refer to them here as **reusable prompt engineering** and **disposable prompt engineering**, each for different applications and requirements. It is important to recognize the difference between these and to know and use these objectives in your daily interactions with the AI.

Reusable prompt engineering

Reusable prompt engineering is designed for scenarios where prompts are repeatedly used in similar contexts. This is common in consumer-facing AI applications, automated systems, and AI-to-machine interactions. The aim here is to create prompts that consistently elicit accurate and relevant responses from AI, regardless of minor variations in input or context.

In reusable prompt engineering, near-perfect accuracy is essential. This is particularly true for machine consumers, where AI responses trigger other functions or processes. Similarly, in B2C applications, high accuracy is crucial to maintain user engagement and prevent frustration or confusion.

The primary challenge in this type of prompt engineering is maintaining stability and consistency in AI responses. This often requires a deep understanding of the AI model's capabilities and limitations. Engineers who build prompts must also consider the variability in user inputs and contexts, ensuring that the AI can handle these variations without significant loss of accuracy.

In reusable prompt engineering, the emphasis is primarily on *how*—crafting prompts to ensure reliable and accurate responses. This focus is critical because the *what* and *why* can often be unpredictable, particularly in scenarios involving a broad and diverse user base. The prompts must be designed to handle a wide range of inputs from an unspecified number of users, each with their unique needs and ways of interacting with the AI system.

The term prompt engineering in the world is used in this context, especially in a narrow sense. It is about how to refine the instructions to the AI in order to extract information from it with a high degree of accuracy. However, in the actual development field, there is no need to spend time refining prompts that are used only once. Prompt engineering in development requires a different context.

Disposable prompt engineering

Disposable prompt engineering is characterized by the creation of one-time-use prompts. These are typically crafted by developers or users for specific, often unique, situations. Here, the emphasis shifts from broad applicability and consistency to specificity and immediate relevance.

This type involves a high degree of creativity and adaptability. Developers create prompts on the fly, tailoring them to specific tasks or problems. This requires a deep understanding of the context and objectives (the why and what) and a flexible approach to interacting with the AI.

In disposable prompt engineering, context is king. The prompts are often designed to address specific issues or to generate unique outputs. As such, the engineer must provide the AI with sufficient context to understand and respond appropriately to the task at hand. In the context of development, you will need to give new instructions to the AI each time you do something creative with each development task. After all, you will find that when you use AIs in your development, you have little need to master each and every type of prompt engineering. What is more important is the context.

In summary, it is important to acknowledge that mastering the intricate techniques of prompt engineering may not be efficient for every goal. Again, for daily tasks requiring fresh ideas and essentially serving as one-off needs, dedicating extensive time to perfecting prompts might not be essential. Conversely, in projects such as developing an app infused with AI, the quality of prompts is crucial. In these instances, it is beneficial to continually refine them to ensure optimal interaction with the AI component. This process often involves trial and error, along with a sophisticated understanding of how the AI model may interpret various prompts.

The importance of context

In AI-powered development, particularly in programming, the context in which a piece of code exists is paramount. Context includes the surrounding information and environment of the code, extending beyond the immediate codebase to encompass project specifications, coding standards, and intended functionality. The effectiveness of AI hinges on its ability to interpret and respond to this context.

The context provided to an AI system determines the relevance and accuracy of its responses and suggestions. In the absence of adequate context, AI tools may generate outputs that are technically correct but misaligned with the project's goals or requirements.

As developers integrate AI into their workflow, it is essential to recognize their role in providing clear and relevant context. This responsibility involves understanding that AI, while powerful, is not infallible or omniscient. It requires input that accurately reflects the problem at hand and the desired outcomes.

Developers should approach AI as a collaborative tool, guiding it through a well-defined context to ensure that its contributions are aligned with project objectives. This involves critically evaluating AI suggestions and adapting them to fit the specific nuances of their projects.

The following would be important to include context:

- **Provide detailed comments**: Incorporate comprehensive comments into the code that explain not just what the code does but also the purpose behind it. This helps AI tools understand the intent behind the code.

- **Use descriptive naming conventions**: Choose variable and function names that clearly indicate their purpose and usage. This aids AI in generating more relevant and readable code.

- **Document code thoroughly**: Ensure that the codebase is well-documented, outlining the broader project objectives, coding standards, and specific functionalities.

- **Frame problems clearly**: When seeking AI assistance, define the problem as specifically as possible. This includes stating the desired outcomes and any relevant constraints or considerations.

Effectively leveraging AI in programming requires a balanced approach that recognizes AI as a powerful assistant but not a complete substitute for human expertise. By providing clear, detailed context and maintaining critical oversight, developers can maximize the benefits of AI-powered tools. This approach ensures that AI serves as a catalyst for enhanced productivity and creativity in software development, complementing human capabilities rather than attempting to replace them.

The paramount importance of context in AI-powered programming cannot be overstated. As AI continues to evolve, its capacity to interpret and utilize context will determine the extent of its impact on software development.

For developers to truly harness the potential of AI in programming, a deep understanding of programming and technology is essential. While prompt engineering significantly amplifies productivity, it is not a standalone solution. The ability to provide clear and detailed context to AI is a skill that synergizes with a developer's technical expertise. Ultimately, the effectiveness of AI tools in augmenting development work hinges on the developer's foundational knowledge and experience in coding. This combination of technical proficiency and skillful prompt engineering is key to maximizing the benefits of AI in software development.

Exploring the capabilities and interaction with AI in coding

This section is dedicated to providing developers with in-depth insights and strategies for effectively leveraging AI within their coding projects, focusing on its features and interaction dynamics. Whether it involves integrating AI for routine coding tasks or utilizing it for the more intricate and imaginative facets of programming, this section intends to offer comprehensive guidance on making AI a transformative element in your coding practices.

Let's explore the expansive capabilities of AI in coding and learn the best practices for interacting with AI tools, enhancing not only the productivity and quality of your projects but also your overall experience as a developer.

Code completion – The foundation of AI-powered coding

Unlike ChatGPT, which requires full context in the prompt for each interaction, code completion in programming environments is deeply integrated with the code editor. AI-powered coding tools dynamically collect necessary data from the code you are writing and seamlessly communicate with the backend LLM. This integration offers an experience akin to pair programming or mob programming with an AI collaborator.

The typical AI tool continuously analyzes the code within the editor, understanding the immediate context to offer relevant suggestions. This contextual awareness is key to the effectiveness of code completion. In AI tools, where context is important, the most important thing is how the context was collected from the editor. Sometimes, humans tend to focus on the accuracy of the model behind it. That is never a mistake; the smarter the AI, the better. However, as AI develops in the future, any tool will be able to perform certain tasks. What will stand out in that case is its excellence as a data collection tool. Therefore, in code completion, it is important to know how the AI-powered coding assistant tool collects information from the editor and to determine whether code completion should take this into account.

As developers type code, an AI-powered coding tool suggests potential code snippets that complete or extend the code. Typically, this functionality is not just about speeding up the typing process; it is about offering intelligent, contextually relevant suggestions that can improve code quality and efficiency.

Here is an example of code completion in action. Let's create a file `calc.js` and write the following in JavaScript:

```
function calculateSum(a, b) {
    // AI Suggestion Here}
```

For example, AI code-completion would complement the contents of a function as follows:

```
function calculateSum(a, b) {
    const sum = a + b;
    return sum;
}
```

The AI model behind code completion has been exposed to a vast array of code, but it is important to clarify that this exposure means it has been "*trained on data*" rather than having fundamentally "*learned*" in the traditional sense. Essentially, it has become adept at recognizing patterns unique to coding through the analysis of these extensive code repositories. By utilizing LLMs, the model can discern patterns, best practices, and common coding paradigms to generate suggestions. As a predictive engine for the next word or sequence in code, the quality of its suggestions is directly influenced by the quality of the input code. In essence, the output quality reflects the quality of the code data it was trained on, highlighting that its capability to provide relevant suggestions depends on recognizing patterns within the training data.

Code generation—the ability of AI-powered coding tools to interpret and respond to natural language—is remarkable. The breakthrough with AI is its capacity to understand natural language as it is presented, offering code suggestions based on that understanding rather than relying on static analysis, as with traditional non-AI code completion tools such as IntelliSense. Developers can detail the functionality, parameters, and expected outcomes of a code segment through comments, directing the AI to generate relevant code.

When we talk about "*code generation*," it includes what was referred to in the previous section as code completion, but here we are discussing it in a broader sense, focusing on generating code from natural language and various types of information.

The effectiveness of this feature depends on the precision and clarity of the instructions provided. Well-defined and explicit comments empower AI-powered coding tools to produce more accurate and suitable code responses.

This is where the importance of your knowledge, experience, and approach to prompt crafting becomes evident. It is crucial to leverage your critical thinking and logical writing skills in a manner that the AI can comprehend.

For example, let's create a JavaScript file named `calc.js`, as follows, and write the comments you want to implement:

```
// Function name: calculateAverage
// Function arguments: numbers (array)
// Return type of the function: number
```

If AI-powered tools can generate code, it will look like the following:

```
function calculateAverage(numbers: number[]): number {
    // calculate the average of the array
    const sum = numbers.reduce((a, b) => a + b);
    return sum / numbers.length;
}
```

Providing examples within other sections of the code or in comments can be extremely helpful. Additionally, one of the strengths of AI-powered coding tools lies in their ability to generate code based on structured examples. This feature proves especially beneficial in situations such as developing models from given data examples.

For instance, consider the following comment:

```
# [{"id": "A1", "name": "Yoshi Yamashita"}]
```

Then, AI can produce the following model. The following example will output Python if you write Python in the file `user.py`, but similarly, if you write a specific language, such as `user.js` or `user.rb`, the same implementation would be carried out for a different language:

```
users = json.loads(json_data)
class User:
    def __init__(self, id, name):
        self.id = id
        self.name = name
```

This indicates that the distance between the definition of the implementation and the implementation itself is getting very close.

When it comes to definitions, table definitions can be turned into SQL queries for database tables, cloud infrastructure definitions can be turned into YAML files for Terraform, and so on.

For example, from a given JSON example, it is possible to generate commands to create a model for Ruby on Rails.

Here is the given JSON example:

```
{
    "name": "Yoshi Yamashita",
    "age": 48,
    "description": "Hello from Tokyo",
    "country": "Japan",
    "title": "Software Engineer",
    "email": yoshiyamashita@example.com
}
```

All you have to do is provide the prompt "*Generate a rails command to create a new user*" for this example, and AI will create a ready-to-use command in CLI as follows:

```
rails g model User name:string age:integer description:text
country:string title:string email:string
```

The code generation capability represents a significant advancement in AI-powered coding. By interpreting descriptive comments and structured examples, AI can generate accurate and functional code, reducing manual coding efforts and enhancing the efficiency of the development process.

Code explanation

AI has the capability to analyze existing code and automatically generate explanations that clarify the code's functionality. This feature proves to be invaluable for understanding code that is not adequately documented or for demystifying complex algorithms for other developers. These generated explanations assist in simplifying complex code into more comprehensible segments, thereby facilitating a better understanding of the logic and intent behind the code for others.

Such a capability is instrumental in reducing the onboarding time for new team members, accelerating the comprehension of code for first-time viewers, and proving useful in scenarios where there is a noticeable gap between the specification and the actual code. Moreover, it enhances the value of the code by providing explanations for previously unmaintained or obscure code, thereby making its functionality clearer.

Here is an example of writing an algorithm in Python by creating a file, `eratosthenes.py`, and specifically considering generating explanations for the Sieve of the Eratosthenes algorithm, which was originally presented without explanation:

```python
def eratosthenes_sieve(n):
    primes = []
    sieve = [True] * (n + 1)
    for p in range(2, n + 1):
        if sieve[p]:
            primes.append(p)
```

```
            for i in range(p * p, n + 1, p):
                sieve[i] = False
    return primes
```

If you write a comment at the beginning of a line, the AI will recognize that you write a comment on every new line, and the AI will automatically complete the rest by simply breaking the line. AI can generate the following comments:

```
# This is a function that calculates prime numbers less than n
def eratosthenes_sieve(n):
    # Primes will hold all the prime numbers found
    primes = []
    # sieve is a list used to track prime numbers
    sieve = [True] * (n + 1)
    # loop through each number in the range 2 to n
    for p in range(2, n + 1):
        # If the number is marked as True in the sieve list
        if sieve[p]:
            # It is a prime number, so add it to the primes list
            primes.append(p)
            # Mark all multiples of this prime number as False
            for i in range(p * p, n + 1, p):
                sieve[i] = False
    # return the list of prime numbers
    return primes
```

In extreme cases, you do not need any specific prompt. Sometimes, all you have to do when you use GitHub Copilot is press *Tab* and *Enter*. However, if more formatting is done, it can go beyond explanation and have various possibilities, such as deriving documentation from code or reverse engineering table definitions from a database migration implementation, for example.

Code explanation by AI significantly elevates the overall quality of code by enhancing its readability and understandability. This feature plays a crucial role in narrowing the gap between intricate code and comprehensive documentation, offering an automated solution to make code accessible and intelligible to a broad spectrum of developers. By saving time and facilitating better code maintenance and collaboration, this capability highlights the transformative influence of AI in the coding process.

Strategies for maximizing AI efficiency

In this section, we delve into strategies aimed at boosting your mastery of AI tools within the realm of programming. By embracing an approach that emphasizes specificity, context awareness, and consistency, you will find significant enhancements in how you interact with AI, leading to streamlined coding processes and improved output quality. Specifically, offering clear, detailed instructions enhances the efficacy of AI tools, enabling them to better align with your expectations. A deep understanding and communication of the working context lead to more precise and applicable AI-generated suggestions. Furthermore, upholding a uniform coding style and adhering to established naming conventions greatly aid AI's interpretation of your code, culminating in superior quality outcomes. These strategies collectively refine your engagement with AI, transforming it into a more efficient and effective partnership in programming.

Moreover, I want to touch upon the iterative process of improving interactions with AI. This process involves the following:

1. Requesting a suggestion from AI

2. Reviewing the results critically

3. Making a decision to accept, reject, or manually adjust the suggestion

4. Applying the change or feedback for continuous improvement (kaizen)

By keeping these three principles in mind at each phase of interaction with AI, you will foster a more productive and harmonious collaboration. These practices blend traditional software engineering principles with the innovative capabilities of AI, ensuring that your code remains both human-friendly and optimized for AI assistance.

Be specific

The clarity and specificity of instructions play a crucial role in the effectiveness of the tool.

AI-powered coding tools are designed to respond to the nuances of the instructions provided by the developer. Their ability to generate useful and accurate code is greatly enhanced when the prompts or comments are specific and clear. The more detailed the instruction, the better the AI can understand the intended outcome. This understanding directly influences the relevance and accuracy of the code suggestions provided by the AI tool.

In the example of a vague prompt, a developer might instruct an AI with a statement such as *"Sort this list."* Such a prompt is unclear because it does not specify the contents of the list or how it should be sorted. The AI, faced with this ambiguity, might struggle to provide an accurate solution. However, when the instruction is more specific, such as *"Sort this list of integers in ascending order,"* it becomes much clearer. This specific prompt gives the AI precise information about the type of data in the list, which is integers, and the desired sorting criterion, which is ascending order. With these details, the AI is better equipped to generate a more accurate and relevant piece of code, aligned with the developer's intent.

The following two points can be considered to elicit better results:

- **Tailoring prompts to the task**: When using AI tools, it is important to tailor the prompts to the specific task at hand. This includes specifying data types, desired outcomes, constraints, and any other relevant details that could impact code generation.

- **Avoiding ambiguity**: Specific instructions help in avoiding ambiguity, ensuring that the AI tool does not misinterpret the task or provide irrelevant code snippets.

Being specific in instructions is a key best practice when working with AI tools in software development. Detailed prompts enable these tools to provide more accurate and useful code suggestions, thereby enhancing the efficiency and effectiveness of the development process. By focusing on clarity and precision in their interactions with AI, developers can harness the full potential of these tools, leading to more productive and successful coding experiences.

Be context-aware

Embracing context awareness is paramount. This approach not only enhances the efficiency with which tools are utilized but also improves the precision of information relayed to AI. Context awareness in software design entails being mindful of the boundaries that delineate work, systems, and processes.

The significance of recognizing these boundaries is highlighted when taking into account the inherent limitations of both humans and AI. Simply put, this underscores that both entities have a finite capacity for processing information and must operate within appropriate contexts to function effectively.

- **Human limitations**: Humans have a cognitive threshold. When information overload occurs, selecting relevant information becomes challenging, leading to what is known as cognitive overload. By being mindful of one's current context and processing information within limited contexts, humans can manage information more efficiently. Humans cannot provide AI with unlimited information, nor can they effectively sift through vast amounts of information received from AI.

- **AI limitations**: Similarly, AI has its own limits in recognition, primarily defined by the token limits of current models. Tokens, the smallest units recognized by AI, such as characters or words, have a numerical limit in AI models at the time of writing. While AI can continue to generate contextually appropriate information, the generation must eventually terminate to ensure the output remains accurate and as intended, necessitating an awareness of AI's performance boundaries.

Here, I provide a practical checklist of items for use during interactions with AI. This checklist is vital for ensuring effective collaboration with AI, focusing on the right context for your development efforts. Getting into the habit of thinking about this in every interaction with the AI will help you have good interactions.

Checklist for every AI interaction:

- **Does AI know it? – Explicit context provision**: Check if the AI is already familiar with the context of your task. If your task ventures beyond AI's pre-existing knowledge, provide additional, detailed context to bridge the gap.

- **Is AI Capable? – Assessing AI limits**: Verify that your expectations align with what AI, such as GPT-4, can realistically achieve. Understanding the capabilities and limitations, especially regarding token counts and context expansiveness, is crucial.

- **How to pass the info? – File and information check**: Ensure you are using the correct files and information with AI. For GitHub Copilot Chat, leveraging context variables such as `#file` and `#editor` to specify the relevant context and using an agent feature such as `@workspace` to expand context can enhance accuracy. Please verify the accuracy of your approach. The implementation of the specific tool is not covered here, but for GitHub Copilot, please refer to the documentation on the latest implementation in the *Further reading* section.

- **How can I optimize It? – Quality management**: Evaluate and adjust the volume of text, characters, and data you are sending to AI. The goal is to optimize the amount of information—increasing what's necessary and reducing what's not—to ensure quality and efficiency.

The importance of being context-aware cannot be overstated—it involves providing information in just the right measure and utilizing prompts and coding techniques to convey intentions with precision. AI-powered development tools such as GitHub Copilot stand as aids for engineers, facilitating the provision of rich context to AI, thus enhancing the tool's utility and effectiveness.

Reflecting on this, it becomes evident that applying these ideas to architecture and programming is not a new concept. This principle aligns with methodologies that have been in practice for a long time. By embracing a domain-driven development approach, one can engage in context-aware design. Additionally, the principle of loose coupling in architecture, which has been explored in various contexts, has evolved from language-specific domain separation to service-oriented architecture and further into microservices architecture.

In summary, incorporating a context-aware approach into AI-powered coding can be considered a good strategy in the era of AI software development. Ultimately, this approach boils down to adopting good, existing architectural practices that are loosely coupled, boundary-conscious, and user-friendly for humans. By focusing on the integration of comprehensive context, allowing AI tools to gain a richer understanding of the project, developers can enhance the precision and usefulness of AI-generated suggestions. This not only enables developers to more effectively handle AI but also makes it easier for anyone to navigate and utilize AI capabilities to their fullest potential.

Be consistent

In an AI-enhanced programming environment, maintaining a consistent coding style and adopting AI-readable naming conventions are pivotal. This section explores how these practices enhance interactions with AI-powered coding tools and contribute to better code quality.

A consistent coding style, encompassing aspects such as indentation, naming conventions, and comment writing, is essential in software development. It not only ensures code readability for human developers but also plays a significant role in how effectively AI-powered coding tools can interpret and suggest code.

For example, the following code in Python could be considered a consistent code:

```
def calculate_area(length, width):
    return length * width
```

This example demonstrates a clear and consistent use of `snake_case` naming and straightforward function naming, facilitating both human understanding and AI interpretation.

In contrast, the following code can be a bad example for AI:

```
def calcSomething(l, w):
    # code goes here
```

In this example, the inconsistent naming and lack of clarity might result in less effective suggestions from AI. If one were to try to complete this content with auto-completion, the AI might be able to give an accurate answer for a simple example such as this, but if there were countless such random, meaningless notations scattered throughout the code base, mistakes could be made.

AI's capability to interpret both natural and programming languages suggests that it reads code not only in its technical syntax but also as a form of natural language. This underscores the importance of clear and meaningful naming conventions in programming. By naming variables and functions in a way that is easily understandable, developers not only aid human comprehension but also enhance the ability of AI models to accurately discern the purpose and context of the code.

For example, effective AI-readable naming conventions involve using specific and descriptive names for variables and functions. This practice extends beyond just aiding human collaborators; it allows AI tools to interpret code with higher accuracy. Such clarity in naming is beneficial in reducing the ambiguity that might otherwise lead to inaccurate or irrelevant code suggestions by AI systems.

Concreteness and context are crucial. Avoid generic names and strive to provide clear context, which can be achieved through methods such as type hinting or adding explanatory comments. These practices significantly enhance the precision of AI-generated suggestions, leading to more relevant and functional code outputs.

At this stage, it is clear that code that is easily understandable by AI is also inherently more comprehensible to humans. In essence, the advent of AI in coding does not always necessitate a reinvention of best practices in software engineering. The principles outlined in respected resources like O'Reilly's *The Art of Readable Code: Simple and Practical Techniques for Writing Better Code* remain relevant and applicable in the AI era. Maintaining these tried and tested practices ensures that code remains accessible and understandable, both for human collaborators and AI tools.

Summary

AI can help you code. However, you may have noticed that no matter how advanced AI gets, the approach to coding does not really change much. All you have to do is be the great engineer that you always have been. Additionally, using AI well will help you improve your skills.

AI will do more than you expect if you approach things with curiosity, so let's work with AI to create a great future, and I hope this chapter will give you a hint.

Further reading

- *GitHub Copilot optimization with prompt crafting and context setting* (https://code.visualstudio.com/docs/copilot/prompt-crafting)

- *The Art of Readable Code: Simple and Practical Techniques for Writing Better Code* by Dustin Boswell and Trevor Foucher (https://www.oreilly.com/library/view/the-art-of/9781449318482/)

Reflection and Conclusion

Let's conclude our journey through the dynamic terrains of Git, GitHub, DevOps, and the burgeoning world of AI in software development. This short chapter not only reflects on the profound transformations these technologies have brought to the developer experience but also gazes forward into the future, pondering the impact and potential of AI in reshaping our approach to software engineering.

Let's reflect together and celebrate what we have learned in this book to drive the next step forward.

We will cover the following main headings in this chapter:

- Reflecting on the journey through Git, GitHub, and DevOps – Enhancing the developer experience
- Embracing AI in development – The next evolutionary step in software engineering
- Concluding remarks

Reflecting on the journey through Git, GitHub, and DevOps – Enhancing the developer experience

As we pause to reflect on our journey, it is evident that our path through the realms of Git, GitHub, and DevOps has been transformative. This journey, more than just a series of steps through technological concepts, has been a deep dive into the quintessence of the developer experience. It is about understanding how developers work, enhancing their impact, and increasing their job satisfaction. Let's take a moment to connect the dots between these key elements, unraveling how each contributes to the grander scheme of software development and team collaboration:

- **Git**: More than just a tool, Git represents a fundamental shift in how we manage and interact with code. It is not just about tracking changes; it is about enabling a fluid, collaborative environment where mistakes can be undone and divergent ideas can co-exist before being seamlessly merged. This foundation in version control is pivotal, as it sets the stage for more advanced practices and methodologies that follow.

- **GitHub**: GitHub acts as a nexus, transforming the solitary act of coding into a collaborative endeavor. Here, the emphasis shifts from just managing code to managing the people and processes behind the code. GitHub, as a collaboration platform, introduces an ecosystem where code review, issue tracking, and documentation converge, creating a more cohesive and transparent workflow. This is where the magic of open source and InnerSource thinking truly comes to life, fostering communities where innovation thrives through collective effort.

- **DevOps**: DevOps is not just a set of practices; it is a cultural shift. Its incorporation underscores a commitment to continuous integration and delivery, where the aim is to shorten the development lifecycle while ensuring high software quality. DevOps encourages a mentality of shared responsibility, automated processes, and frequent, reliable releases, all underpinned by the principles we have learned in Git and GitHub.

- **Developer experience**: While many books on DevOps conclude their discussion at this point, our focus extends to the broader, more holistic aspect of the developer experience within an organizational context. This aspect is crucial. Improving the developer experience is about creating an environment where developers feel valued, can work efficiently, and have the autonomy to make significant decisions. This involves enhancing both the tangible and intangible aspects, from streamlined workflows and effective tools to fostering a culture of open communication and appreciating individual expertise. The developer experience is deeply intertwined with the tools and practices of Git, GitHub, and DevOps. In Git, it is about empowering developers with control and flexibility. In GitHub, it is about fostering collaboration and community. In DevOps, it is about ensuring that the entire software lifecycle, from coding to deployment, is smooth and efficient.

As we look back, it is clear that the journey through Git, GitHub, and DevOps is not just about mastering tools or technologies. It is about embracing a philosophy that places the developer experience at the forefront. It is where each element—version control, collaboration, and operational efficiency—plays a critical role, and when harmonized, they lead to a more productive, satisfying, and impactful development environment. This journey, therefore, is not just a technical progression but a cultural evolution.

Embracing AI in development — The next evolutionary step in software engineering

We now turn our attention to a transformative force that is reshaping the industry: AI. This transition into the realm of AI marks a paradigm shift, not just in how we develop software but in how we perceive and interact with technology as a whole. Now let's think together about how AI is revolutionizing development, urging us to embrace learning and innovation and ultimately guiding us toward a future where technology and human ingenuity coalesce.

AI is not just another tool in the developer's arsenal; it represents a fundamental shift in the development process. With AI's ability to generate code, the landscape of development is undergoing a seismic change. In my opinion, this revolution is not about replacing human developers but enhancing and augmenting their capabilities. AI empowers developers to focus on creative problem-solving and strategic thinking, leaving some of the routine coding tasks to AI

The advent of AI in development is a call for continuous learning and adaptation. If curiosity has always been the engine of human progress, it is the same here in the age of AI. Embracing AI in development is not just about learning new technologies; it is about cultivating a mindset of exploration and innovation. With AI, the boundaries of what is possible are constantly expanding, offering endless opportunities for those willing to explore and learn.

The history of technology is replete with moments of apprehension and excitement, from the internet revolution to the rise of open source and the advent of cloud computing. Each of these milestones brought concerns about job displacement, but they actually opened new horizons for innovation and growth. In that way, the number of jobs has increased, not decreased. AI, much like its predecessors, can be not a harbinger of job obsolescence but a beacon of evolution.

This progression perhaps reflects our inherent human desire to continually advance, refusing to remain stagnant. In a capitalist framework, this drive toward constant innovation and improvement seems almost inevitable. We have collectively chosen to innovate and evolve. However, the conversation around AI extends beyond technological implications to ethical and regulatory considerations. As AI becomes more pervasive, calls for regulation are growing louder. The path forward may be uncertain, but it is a path that we, as a collective society, are charting together.

Incorporating AI into the developer's toolkit offers a myriad of opportunities to improve efficiency, automate mundane tasks, and foster innovation in creating new software solutions. For developers, AI can streamline the coding process, identify bugs more quickly, and personalize the development experience, thereby enhancing productivity and job satisfaction. Furthermore, developers can enhance their learning curve by interacting with AI, making it not just a tool for increasing productivity but also a powerful ally in learning. As developers harness AI, they not only adapt to the evolving technological landscape but also play a pivotal role in shaping it. This transition underscores the importance of upskilling and embracing new tools and methodologies, ensuring developers remain at the forefront of innovation.

As we stand at this juncture, the message is clear—AI is not just a technological phenomenon; it is a transformative force that we must embrace collectively. Let us step into this new era with optimism and determination, recognizing that AI is a tool that amplifies our capabilities and expands our potential. It is time to explore, innovate, and evolve with AI as our ally. This is not just a journey of technological advancement but a journey of human growth and development. Let's embark on this exciting path together, embracing the challenges and opportunities that AI presents, and in doing so, redefining the future of software development!

Concluding remarks

As we reach the conclusion of this book, I extend my heartfelt gratitude to you for embarking on this journey with me. From the fundamentals of Git and GitHub to the expansive world of DevOps and the groundbreaking realm of AI, our exploration has spanned the multifaceted landscape of modern software development.

One of the core objectives of this book has been to illustrate how modern development methods such as DevOps integrate seamlessly into the broader context of the developer experience. This is not a mere discussion of productivity or satisfaction; it is an invitation to view development as a holistic, interconnected process where management, collaboration, and technical proficiency converge.

A significant theme of this book is the redefinition of failure within the DevOps context. Failure, rather than being a setback, is an opportunity for growth, learning, and improvement. It is about establishing guardrails for safe experimentation, embracing early failures, and fostering a culture where collaboration and creativity are paramount. This philosophy extends beyond code to include documentation and knowledge sharing, leveraging tools such as Git as repositories of collective wisdom.

Again, as we look toward a future shaped by AI, let us approach it not with apprehension but with optimism and a desire to innovate. AI is not a threat but a companion in our journey toward making the world a better place through technology. This book encourages you to set aside fears and embrace a future where collaboration, creativity, and technology intersect to enhance satisfaction and heighten the impact of our work on society.

In conclusion, I urge you to utilize this book as one of the toolkits to conquer fears – the fear of failure and the fear of embarrassment. Embrace technologies such as Git, automation, and AI-assisted collaboration to broaden your horizons and rediscover joy in your work. By doing so, you will find yourself with more time to engage in essential, creative tasks.

Please remember, at its core, everything is about collaboration. Rarely can things be accomplished alone; most achievements are the result of collaboration among many. While this book may have introduced you to various technologies, it is also a guide to best practices for collaboration. Whether it is with your colleagues or someone in the open source community you are yet to meet, use this knowledge to enhance and deepen your collaborative efforts.

Together, let's embrace change, explore new possibilities, and enjoy the art of development and collaboration!

Yuki Hattori

Index

packtpub.com

Subscribe to our online digital library for full access to over 7,000 books and videos, as well as industry leading tools to help you plan your personal development and advance your career. For more information, please visit our website.

Why subscribe?

- Spend less time learning and more time coding with practical eBooks and Videos from over 4,000 industry professionals

- Improve your learning with Skill Plans built especially for you

- Get a free eBook or video every month

- Fully searchable for easy access to vital information

- Copy and paste, print, and bookmark content

Did you know that Packt offers eBook versions of every book published, with PDF and ePub files available? You can upgrade to the eBook version at packtpub.com and as a print book customer, you are entitled to a discount on the eBook copy. Get in touch with us at customercare@packtpub.com for more details.

At www.packtpub.com, you can also read a collection of free technical articles, sign up for a range of free newsletters, and receive exclusive discounts and offers on Packt books and eBooks.

Other Books You May Enjoy

If you enjoyed this book, you may be interested in these other books by Packt:

Automating DevOps with GitLab CI/CD Pipelines

Christopher Cowell, Nicholas Lotz, Chris Timberlake

ISBN: 978-1-80323-300-0

- Gain insights into the essentials of Git, GitLab, and DevOps
- Understand how to create, view, and run GitLab CI/CD pipelines
- Explore how to verify, secure, and deploy code with GitLab CI/CD pipelines
- Configure and use GitLab Runners to execute CI/CD pipelines
- Explore advanced GitLab CI/CD pipeline features like DAGs and conditional logic
- Follow best practices and troubleshooting methods of GitLab CI/CD pipelines
- Implement end-to-end software development lifecycle workflows using examples

Automating Workflows with GitHub Actions

Priscila Heller

ISBN: 978-1-80056-040-6

- Get to grips with the basics of GitHub and the YAML syntax
- Understand key concepts of GitHub Actions
- Find out how to write actions for JavaScript and Docker environments
- Discover how to create a self-hosted runner
- Migrate from other continuous integration and continuous delivery (CI/CD) platforms to GitHub Actions
- Collaborate with the GitHub Actions community and find technical help to navigate technical difficulties
- Publish your workflows in GitHub Marketplace

Packt is searching for authors like you

If you're interested in becoming an author for Packt, please visit `authors.packtpub.com` and apply today. We have worked with thousands of developers and tech professionals, just like you, to help them share their insight with the global tech community. You can make a general application, apply for a specific hot topic that we are recruiting an author for, or submit your own idea.

Share your thoughts

Now you've finished *DevOps Unleashed with Git and GitHub*, we'd love to hear your thoughts! Scan the QR code below to go straight to the Amazon review page for this book and share your feedback or leave a review on the site that you purchased it from.

`https://packt.link/r/1835463711`

Your review is important to us and the tech community and will help us make sure we're delivering excellent quality content.

Download a free PDF copy of this book

Thanks for purchasing this book!

Do you like to read on the go but are unable to carry your print books everywhere?

Is your eBook purchase not compatible with the device of your choice?

Don't worry, now with every Packt book you get a DRM-free PDF version of that book at no cost.

Read anywhere, any place, on any device. Search, copy, and paste code from your favorite technical books directly into your application.

The perks don't stop there, you can get exclusive access to discounts, newsletters, and great free content in your inbox daily

Follow these simple steps to get the benefits:

1. Scan the QR code or visit the link below

https://packt.link/free-ebook/9781835463710

2. Submit your proof of purchase
3. That's it! We'll send your free PDF and other benefits to your email directly

www.ingramcontent.com/pod-product-compliance
Lightning Source LLC
Chambersburg PA
CBHW080631060326
40690CB00021B/4889